LIVING & WORKING
ABROAD

THE DEFINITIVE GUIDE TO
SUCCESSFUL RELOCATION

Compiled by
Merricks Media Ltd
3 & 4 Riverside Court
Lower Bristol Road
Bath, BA2 3DZ
Tel: 01225 786800
redguides@merricksmedia.co.uk
www.redguides.co.uk

Managing Editor Daphne Razazan
Editor Joanna Styles
Assistant Editor Leaonne Hall
Researcher Helen Hill

Edited and designed by Bookwork Ltd

Managing Director Lisa Doerr
Publisher John Weir
General Sales Manager Keith Burnell
Special Projects Manager Ali Stewart

Sales Executive Barney Pearson
Production Manager Graham Prichard
Advertisement Design Becky Hamblin
Production co-ordinator Sarah Dimelow

 is a trademark of
Merricks Media Ltd

Cover image © **Simpson Travel** All rights reserved.

Printed and bound in the UK by Polestar.

Copyright © 2005 **Merricks Media Ltd**
ISBN 1-905049-05-6 British Library Cataloguing in Publication Data.

A catalogue record for this bookazine is available from the British Library.

This version of **Living & Working Abroad** is exclusive to WHSmith.

Joanna Styles

Joanna Styles relocated to Spain 16 years ago, and she now lives and works on the Costa del Sol. Joanna is a freelance writer, and has contributed to and written numerous relocation guides including *Living and Working in the EU*, *Costa del Sol Lifeline* and *The Best Places to Buy a Home in Spain*.

Welcome

IT'S TIPPING DOWN WITH RAIN (AGAIN) AND IN THE TIME IT'S taken you to crawl ten miles down the motorway you could have been half-way to Spain. Tomorrow will be the same and so will the day after, and you just can't help wishing you were somewhere else – abroad.

Every year, more and more of us dream of relocating overseas in search of blue skies and the sun, cheaper property, perhaps a better salary and a taste of foreign "exotica". It all seems so easy in today's more accessible world – you can fly anywhere quickly, apply for a job anywhere with a click and even "stroll" through most of the world's cities via web cams. But, although dreaming of a fat salary in a balmy climate is all very well, relocation is never that simple and to make it work you need authoritative information and advice. This is where *Living & Working Abroad* steps in.

Here, you have detailed and up-to-date information about what it's really like to live and work overseas. Not only does the guide highlight relocation hotspots so you can follow in the success of others, it also gives you the low-down on everyday life as well as essential facts on those all-important matters such as taxes, healthcare and property, plus information on the job market and what's available for expat employees. And you can read about the experiences of people who've already "been there and done it".

So, if you fancy joining them and starting afresh overseas, buying this guide should be your first move. With its help, your move abroad will probably be easier and more successful.

Anna Styles

Editor

GW00696615

Contents

OVERVIEW

We uncover why thousands of people are looking to live and work abroad, with a special focus on working within the EU

COUNTRY GUIDE

We give you all the information you need on living and working in your chosen country

UP-AND-COMING COUNTRIES

We pinpoint the countries destined to become major centres for relocators looking for a fresh start and a new, challenging career

Singapore offers a wealth of jobs and a great social scene

CONTENTS

REAL LIFE STORIES

We did it!

True tales of people who have taken the plunge and started a new life and career abroad

Rob and his family find a new lease of life in Australia

Chris shares her experiences of running a business in Japan

BUYER'S REFERENCE

Quick-reference facts, figures and contact details in our easy-to-read directory

131

Our property guide helps you find your perfect pad in the New Zealand sunshine

Panel of experts

Our team of experts has a wealth of knowledge from the property and financial sectors as well as experience of living and working abroad

JOE BINDLOSS

Joe Bindloss is an author and journalist based in north London. Joe has written more than 20 travel guidebooks for *Lonely Planet*, *Time Out* and other publishers, and he has lived and worked in Europe, USA, Australia and Asia. His specialist subjects are travel, careers and education. Joe wrote the section on the USA.

SIMON CONN

Simon Conn has worked in the financial services sector for 24 years, and is Managing Director of Conti Financial Services Ltd, the UK's leading overseas mortgage brokers, who assist clients to raise finance in more than 25 countries.
■ Tel: 01273 772811
■ Email: enquiries@contifs.com
■ Website: www.mortgagesoverseas.com

PAUL OWEN

Sales and Marketing Director at VEF French Property, Paul is regarded as the leading market commentator in the media. He has had articles published in the national press, and made several television appearances.
■ Tel: 0207 515 8660
■ Website: www.vefuk.com

DES ROWSON

Des Rowson is one of DLR Properties' UK partners. DLR Properties Overseas and their partnership office in Spain, Old Tower Properties S.L., have been selling properties on the Costa Blanca for 15 and 20 years respectively.
■ Tel: 0120 630 3049
■ Website: www.dlr-properties.co.uk

BRIAN SCUDDER

Brian Scudder has lived in Dubai for nine years. He launched the region's first business magazine, Gulf Business, in 1996 and launched *Time Out Dubai* in 2001. Brian was enticed into practising the dark arts of Public Relations and Marketing by Ray and Emma Hogan, at Oryx Real Estate's inception two years ago. Brian speaks English, French and "dodgy" Arabic.

RIN SIMPSON

Rin Simpson was born in South Africa and has since lived in England and Japan. She is currently doing a postgraduate diploma in magazine journalism at Cardiff University. Rin has always had a passion for travel and foreign cultures. Her dream is to visit every country on the map, starting in South America. Rin wrote the sections on South Africa, Japan and Canada.

JOANNA STYLES

Joanna Styles relocated to Spain 16 years ago and lives on the Costa del Sol. Joanna is a freelance writer and has contributed to numerous relocation guides including *Living and Working in the EU*, *Costa del Sol Lifeline* and *The Best Places to Buy a Home in Spain* by Survival Books. Joanna wrote Why live abroad? and The EU jobs market.

LINDA TRAVELLA

Linda Travella is director of Casa Travella, and has been selling property in Italy for 18 years. She is seen as a leading expert on Italy, and has appeared in six episodes of ITV's *I Want That House* and on BBC Breakfast television.
■ Tel: 01322 660988
■ Website: www.casatravella.com

ADAM WARING

Adam Waring has worked as a journalist for the past 15 years, both in the UK and in Australia, where he lived in Sydney for four years. Adam has travelled extensively through South America, Europe, Asia, Africa and, of course, Australia. Adam wrote the sections on Australia, New Zealand, Italy, Malaysia, Singapore and Ireland.

How to use this guide

In our up-to-the-minute guide you'll find a wealth of information and advice on every aspect of moving abroad, from obtaining a visa to finding a home

Whether you're looking for a change of lifestyle abroad or being relocated through your company, the *Red Guide to Living & Working Abroad* will help you to plan your move and give you the practical advice and information you need. The guide contains an illustrated A–Z of the most popular countries for relocation, with detailed profiles for each one, plus special features on up-and-coming countries and the EU jobs market.

Living in

A cultural and economic overview of each country, giving a real flavour of what it's like to live there, with information on everything from healthcare and education to the economy, food and drink and expat communities

■ Climate charts

■ Cost of living index   ■ Fact file   ■ Travel file

The EU jobs market
A special feature on key employment opportunities within the EU

Real life stories
Find out how other people have made the move and adjusted to life in another country with our inspirational case studies

■ Q&A format for easy reference   ■ Invaluable hints and tips

■ Advice on permits

Up-and-coming
A round-up of countries that are becoming increasingly popular with relocators and that are likely to provide significant job opportunities

■ Fact-packed country profiles

Working in
A guide to the labour market, key job opportunities, business etiquette and how to go about finding a job

■ Useful websites for job hunters

■ Practical advice on visas and permits

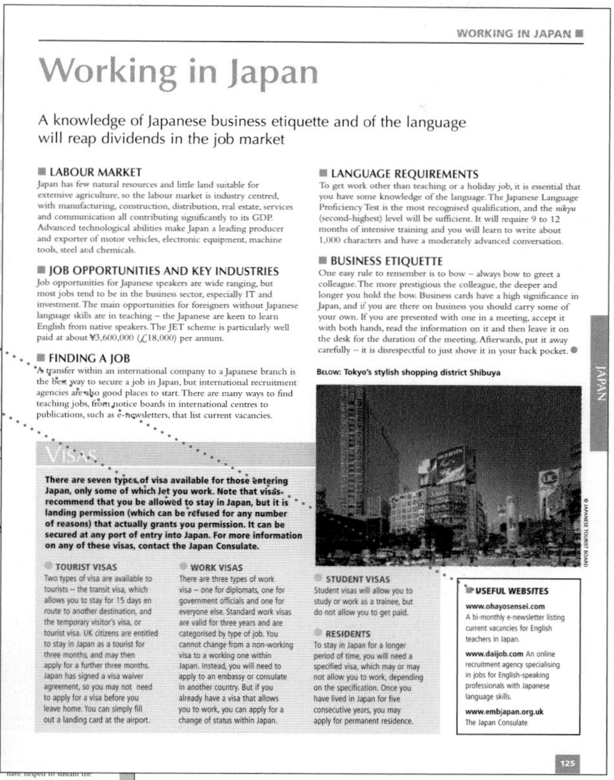

Working in Japan

A knowledge of Japanese business etiquette and of the language will reap dividends in the job market

■ LABOUR MARKET
Japan has few natural resources and little land suitable for extensive agriculture, so the labour market is industry centred, with manufacturing, construction, distribution, real estate, services and communication all contributing significantly to its GDP. Advanced technological abilities make Japan a leading producer and exporter of motor vehicles, electronic equipment, machine tools, steel and chemicals.

■ JOB OPPORTUNITIES AND KEY INDUSTRIES
Job opportunities for Japanese speakers are wide ranging, but most jobs tend to be in the business sector, especially IT and investment. The main opportunities for foreigners without Japanese language skills are in teaching – the Japanese are keen to learn English from native speakers. The JET scheme is particularly well paid at about ¥3,600,000 (£18,000) per annum.

■ FINDING A JOB
A transfer within an international company to a Japanese branch is the best way to secure a job in Japan, but international recruitment agencies are also good places to start. There are many ways to find teaching jobs, from notice boards in international centres to publications, such as e-newsletters, that list current vacancies.

■ LANGUAGE REQUIREMENTS
To get work other than teaching or a holiday job, it is essential that you have some knowledge of the language. The Japanese Language Proficiency Test is the most recognised qualification, and the *nikyu* (second-highest) level will be sufficient. It will require 9 to 12 months of intensive training and you will learn to write about 1,000 characters and have a moderately advanced conversation.

■ BUSINESS ETIQUETTE
One easy rule to remember is to bow – always bow to greet a colleague. The more prestigious the colleague, the deeper and longer you hold the bow. Business cards have a high significance in Japan, and if you are there on business you should carry some of your own. If you are presented with one in a meeting, accept it with both hands, read the information on it and then leave it on the desk for the duration of the meeting. Afterwards, put it away carefully – it is disrespectful to just shove it in your back pocket. ●

Below: Tokyo's stylish shopping district Shibuya

VISAS
There are seven types of visa available for those entering Japan, only some of which let you work. Note that visas recommend that you be allowed to stay in Japan, but it is landing permission (which can be refused for any number of reasons) that actually grants you permission. It can be secured at any port of entry into Japan. For more information on any of these visas, contact the Japan Consulate.

■ TOURIST VISAS
Two types of visa are available to tourists – the transit visa, which allows you to stay for 15 days en route to another destination, and the temporary visitor's visa, or tourist visa. UK citizens are entitled to stay in Japan as a tourist for three months, and may then apply for a further three months. Japan has signed a visa waiver agreement, so you may not need to apply for a visa before you leave home. You can simply fill out a landing card at the airport.

■ WORK VISAS
There are three types of work visa – one for diplomats, one for government officials and one for everyone else. Standard work visas are valid for three years and are categorised by type of job. You cannot change from a non-working visa to a working one within Japan. Instead, you will need to apply to an embassy or consulate in another country. But if you already have a visa that allows you to work, you can apply for a change of status within Japan.

■ STUDENT VISAS
Student visas will allow you to study or work as a trainee, but do not allow you to get paid.

■ RESIDENTS
To stay in Japan for a longer period of time, you will need a specified visa, which may or may not allow you to work, depending on the specification. Once you have lived in Japan for five consecutive years, you may apply for permanent residence.

■ USEFUL WEBSITES
www.ohayosensei.com
A bi-monthly e-newsletter listing current vacancies for English teachers in Japan.
www.daijob.com An online recruitment agency specialising in jobs for English-speaking professionals with Japanese language skills.
www.embjapan.org.uk
The Japan Consulate

JAPAN

125

Finding a home
A snapshot guide to the property market and how to go about renting and buying

■ Advice on taxation

Finding a home

New Zealanders are a nation of homeowners, with more than 75 per cent owning their own home

HOUSES TEND TO BE DETACHED AND ON LARGE, 1,000-square-metre plots, even in city suburbs. This goes back to the early days of the colony, when land was granted to settlers in quarter-acre plots. Buildings tend to be constructed from simpler materials than a traditional in Europe. Weatherboard walls and corrugated tin roofs are the norm, but while this may seem flimsy and primitive, it suits the climate and such buildings are better able to withstand New Zealand's frequent earthquakes.

In the city centres, properties are more compact and apartment blocks are common. Property is cheaper than in the UK, but Auckland is significantly pricier than the rest of the country.

Renting
There are a limited number of rental properties available in New Zealand, and they tend to get snapped up quickly. The Ministry of Housing issues standard tenancy agreements, which you can rely on as being fair to both parties. A bond, equivalent to up to four weeks' rent, is paid to the Tenancy Services Department, who refund it to you, less any damage, on termination of the contract.

Buying
The first step is to make a formal offer in writing. Then, once surveys and searches prove satisfactory, a price is agreed upon, a contract is signed and a ten per cent deposit is paid. This legally binds you to go through with the purchase or forfeit the deposit. The title search is carried out by the Department of Survey and Land Information, which is very efficient – so much so that the services of a lawyer are not strictly necessary. Mortgages are generally straightforward to obtain, and there will be a variety of fixed- and broken competing for your custom and offering a dazzling choice of products. Mortgages can be 90 per cent of the purchase price and can last for up to 25 years. Repayments are usually limited to about 30 per cent of your income, which is combined for a couple.

Restrictions on foreign buyers
Non-residents may buy a property on a plot of land up to 4,074 square metres in size. For larger plots, permission is required from the Land Value Tribunal or District Land Registrar. If you have been granted residency, then such restrictions apply.

Property tax
New Zealand uses a rates system by which properties are assessed a rateable value depending on size and location. Expect to pay between $1,000 (£380) and $2,500 (£760) per year for a three-bedroom home. The money is used for local authority services.

TAXES
In order to work in New Zealand, you need to apply for an IRD number from the Inland Revenue Department. You should do this as soon as you start work, or preferably before, because if you don't give your employer an IRD number, you will be taxed the higher non-declaration rate of 45 per cent. You can download the form from www.ird.govt.nz and will usually be issued with your IRD number within a week. The tax year runs from 1 April to 31 March, and tax returns have to be filed by 7 July. Until recently, everyone who worked in New Zealand had to fill in a tax return; however, the system has been overhauled. Now, most employees have tax deducted at source by their employers as part of a PAYE scheme and, if no other income is received, it is not necessary to file a tax return.

In addition to the above, there are various allowances (called "rebates") that you can deduct from your gross salary to reduce your tax bill.

NEW ZEALAND

Up to $38,000	19.5% ($0.195 per dollar)
$38,001 to $60,000	33% ($7,410 + $0.33 per dollar over $38,000)
Over $60,001	39% ($14,670 + $0.39 per dollar over $60,000)

The equivalent tax on a salary of £29,000 would be: $67,000 – $14,670 = (1,000x0.39 = 2,730) = $17,400 or 26% of income.

AVERAGE RENTAL/SALE PRICES

	2-bed apartment rentals	2-bed apartment sales	4-bed house sales
Auckland	$1,370 (£525)	$330K (£125K)	$825K (£275K)
Christchurch	$960 (£365)	$340K (£129K)	$465K (£177K)
Wellington	$950 (£361)	$234K (£89K)	$370K (£141K)

Above: New Zealand boasts stunning scenery and mountain ranges

138

Employment hotspots

With an economy heavily reliant on tourism, France has many job openings for those with a working knowledge of French

1 Paris
Glamorous and cosmopolitan, Paris is one of the world's great cities, both culturally and architecturally. It is a haven for artists and writers, and the streets are lined with cafés, bars and restaurants.

A quarter of France's manufacturing industry is situated in Paris – chemicals, pharmaceuticals, computer software and electrical equipment. More than 8,000 foreign companies are based here and La Défense business centre is home to ELF, Esso and IBM. Sixty-five per cent of jobs are in the business sector, and 138,600 are employed in tourism. Disneyland, to the east of the city, is a major employer. Paris is also a centre of art and publishing.

Property prices are high, but you will get a better deal in areas such as Montmartre and Montparnasse. Prices start at €579,000 (£400,000) for a two-bedroom apartment and €1,050,000 (£725,000) for a four-bedroom house.

KEY FACTS
■ **Population:** 2.15 million
■ **Airport:** Paris Charles de Gaulle, Tel: 00 33 1 48 62 12 12
■ **Medical:** Clinique Internationale du Parc Monceau, Tel: 00 33 1 48 88 25 25
■ **Schools:** British School of Paris, Tel: 00 33 1 34 80 45 90 ■ Lycée International de Saint-Germain-en-Laye (American School), Tel: 00 33 1 34 51 74 85
■ **Rentals:** There is excellent rental potential for long and short-term lets
■ **Pros:** Public transport is excellent ■ There are job opportunities for foreigners who speak French
■ **Cons:** Property prices are high ■ The cost of living is also very high.

Above: Many buyers are attracted by the traditional French lifestyle

2 Côte d'Azur
Province of the Côte d'Azur are beautiful and varied, with sophisticated resorts, fields of lavender, gorges, rivers and unspoiled villages. Cannes is most famous for its film festival, and Grasse is perfume capital of the world. The French Riviera has many beaches, golf courses and casinos, which attract tourists and celebrities alike.

The economy in Cannes, St Tropez and Nice is based on tourism, which has encouraged a thriving property market. Tourism accounts for 16 per cent of the region's jobs, and the Côte d'Azur also boasts Europe's silicon valley at Sophia Antipolis, which is home to 1,200 companies.

A two-bedroom apartment in Nice will set you back €242,000 (£167,000). A four-bedroom house costs about €654,800 (£452,000).

KEY FACTS
■ **Population:** 4,506,151
■ **Airport:** Toulon/Hyères Airport, Tel: 00 33 4 9400 8383 ■ St Tropez Aéroport du Golfe, Tel: 00 33 4 9449 5779
■ **Medical:** Centre Hospitalier Universitaire de Nice, Tel: 00 33 4 9203 7777 ■ Centre Hospitalier du Pays d'Aix, Tel: 00 33 4 4233 5000
■ **Schools:** The International School of Nice, Tel: 00 33 4 9321 0400 ■ Mougins School, Tel: 00 33 4 9390 1547
■ **Rentals:** The Côte d'Azur is the world's most popular tourist destination ■ You are guaranteed year-round rental income and can charge high prices
■ **Pros:** There is plenty to see and do, from glitz and glamour to relaxing on the beach ■ The weather is fantastic ■ Regular budget flights to the region
■ **Cons:** Property and the cost of living are sky-high ■ The area can get very busy.

85

Employment hotspots
The top places to work in each country, offering a quick-reference guide to economic activity, employment opportunities and the property market

■ Informative city profiles

■ Key facts cover everything from population and airports to schools and hospitals

---

Property price guides
An illustrated selection of typical properties to rent and to buy

■ Apartments to rent

■ Property prices in local currency and sterling

■ Houses for sale

■ Estate agents' codes, listed in Index to Agents on p. 193

Property price guide

Ireland's property market focuses on Dublin, where property can be expensive. However, if you are willing to look elsewhere you can find some real bargains.

APARTMENTS FOR RENT

| The rental market is booming, with something to suit all budgets | €1,000 PER MONTH | €1,200 PER MONTH | €1,200 PER MONTH | €1,700 PER MONTH |
| | 1-BED MONKSTOWN | 2-BED DUBLIN | 2-BED DUBLIN | 3-BED DUBLIN |

APARTMENTS FOR SALE

| €200,000 | €250,000 | €360,000 | €370,000 |
| 2-BED CLONDALKIN | 1-BED DUBLIN | 2-BED LUCAN | 2-BED DUBLIN |

HOUSES FOR SALE

| €710,000 | €810,000 | €1,500,000 | €2,590,000 |
| 4-BED DUBLIN | 3-BED DUBLIN | 3-BED DUBLIN | 3-BED DUBLIN |

IRELAND

Quick-reference matrix
Useful facts and figures for every main country, from the size of expat communities to interest rates

---

Country matrix

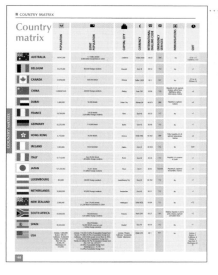

Country matrix	POPULATION	EXPAT POPULATION	CAPITAL CITY	CURRENCY	INTERNATIONAL DIALLING CODE	EMERGENCY SERVICES	IMMUNISATIONS	GMT
AUSTRALIA								
BELGIUM								
CANADA								
CHINA								
DUBAI								
FRANCE								
GERMANY								
HONG KONG								
IRELAND								
ITALY								
JAPAN								
LUXEMBOURG								
NETHERLANDS								
NEW ZEALAND								
SOUTH AFRICA								
SPAIN								
USA								

COUNTRY MATRIX

HOW TO USE THIS GUIDE

Why live abroad?

Moving abroad can be an invigorating experience, whether you're looking for a change of lifestyle or relocating to a new job

LEFT: The global manufacturing industry is shrinking as the services sector continues to grow

"In today's global environment, a spell overseas is considered to be one of the best career moves you can make"

G LOBALISATION IS ONE OF TODAY'S watchwords, and the advent of the Internet and faster communications have "shrunk" the world. Never before have we been able to move around the globe so easily, quickly and cheaply, and never before have we had so much knowledge at our fingertips about other countries and their lifestyles. Moving overseas is far from a new phenomenon – more than 14 million British nationals have left the UK for a new start abroad since the 1950s. But, perhaps not surprisingly, relocation abroad is on the increase, and 2002 saw record emigration figures from the UK. Perennially favourite overseas destinations include the EU (accounting for more than one-third), Australia, the USA, New Zealand and the Middle East.

Reasons for moving abroad are diverse and depend very much on the individual's personal circumstances, although the main reason among relocators of working age is employment. Some people make the move having already found a job and signed a contract or been relocated by their company. Others may intend to look for

employment once they arrive, although this is usually possible only within the EU.

Other reasons commonly stated by people who have to decided to emigrate include a change of lifestyle and a better climate – the more relaxed Mediterranean and Australian ways of life are big favourites, and thousands of northern Europeans relocate southwards every year. A larger income is also a great incentive – salaries in many countries are higher than in the UK, and some have the added advantage of zero taxation. Family reunification is often the reason with those moving to Australia, Canada or New Zealand. It is not uncommon to come across expats who have moved abroad after a bereavement, divorce or personal tragedy, and many UK retirees choose to spend their well-earned rest abroad.

Living and working abroad is a unique experience, one that enriches not only your CV but also your personality. A taste of a different culture and way of life, and meeting new people, can enhance your "life skills" and increase your confidence. In today's global environment, a spell overseas is considered by many chief executives to be one of the best career moves you can make, and many expats take to it so much that they become permanent residents in their new country.

But moving abroad isn't for everyone, and relocation is not an easy ride. No one adapts to a new life overnight, and many expats are badly prepared for the culture shock. So, before taking the plunge, do plenty of research and planning. The box opposite gives you some advice as to what you should think about before you go. ●

THINGS TO THINK ABOUT BEFORE YOU MOVE

WHICH COUNTRY?

■ Distance from friends and family
Relocating abroad, especially if you're single, can be a lonely experience. If you feel you'll need support from your loved ones, choose a nearby country with good telephone communication.

■ Distance from the UK Opting for a country close to the UK will allow you to pop back occasionally, and your friends and family can visit you. Long-haul destinations, especially Australia and New Zealand, mean that visits to and from the UK are likely to be few and far between.

■ Climate The weather in the UK is notoriously bad, but don't assume you'll find the perfect climate abroad. Seemingly warm, sunny countries can be stiflingly hot in the summer or suffer days of torrential rain. Winters can be cold anywhere in Europe (even in southern Spain and Greece), and last for months in northern parts.

■ Language This is an important consideration in non-English-speaking countries. Your chances of getting a job, finding accommodation and making a success of your stay abroad are much higher if you speak the local language. Before you relocate, take a crash course in the language and keep up lessons once you arrive.

■ Health Check out the standard of healthcare and facilities. Most countries have a state healthcare scheme, but facilities in many are poor. Private healthcare is generally good worldwide, but can you afford it? Find out whether you need vaccinations before you go and what precautions you need to take once you arrive.

■ Education If you are relocating with children of school age, you will need to consider the pros and cons of the country's state education system (if foreigners are eligible) and the private system. International schools are the only practical option in some countries, but fees are usually high.

■ Insurance You will probably need various types of insurance. Private health insurance is a must in many countries, so work out whether you can afford it. Travel insurance is essential, as is household insurance (contents only if you're renting). A life insurance policy is a good idea for relocators with partners or a family. Shop around for the best policies and read all the small print.

■ Pets Importing a pet is usually subject to strict regulations, including quarantine. If you plan to return to the UK with your pet, don't forget that regulations here are among the most stringent in the world!

EMPLOYMENT

■ How easy is it to find work? Look at the job market and growth industries in your chosen country. Don't forget to find out how easy it is to change jobs once you are there – some countries issue job-specific work permits only.

■ Visas and permits Most countries have strict immigration policies for migrants, and it is almost impossible to take up employment "on spec" without a work permit. This usually involves obtaining a visa – which often takes several months, so plan ahead. UK nationals don't usually need a work permit within the EU.

■ Working conditions Before you sign a contract, ask about the country's employment conditions. Look at the length of the working week, holiday entitlement, dismissal regulations, union membership and pension rules. Find out what benefits and allowances you are entitled to under the country's social security scheme.

■ Taxation Income tax rates vary greatly. Find out how much tax you will pay on your earnings, if there are special rates for foreign workers and whether you will need to file an annual tax return.

ACCOMMODATION

■ Renting When you first arrive this is the best option, offering flexibility, short-term commitment and minimum financial investment. Most large cities have a shortage of rental accommodation, which is often only apartments. Ask about costs, deposits, furnishings and contracts. Finding a place to live can take a while, so plan ahead.

■ Buying This is usually a worthwhile option only if your stay is long-term. Some countries do not allow foreigners to buy property, and associated costs are at least five per cent in most. Property, however, is one of the best investments worldwide.

■ Shipping your belongings If you are lucky, your new employer will pay for your relocation costs. If this isn't the case, work out what shipping costs will be. Many countries allow new residents to import personal goods duty-free, but you still have to get them there. Shop around for relocation quotes. Unless you are relocating long-term, it is usually cheaper to buy new once you arrive.

© BECKY HAMBLIN

LEFT: Before you splash out and buy a new home, it's best to rent somewhere first

BELOW: Make sure you consider the implications of finding work if you don't speak the language

© SOUTH AFRICAN TOURIST BOARD

The EU jobs market

The expanding European Union offers a wide range of employment opportunities, especially for those with foreign language skills

THE EU CONSISTS OF 15 ORIGINAL countries (Austria, Belgium, Denmark, Finland, France, Germany, Greece, Ireland, Italy, Luxembourg, Netherlands, Portugal, Spain, Sweden and the UK), which are known as the EU15, plus ten new members (Czech Republic, Cyprus, Estonia, Hungary, Latvia, Lithuania, Malta, Poland, Slovakia and Slovenia). It has a population of more than 455 million, and is the world's largest and most diverse single market. In 2007, the EU is set to expand still further when Bulgaria, Romania and possibly Croatia join. Within its vast territory, the EU offers a world of opportunities for employment. Professionals with language skills and practical experience are in highest demand, but there are job opportunities in all sectors and at all levels across its member states.

ABOVE: As the EU grows, so does the workers' freedom of movement

Unemployment

Unemployment figures across the EU are by no means uniform. The average is 8.9 per cent (January 2005), but this hides huge variations from one member state to another – compare Poland's high 18.3 per cent or Slovenia's 16.9 per cent with 4.3 per cent in Ireland and 4.5 per cent in Austria. Percentages within countries may also vary greatly from one region to another.

Freedom of movement

The EU single market's main characteristics are its "Four Freedoms", the most important of which is the "Freedom of Movement of People". This allows EU nationals to live, work or set up a business anywhere in the EU without needing to apply for visas or work permits. The only restriction is that foreigners may not work in the civil services or armed forces in certain countries. Otherwise, EU nationals are free to choose from a wide range of countries, employment opportunities, lifestyles and cultures. Bureaucratically, it is easy to move around from one EU state to another and, therefore, the chance to enrich your CV with overseas experience has never been greater.

Another significant advantage is that most states are within easy reach of each other – the majority of EU capitals are within three hours flight. With the advent of the ever-widening network of cheap no-frills flights, it is now feasible to have your workplace in several different cities. Commuting between countries is also possible, and every day many hundreds

of employees cross borders to work in the country next door. For example, in Luxembourg, many workers live across the border in France to take advantage of high salaries in Luxembourg and cheaper accommodation in France.

Permits

Freedom of movement applies across most of the EU, and by 2007 it is expected that most restrictions on employment will have been lifted. Until then, the following regulations apply:

EU15 plus Cyprus and Malta: EU nationals are free to work in these states without a work permit. You may need to apply for a residence permit if you plan to stay for longer than three months, but this is usually a straightforward process. Residence permits are no longer necessary for EU nationals working in France or Spain.

New member states: Until at least mid-2006, EU15, Cypriot and Maltese nationals will still require a work permit to work in the Czech Republic, Estonia, Hungary, Latvia, Lithuania, Poland, Slovakia and Slovenia, and a visa may also be necessary. It is a good idea to contact the country's embassy in the UK for up-to-date information before you travel. EU nationals are, however, given priority over other nationalities both in finding employment and applying for work permits.

"Within its vast territory, the EU offers a world of opportunity for employment"

"The EU is, undoubtedly, one of the most exciting places in the world to work"

The EU's most prominent industries

The diverse nature of the EU and its member states means that opportunities are available for all ages, skills and qualifications – from fruit picking to investment banking, and from nursing to interpreting, with just about everything in-between. The job market caters for casual, temporary and permanent posts. Vacancies vary from one country to another, but if you have certain skills to offer, finding employment shouldn't be difficult.

Construction

The construction industry is one of the main engines behind the EU economy. It employs more than 127 million workers in the EU15 alone (about 8 per cent of the total workforce) and is a major growth industry, particularly in new member states, where the property markets are taking off. Construction is also one of the least regulated industries – unions claim that millions of construction workers are employed illegally. Job opportunities are available at all levels, from casual manual labourers to architects, and also in related fields such as engineering and health and safety.

Finance

Finance is a massive growth industry. Several EU countries have important financial centres, including Frankfurt, Luxembourg, Paris and Cyprus, where there are countless opportunities in the fields of auditing, financial advice and investment banking. The outlook is also good in the new member states, where the banking and financial sectors are in their infancy and growing. The finance industry is one of highest paid in the EU and jobs often come with numerous perks.

ICT

Information and Communication technologies (ICT) skills and qualifications provide a passport to jobs worldwide, and there is currently a shortage in the EU. Some member states, including Germany and Ireland, have introduced "fast-track" admissions for foreigners with ICT skills. The Baltic States have exceptional opportunities in the ICT sector and are tipped to be at the forefront of the EU. ICT jobs are generally well paid.

Management and personnel

Opportunities for graduates with management and personnel skills are available in most EU countries. It is a great advantage if you can speak the local language, and Master of Business Administration (MBA) qualifications are in high demand in the new EU states. There is a particular shortage of business consultants in Poland.

TEFL

English is the lingua franca of EU business, and the ability to teach English as a foreign language (TEFL) is in great demand. There are plenty of opportunities for professionals with TEFL qualifications, particularly in the new member states. TEFL is often poorly paid and the working hours are unsociable, but you may be able to supplement your income with private teaching. Taking a TEFL post can be a good way to enter a country before seeking alternative employment.

Tourism

France, Spain and several other EU countries are among the most popular tourist destinations in the world, and income from tourism constitutes a large part of many member states' GDP. Opportunities for employment in tourism are enormous. Jobs tend to be seasonal, but if you're flexible about where you work and when, tourism can provide year-round employment. Tourism "know-how" is in great demand in the new member states, many of which are expanding their tourist industry.

Translating and interpreting

There are 27 languages spoken within the EU, so professionals with language skills are always in demand in most sectors. Interpreting is usually well paid, although to be successful you need to be fluent in at least three languages. Translating is not as well paid. Languages spoken in the new member states are in particular demand.

BELOW: Banking and finance are massive growth industries

© POLISH TOURIST BOARD

Company relocation

Many business experts believed that the expansion of the EU in May 2004 would result in large numbers of companies relocating or outsourcing parts of their manufacturing process to the new member states. Labour costs there are considerably cheaper, representing vast savings for employers.

In recent months, there have indeed been several highly publicised relocations. General Electric transferred its European headquarters from London to Budapest, Samsung moved its factories from Spain to Slovakia and Philips relocated many factories from Western Europe to Poland.

Multinational companies such as IBM, Nokia, Siemens and Tesco (now the largest retailer in Slovakia) have set up factories and offices in the Czech Republic, Estonia, Hungary and Poland, and headquarters of large international firms can be found in Budapest, Prague, Tallinn and Warsaw.

As a consequence, new member states are becoming key players in European business. The Czech Republic is emerging as one of Europe's largest manufacturing sectors, Hungary has become a major logistics centre, Slovakia has booming automobile and aviation industries and the small island of Malta is rapidly gaining a reputation as one of the world's up-and-coming financial and insurance centres.

However, recent surveys conducted among company directors in the UK and Ireland indicated that 80 per cent of British and 65 per cent of Irish companies had no intention of outsourcing to the new member states.

Migrant patterns

Many experts predicted that the expansion of the EU would lead to an influx of immigrants to the West from the new member states, seeking better-paid employment. To prevent this, the EU15 (excluding Ireland, Sweden and the UK) imposed work permit restrictions on new member states.

Almost a year after expansion, however, no EU15 state has had to cope with large numbers of immigrants from the new states and most new arrivals have found employment. Migration experts predict that, over the next decade, about one per cent of the EU15 population will be from the new member states. They are unanimous in their claim that the EU, with its ageing population and falling birth rate, needs vast numbers of immigrant workers to sustain its economy.

Quality of life

Salaries are generally higher in the north and west of the EU, and the top payers are Luxembourg, Ireland, Denmark and the Netherlands. Salaries in other countries vary greatly. Multinational firms in

large cities tend to pay well, but jobs in many southern EU countries and new member states are poorly paid.

High costs of living and taxation may offset high wages. Taxation is high in the Scandinavian countries, Austria and Belgium and the most expensive cities are London, Copenhagen, Milan, Dublin and Paris. Greece, Slovenia and Cyprus are the cheapest countries. If a high standard of living features on your list of priorities, you should consider the Scandinavian countries, Amsterdam, Luxembourg, Vienna and Dublin, although most of the EU15 states have good standards of living.

The EU is undoubtedly one of the most exciting places in the world to work. It offers its members maximum flexibility about where they can work and what they can do – an opportunity that is almost impossible to find elsewhere. It is therefore hardly surprising that more than one-third of the UK's migrants choose to relocate there. Why not join them? ●

ABOVE: Traditional family-run businesses and multi-national corporations can be found throughout the EU

INSET: Smaller communities will require employees to have language skills

Country guide

A comprehensive guide to living and working in the 22 most popular countries for relocators

COUNTRY GUIDE

Australia

Enjoy an outdoor lifestyle with sun, sea and surf

© AUSTRALIAN TOURIST BOARD

FACT BOX

- **Population** 19,913,144
- **Population growth rate** 0.9%
- **Economic growth rate** 3%
- **Inflation rate** 2.8%
- **Capital** Canberra
- **Hotspots** Sydney, Melbourne, Brisbane, Perth and Adelaide
- **Average house price** (4-bed) $567,000
- **Average rental price** (2-bed) $1,440

Living in Australia

A popular destination for British relocators, Australia offers virtually year-round sunshine and a relaxed way of life

FACT FILE

AREA	7,686,850km²
POPULATION	19,913,144
CAPITAL	Canberra
LIFE EXPECTANCY	80 years
LITERACY	100%
GOVERNMENT	Democracy
GDP PER CAPITA	US$29,000
UNEMPLOYMENT RATE	6%
CURRENCY	Australian dollar (AUS$)
EXCHANGE RATE	AUS$ = £0.40; £1=AUS$2.50
LANGUAGES	English, native aboriginal languages

COST OF LIVING

PETROL (1L)	AUS$1.08
WINE (0.75L)	AUS$7.50
MEAL (3-COURSE)	AUS$28
BEER IN PUB (375ML)	AUS$5
LOAF OF BREAD (650G)	AUS$2
MILK (1L)	AUS$0.43

CLIMATE

Average monthly temperature °C

SYDNEY		LONDON
21	Dec	7
20	Nov	10
18	Oct	14
16	Sept	19
14	Aug	21
12	July	22
13	June	20
15	May	17
19	April	13
21	March	10
23	Feb	7
23	Jan	6

Average monthly rainfall mm

SYDNEY		LONDON
75	Dec	81
80	Nov	78
75	Oct	70
65	Sept	65
75	Aug	62
100	July	59
125	June	58
120	May	57
120	April	56
130	March	64
110	Feb	72
100	Jan	77

IN TERMS OF LAND MASS, AUSTRALIA IS enormous. At 7.68 million square kilometres, it's comparable in size to the whole of Western Europe or the USA, but its population is less than 20 million. There's a reason for this: much of the interior of the country is harsh, uninhabitable desert, so the vast majority of people live within 20 kilometres of the coast.

The population is most densely concentrated in the southeastern corner where Sydney and Melbourne are situated. Other major cities are Adelaide on the south coast, Brisbane on the east, and the isolated city of Perth, on the west coast.

Politics and economy

Australia's government is a democratic one, headed by the prime minister John Howard, in office since 1996. A federal state system, Australia still recognises the British monarch as soverign, although today this is a relatively symbolic gesture. The Australian economy has taken a battering in recent years with its tourist industry badly affected by the SARS epidemic and its business sector hard hit by the collapse of several major companies. Yet the economy has remained stable, supported by residential and commercial construction.

Australia is a moderately safe country, but drug-related burglaries are a problem in the cities, althoguh violent crime is rare, and it is generally safe to walk in the cities late at night.

Climate

The climate varies significantly, from tropical in the north to temperate in the south. Most places are agreeably sunny for much of the year. Sydney, Melbourne and Perth all have hot and sometimes humid summers. Adelaide has a milder climate and is popular with British immigrants for this reason. In Darwin and the "top end", the seasons are restricted to hot and wet, or hot and dry.

Education

Australia has one of the highest standards of education in the world, with about 80 per cent of school students going on to higher education. Forty-two per cent of the working-age population has a university degree, diploma or trade qualification. Generally children start school at about five years old and, by law, have to remain in education until 15 years old. Primary education usually lasts six or seven years, and secondary education begins in "Year 7" and ends in "Year 12", with a Senior Certificate of Secondary Education (the precise name varies between states). Roughly equivalent to A levels, this covers a broad base of subjects and is a mix of classroom studies, written assessments and exams.

Healthcare

Australia has an advanced public healthcare system called Medicare. British nationals, and people from many other countries, are automatically covered under reciprocal agreements, so it's not strictly necessary to purchase private health insurance, although it is available. Medicare is funded by the Medicare levy, a 1.5 per cent income tax.

Lifestyle

The relaxed "beach and barbie" lifestyle is what attracts many people to Australia, and once

BELOW: Dunk Island on the Great Barrier Reef

© AUSTRALIAN TOURIST BOARD

ABOVE: Ayers Rock, the world's largest monolith, is situated at the entrance of Kata Tjuta National Park

AIR All the state capitals have an international airport, with Sydney, Melbourne and Perth all serviced by long-haul flights. There are no direct flights from the UK; a stopover usually takes place in Southeast Asian hubs such as Singapore, Bangkok or Hong Kong. Even the quickest flights from the UK will take a shade under 24 hours. There are plenty of options, and as a general rule the cheaper flights will require more stopovers. The most direct flights are offered by national flag carrier **Qantas** (www.qantas.co.uk; 0845 7 747 767), which has a code-sharing arrangement with **British Airways** (www.ba.com; 0870 850 9850). **Virgin Atlantic** (www.virgin-atlantic.com; 0870 380 2007) flies only to Sydney. Many of the Southeast Asian airlines also offer fairly direct flights to Australia including **Singapore Airlines** (www. singaporeair.com; 0870 6088886), **Thai Airways** (www.thaiair.com; 0870 60 60 911) and **Malaysia Airlines** (uk.malaysiaairlines.com; 0870 607 9090).

Because Australia is such an enormous country, flying is the most practical method of travelling interstate. (Perth to Sydney by road is a 4,425-kilometre journey and takes several days.) Recent years have seen the appearance of budget airlines – notably Richard Branson's **Virgin Blue** airline – which has reduced the cost of plane travel dramatically.

ROAD In Australia, they drive on the left, as in the UK. Officially, you should retake your driving test within six months of taking up residence in Australia to obtain an Australian licence. However, you can register and insure your vehicle without an Australian licence.

Each state has its own system and requirements for registering vehicles. If you buy a car that's registered in a different state from the one in which you reside, you have to re-register it in your home state – the alternative is an annual journey back to the original state to re-register the vehicle. You buy the registration certificate "rego" from an insurance company and it includes compulsory third-party insurance. It will cost several hundred dollars. This covers you for causing injury or death to a third party, but not for damage to property. You should therefore always ensure that you also obtain additional insurance for this.

GETTING AROUND A national bus network, run by Greyhound Pioneer, and several smaller operators offer inter- and intrastate routes. Although a train network links the major cities, it's far from extensive and is the slowest way to travel. All the major cities have good bus and/or train public transport networks. Melbourne also has trams and Sydney has ferries.

immigrants have settled in, it's easy for them to while away the weekends relaxing with friends. It's a very active country offering many outdoor pursuits. Hiking through the wilderness, or "going bush", is popular, as are watersports, such as sailing and scuba diving. Surfing is for many a way of life.

"Australia is a multicultural place with more than a quarter of the population fluent in a second language. It's an easy society into which to integrate"

Australians are fanatical about their sports, particularly cricket, rugby league and Australian rules football.

Food and drink
Although Australia doesn't have much of a cuisine it can call its own, the multicultural influx means that there are restaurants catering for every taste in even the smallest towns. Eating out is cheap and relaxed. Most restaurants allow you to bring your own alcohol – known as BYO – and the corkage charge, when levied, is normally less than a dollar.

Australian wine has really made its mark internationally in the past decade or so. There are many wine-growing areas in southern and eastern Australia, which provide ideal growing climates. Prices for wine start at just a few dollars a bottle from the local "bottle shops".

Expat communities
Of course, a big draw for British and Irish migrants is the fact that English is the native tongue, thanks to Australia's British colonial history. But modern Australia is a multicultural place with more than a quarter of the population fluent in a second language. It's an easy society into which to integrate (the majority of Australians are a mere generation or two removed from their European roots), and although "pommie-bashing" is a popular pastime, it's usually good-natured.

Pets
There are stringent quarantine procedures for pets going into Australia. Dogs and cats from the UK must go into quarantine for 30 days. You will be liable for all quarantine costs, (the cost does go down for additional animals) although you will be liable for any additional veterinary care that may be required. Certain breeds of "dangerous" dogs, including pit-bull terriers, cannot be taken into the country. Your pets will have to be microchipped and you will have to provide vaccination certificates for a range of common diseases. Animals may arrive in Australia only via Sydney, Melbourne or Perth airports. The Department of Agriculture, Fisheries and Forestry (www.affa.gov.au) is responsible for all matters. ●

Name: Rob and Sanchia Pegley
Job: Editorial Director
Where: Sydney

AUSTRALIA

Emigrating to Australia

Rob, Sanchia and their three children decided the Aussie lifestyle was just what they needed

ON THEIR RETURN TO THE UK AFTER HAVING lived and worked in Australia for three years, Rob and Sanchia Pegley decided to emigrate permanently to the land down under with their three young children. We asked Rob all about it.

Q: Where did you move to and what is the job you are doing?
A: We have moved to the Northern Beaches area of Sydney, where I am working as editorial director for a small consumer publisher of specialist magazines.

Q: Why did you decide to move to Australia?
A: The lifestyle here just cannot be compared to the UK. Every weekend is like a holiday, either at the beach, up at the park or having a barbecue, rather than in a shopping centre or watching television. It is also a far healthier environment in Australia than in the UK. People are outside more often, playing sport or eating and socialising, and everybody is incredibly friendly and easy going. "No worries" is not just something you say here, it is a whole attitude to life.

On the practical side, living here is also cheaper than the UK in terms of everyday items such as the weekly shopping or eating out. The food and wine culture here is fantastic.

Q: How have the family adapted to living in Australia?
A: We have three children: Noah will be five in March and our twin girls, Tean and Iona, will be three in May. They all love it here; the standard of life they have now is incredible. Since we've been here they have spent almost every day on the beach, in the pool or in the park. In the UK, they used to spend a lot of time indoors going crazy! The children have become much healthier and more outgoing in the four months that we have been here. Noah has asthma and needed to use an inhaler every day in the UK. Here he hardly ever uses it. He has also settled in really well at kindy. He will start school a year later than he would have done in the UK.

Settling in has been made even easier because when we went back to the UK, we kept in touch with some people whom we had spent time with when we had lived in Australia previously.

Q: What kind of property are you living in?
A: We are renting a property at the moment. It is a large semi-detached house with three bedrooms, including an en-suite, on the Northern Beaches of Sydney. Rental property is very easy to find in Sydney

Q: How do property prices compare to the UK?
A: Property prices vary according to your location. In the Northern Beaches where we live in Sydney they are probably similar to London prices, but you get some great houses with ocean views and pools for your money. Sydney in

LEFT: Rob and Sanchia felt their children would enjoy a better quality of life in Australia

ABOVE: Australia boasts a healthy lifestyle, and Rob believes it gives the family a positive outlook

general can be pretty expensive, and you will need to move well into the outskirts and away from the coast to find cheaper places. If you move anywhere but Sydney then you will get great value for your money. You can get a three-bedroom cottage in the Blue Mountains for around $337,400 (£140,000). Wherever you buy, you generally get more space than you would in the UK, including bigger rooms and wider roads. It's a big country with not that many people in it!

"It is a healthier environment than in the UK. People are outside more often, playing sport or socialising, and everyone is incredibly friendly and easy going"

Q: What are the advantages of working in Australia?
A: The job I first took here was similar to the one I had in the UK, although the pay was initially not as good. If there is an advantage for me personally working in Sydney, it is that the magazine arena is much smaller, and you feel that career progression is possibly easier. In the UK, I didn't know any of the MDs in London, whereas here I'm on first name terms with the MDs of all of the top five publishers.

Q: How easy was it to find work in Australia?
A: I had a job secured before we left the UK, which I found through one of the Australian online job sites. Since then I have obtained another job, which has taken me back to my preferred salary level. I applied for a lot of jobs from the UK before I found one, and I would say that if you can afford it, it would be easier just to come out, and find a job when you are here. I'm lucky in that I've got permanent residency so I can move from job to job with no restrictions. Also, because I worked out here for three years previously, I have lots of contacts and a reasonable reputation.

Q: How does the work ethic and etiquette vary in Australia compared with the UK?
A: It is very similar. There is a misconception that Australians don't work as hard as people in the UK, but in my experience that is not the case. They generally arrive at work earlier and leave earlier because they are healthier and their life doesn't revolve around the pub, although they do like a drink on a Friday evening! I have found them to be very professional, hard-working and organised.

Q: Any final thoughts?
A: I would say that some of the best things about living in Australia are that people have a more positive attitude. Living here feels like the few weeks during the UK summer when the sun shines and everyone is nice to each other! I find that in the UK I can feel quite negative, but when I am here I have a far more positive attitude. Also, people really live here rather than just exist. ●

Top tips

● Securing a visa to live and work in Australia is a complex process, and it is essential to ensure you do your research, find a reliable visa specialist and leave yourself enough time to sort out your visa. Many people also recommend you take copies of all documentation and paperwork relating to your visa application.

● Always ensure you visit the area you are thinking of moving to, and spend time there before you take the plunge and uproot yourself and your family.

● Try to ensure your job is secured prior to departure – obtain this in writing, and if moving with your family, ensure you have found a school for your children and enrolled them in it.

● Obtain a tax file number; you will need this to open a bank account and before you can commence work.

● Open an Australian bank account. You should do this within six weeks of arrival and you can use your passport as ID.

Who moves there?

Traditionally a magnet for families and gap-year students, Australia is now attracting young skilled professionals

"One of the most common reasons people give for moving to Australia is to give their children a better quality of life"

OVER THE LAST COUPLE OF YEARS, THERE has been an 18 per cent increase in the number of British people choosing to live in Australia (about 8,580 in 2004), with 40,000 applying for a 12-month work visa every year. British relocators account for ten per cent of Australia's permanent immigrant population, and 14 per cent of Australia's five million visitors are UK residents.

Who moves there?

Between 2002 and 2003, 52 per cent of Australia's population growth came from immigration; New South Wales received 40 per cent of immigrants, who exceeded the number of locals resident in the area. More than 90,000 permanent settlers entered the country and 13 per cent of those were British. Traditionally, families are seen as the largest proportion of immigrants, but an Australian census for 2002 puts the largest population bracket for immigrants as those aged 20 to 24. Seventy per cent of working-holiday visas are accounted for by 22- to 26-year-olds. Gap-year work opportunities, such as seasonal work within the tourist industry and bar work, draw a huge proportion of young people, but the largest growth area for relocators is people under the age of 31. Twenty per cent of all 30-plus-year-olds

living in Australia are immigrants, and this is reflected in the growing job opportunities in ICT (Information Communication Technology) industries. The student bracket of 18- to 22-year-olds also accounts for a large proportion of immigrants because Australian universities rank among the best in the world.

Why move there?

People are buying property in Australia for a number of reasons. The hosting of the 2000 Olympic Games in Sydney and the 2003 Rugby World Cup revitalised Australia as a desirable destination for UK buyers, although it has never been out of the top five. The four major cities – Melbourne, Sydney, Brisbane and Perth – have all been labelled as desirable locations.

One of the most common reasons people give for wanting to move to Australia is to give their children a better quality of life. The climate, with its guaranteed warm summers, and the laid-back approach to life are attractive to British buyers. Australia has more than 7,000 beaches and enjoys an unrivalled and extremely healthy outdoor lifestyle.

Other equally important reasons for its popularity are the lack of any language barrier (it is easier for children to adjust in a country when they can speak the language), the excellent value of property and a good exchange rate for the pound to the Australian dollar. For the price of a flat in the UK, you can buy a four-bedroom house complete with swimming pool in Melbourne.

Australia also enjoys a low population density, with only 2.5 people per square kilometre compared with the UK's 383 people. ●

LEFT: **A unique heart-shaped island in the famous Great Barrier Reef**

Working in Australia

A prosperous country, Australia welcomes hard-working immigrant employees under the Skilled Migration Program

■ ECONOMY

Australia's economy is largely based on the service industries. Only 6.5 per cent of the land is suitable for cultivation, but the country is able to produce much of its own meat and cereals and there are several wine-producing regions. Australia doesn't have much of a manufacturing base, due to its relatively small population and its proximity to Southeast Asian countries, which have lower costs.

■ JOB OPPORTUNITIES AND KEY INDUSTRIES

In addition to the usual array of service jobs, certain professions, such as nurses, doctors, chefs and panel beaters, qualify for bonus points on the Skilled Migration Program. Australia is particularly short of IT professionals.

■ MAIN EMPLOYMENT CENTRES

Sydney and Melbourne could be called the service centres of the southern hemisphere, but the states of Western Australia and Queensland have seen the most new jobs created in recent years. There are government initiatives to attract workers, particularly in the medical and teaching professions, to more rural areas.

■ FINDING A JOB

All major cities have employment agencies, and there are several jobs sites where you can begin your search before you leave British shores. It's worth registering your CV with many sites because it's normally a free service for jobseekers. ●

©AUSTRALIAN TOURIST BOARD

ABOVE: **The Melbourne skyline at night**

■ USEFUL WEBSITES

www.australia-migration.com Australian migration specialist
www.immi.gov.au Australian Immigration Service's website
www.seek.com.au Claims to be the biggest Australian jobs site. You can put your CV on here, and the site will automatically match it with employers.
jobsearch.gov.au Run by the Australian government, this is more like an on-line job centre than an employment agency.

VISAS AND PERMITS

**Things have changed dramatically since the "populate or perish" days after the Second World War, when Australia operated a mass immigration policy. Nowadays, Australia's immigration policy is more concerned with keeping people out. Emigrating to Australia is a long, complicated and expensive affair, and success is far from guaranteed.
For the majority of people looking for permanent residency in Australia, there are two main routes: sponsorship or application under the Skilled Migration Program.**

● SPONSORSHIP

If you are to be sponsored by an employer, the employer must show that they've been unable to fill the position with an Australian resident. There are various categories of family sponsorship, such as Australian residents sponsoring their parents, parents sponsoring children, and even sibling sponsorship. You can apply for a spouse visa if you're married to (or live in a de facto relationship with) an Australian. If your partner is applying for residency through his or her job, you can be included automatically in that application.

● SKILLED MIGRATION PROGRAM

If you don't have a sponsor, you can apply under the Skilled Migration Program, otherwise known as the "points system" because points are allocated to factors such as profession, age and education. The greater the shortage of workers of a particular profession, the higher the number of points awarded. Check your profession against the Skilled Occupations List. If it's not on the list, you won't be able to apply under the system. You also need to be under 45 years of age. The cost to apply under this system is $1,845 (£743), and you'll have to pay for medicals, police character checks and other expenses. This is non-refundable, so you should be absolutely certain of your chances before going ahead. You can obtain further information from (and even submit your application to) the Australian Immigration Service website (www.immi.gov.au). There are also a number of private visa consultants who offer a free online consultation – see page 184 for some useful contacts. You can lodge your application directly with the Australian Immigration Service, but you're likely to get a faster and easier ride if you use an Australian immigration lawyer. He or she will be able to advise you of the best way forward in your particular case, and will be able to assist, even if you don't immediately qualify. Once you've been awarded residency, you must move to Australia within a certain time, and spend at least two of the following four years in the country. Then you're eligible to apply for full Australian citizenship.

Finding a home

Australian property is generally excellent value and the market is currently booming in all the major hotspots

AUSTRALIA HAS A HIGH RATE OF HOME ownership at about 70 per cent. Sydney is the most expensive place, followed by Melbourne and the other state capitals.

Renting

It can be tricky to find good rental accommodation due to the high proportion of home ownership; the rental market tends to centre round apartments. Most properties are let through agents, who charge a fee of a week's rent for a six-month lease and two weeks' rent for a year's lease. You also have to pay a bond of four weeks' rent, which is held by the Rental Bond Board. You get this back on leaving, less any damages.

Buying

For those staying long-term, buying is the cheaper option. Once you've found a property, you can secure it with a "holding deposit". This is fully refundable should you decide not to go ahead. When you sign the Contract of Sale, you have to pay a ten per cent deposit. This is forfeited should you pull out. Once the contract is signed, the searches take place. If they are satisfactory, contracts are exchanged and the sale goes through. In some states, there is a "cooling off" period during which you can pull out within a few days of exchange of contracts.

The associated costs of buying a property – including Stamp Duty, Land Transfer Registration, legal fees and mortgage fees – vary from state to state, but generally, the more expensive the property, the higher the fees will be. Reckon on adding around five per cent to the property price.

Restrictions on foreign buyers

For non-residents or temporary residents, approval to buy a property must be granted by the Foreign Investment Board. Those granted full residency have no such restrictions.

Property tax

Property tax is called Council Rates in Australia and is charged by local authorities for local services. The amount can vary enormously. In some states, Land Tax is payable, based on the value of the land, disregarding any buildings on it. ●

ABOVE: A bustling Brisbane market

TAXES

In order to work in Australia, you will need a Tax File Number. Applying for this is a simple process that can be done online from the UK once you have been granted residency. You can access the website at:
http://ato.gov.au/individuals/content.asp?doc=/content/38760.htm
You can also apply by post. You'll need to supply an address for the information to be sent to. Forms are available from tax offices in Australia, or online from the Australian Taxation Office website (although if you can get online, you really ought to register online, too!).

There is a scalable income-tax system in Australia. For the year 2004/2005, the tax breakdown was as follows:

Up to $6,000	**0%**
$6,000 to $21,600	**17% ($0.17 per dollar over $6,000)**
$21,601 to $58,000	**30% ($2,652 + $0.30 per dollar over $21,600)**
$58,001 to $70,000	**42% ($13,572 + $0.42 per dollar over $58,000)**
Over $70,000	**47% ($18,612 + $0.47 per dollar over $70,000)**

In addition to this, there is a Medicare levy on taxable income to support Australia's version of the National Health Service. This is typically 1.5% of taxable income, although this varies depending on your circumstances. Tax is paid at source by your employer, but work-related deductions can reduce this figure. The total payable on a salary of $62,000 (£25,000) would be: tax $15,252; Medicare $930 = $16,182 or 26% of income. For non-residents, there is no $6,000 tax-free threshold, but there's no requirement to pay the Medicare levy.

AVERAGE RENTAL/SALE PRICES

Hotspot	2-bed apartment rentals	2-bed apartment sales	4-bed house sales
Sydney	$1,800 (£738)	$420K (£172K)	$694K (£285K)
Melbourne	$1,260 (£523)	$294K (£122K)	$486K (£202K)
Brisbane	$1,440 (£598)	$336K (£139K)	$555K (£230K)

Employment hotspots

From Sydney to Perth, each Australian city has something different and exciting to offer, and you are never far away from a beach...

1 Sydney

Founded as a penal colony in 1788, Sydney has become a cultured and cosmopolitan city with a magnificent harbour dominated by its opera house. It's responsible for 25 to 30 per cent of Australia's economy.

Jobs vary from bar work to banking or finance. There has been a 55 per cent increase in the number of people employed in legal and accounting sectors, IT has skyrocketed and the tourism industry is booming.

Due to land shortage and the rising demand for homes, the city is a low–risk centre for property investors. Trends have turned towards apartments over houses, so family homes are difficult to find and expensive. Property in the city centre and inner city suburbs is 40 per cent cheaper than that on the coast.

KEY FACTS
- **Population:** 4,000,000
- **Airport:** Sydney Airport Corporation Limited, Tel: 00 61 296 679 111
- **Medical:** Sydney Private Hospital, Tel: 00 61 297 970 555
- **Schools:** Abbotsford Public School, Tel: 00 61 971 6220/9713 6419
- **Rentals:** Healthy market driven by long-term rentals and safe investment ▧ Buy-to-let market is strong
- **Pros:** Number one Australian city for investors and developers ▧ Packed with bars, restaurants, clubs, museums and galleries ■ Plenty of jobs available in different fields
- **Cons:** Property is the most expensive in Australia ▧ Expensive for family living.

2 Melbourne

This is Australia's second largest city and the most European. Popular areas are the Riverside and Bayside, and there are new

ABOVE: **From Sydney Harbour Bridge there are magnificent views of the bay**

developments at Southgate, New Quay and the Docklands. This is a sociable city renowned for its sport and culture, with numerous galleries, museums, gardens, cafés and bars.

In 2001, business investment in Melbourne grew at twice the national rate. Aerospace industries, car-manufacturing, financial services, IT and tele-communications are all strong industries here. Television and film production is prominent.

Apartments are over-supplied and more expensive than houses, so investment may not be the best option at present. For those relocating, property is affordable and 30–35 per cent cheaper than in Sydney.

KEY FACTS
- **Population:** 3,200,000
- **Airport:** Melbourne International Airport, Tel: 00 61 321 723 6227
- **Medical:** The Royal Melbourne Hospital, Tel: 00 61 393 872 211
- **Schools:** Melbourne High School, Tel: 00 61 870 368 4500
- **Rentals:** Long-term rentals are the trend ▧ Demand is in apartments

- **Pros:** Houses are cheaper than apartments ▧ Unemployment rates are low
- **Cons:** Apartments market is unstable and the bottom may fall out of it soon ▧ Jobs market is fairly restrictive, with seasonal work offering some of the main opportunities.

3 Brisbane

Brisbane was created in the early 19th century as an alternative penal colony to Sydney. It is now Australia's third largest city with a large expat community. It is a relaxed city, and is an easy place to find temporary work.

A wide range of jobs are available, especially in IT. Manufacturing has grown by 2.3 per cent, and opportunities are arising in aviation and biotechnology. The tourist sector is healthy – the nearby Gold Coast is a tourist magnet.

Housing costs are 20 per cent cheaper than in Sydney, and 96 per cent of properties are occupied. Analysts think prices will rise by up to 50 per cent over the next four years.

KEY FACTS
- **Population:** 1,500,000
- **Airport:** Brisbane Airport, Tel: 00 61 734 063 000
- **Medical:** Royal Brisbane Hospital, Tel: 00 61 732 538 222
- **Schools:** Brisbane Grammar School, Tel: 00 61 738 345 200
- **Rentals:** Demand is high for long-term rentals because this is Australia's fastest growing city ▧ Short-term rentals market is not healthy ▧ Lettings market is primarily domestic
- **Pros:** Jobs market is diverse and the economy is expanding ▧ Property is affordable and is constantly increasing in price ▧ Plenty of jobs available
- **Cons:** Climate is quite wet for Australia ▧ The city is a jumble of old and new with no real structure and many high rise buildings.

OTHER HOTSPOTS
- **Perth:** Recognised as offering property 40 per cent cheaper than Sydney, Perth remains one of the cheapest entry points into the Australian market
- **Adelaide:** Low cost of living and cheap real estate. ●

AUSTRALIA

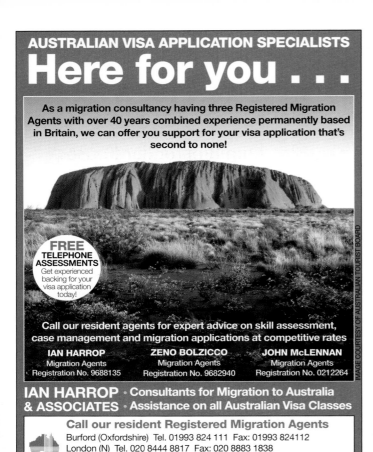

Property price guide

With stunning harbourside apartments and luxury multimillion-dollar houses, Australia is ideal for the affluent investor

APARTMENTS FOR RENT

Riverside apartments with fabulous views of the harbour

$1,800 PER WEEK

2-BED SYDNEY

£740 PER WEEK
- Fully furnished ✔
- Pool ✔
- Parking ✔   CODE RAY

$2,280 PER WEEK

2-BED SYDNEY

£910 PER WEEK
- Fully furnished ✔
- Pool ✘
- Parking ✘   CODE RAY

$2,700 PER WEEK

2-BED SYDNEY

£1,100 PER WEEK
- Fully furnished ✔
- Pool ✔
- Parking ✔   CODE RAY

$3,800 PER WEEK

3-BED SYDNEY

£1,520 PER WEEK
- Fully furnished ✘
- Pool ✔
- Parking ✔   CODE RAY

APARTMENTS FOR SALE

Modern waterfront apartments with fittings

$169,000

1-BED SYDNEY

£70,125
- Fully furnished ✔
- Pool ✘
- Parking ✔   CODE RAY

$199,000

2-BED, SYDNEY

£82,573
- Fully furnished ✔
- Pool ✘
- Parking ✔   CODE RAY

$619,000

2-BED SYDNEY

£254,000
- Fully furnished ✘
- Pool ✔
- Parking ✔   CODE RAY

$675,000

2-BED SYDNEY

£277,000
- Fully furnished ✘
- Pool ✘
- Parking ✔   CODE RAY

HOUSES FOR SALE

Luxurious homes ranging from affordable to costly

$695,000

4-BED SYDNEY

£285,000
- Fully furnished ✘
- Pool ✘
- Parking ✔   CODE RAY

$1,300,000

4-BED SYDNEY

£520,000
- Fully furnished ✘
- Pool ✘
- Parking ✔   CODE RAY

$2,700,000

4-BED SYDNEY

£1,080,000
- Fully furnished ✘
- Pool ✔
- Parking ✔   CODE RAY

$5,000,000

PLOT OF LAND BRISBANE

£2,000,000
- Fully furnished ✘
- Pool ✘
- Parking ✔   CODE RAY

AUSTRALIA

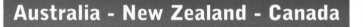

The Benelux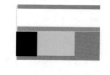

Small yet prosperous, with a high standard of living

FACT BOX

BELGIUM
- **Population** 10,348,276
- **Capital** Brussels
- **Economic growth rate** 1.1%
- **GDP per capita** US$29,100

LUXEMBOURG
- **Population** 462,690
- **Capital** Luxembourg City
- **Economic growth rate** 1.2%
- **GDP per capita** US$55,100

NETHERLANDS
- **Population** 16,381,199
- **Capital** Amsterdam
- **Economic growth rate** -0.7%
- **GDP per capita** US$28,600

FACT FILES

■■■ BELGIUM

AREA	30,528km²
MERCER COST OF LIVING	82.1
LIFE EXPECTANCY	78.44 years
LITERACY	98%
GOVERNMENT	Constitutional Monarchy
CURRENCY	Euro (€)
EXCHANGE RATE	€1 = £0.69; £1 = €1.45
LANGUAGES	Dutch (Flemish), French, German

■■■ LUXEMBOURG

AREA	2,586km²
MERCER COST OF LIVING	84.3
LIFE EXPECTANCY	87.58 years
LITERACY	100%
GOVERNMENT	Constitutional Monarchy
CURRENCY	Euro (€)
EXCHANGE RATE	€1 = £0.69; £1 = €1.45
LANGUAGES	Lëtzebuergesch, German, French

■■■ NETHERLANDS

AREA	41,526km²
MERCER COST OF LIVING	88.1
LIFE EXPECTANCY	78.68 years
LITERACY	99%
GOVERNMENT	Constitutional Monarchy
CURRENCY	Euro (€)
EXCHANGE RATE	€1 = £0.69; £1 = €1.45
LANGUAGES	Dutch, Frisian

CLIMATE

BRUSSELS		LONDON	BRUSSELS		LONDON
6	Dec	7	88	Dec	81
9	Nov	10	75	Nov	78
15	Oct	14	83	Oct	70
21	Sept	19	63	Sept	65
22	Aug	21	80	Aug	62
23	July	22	95	July	59
22	June	20	76	June	58
18	May	17	55	May	57
14	April	13	60	April	56
10	March	10	53	March	64
7	Feb	7	61	Feb	72
4	Jan	6	66	Jan	77

Average monthly temperature °C   Average monthly rainfall mm

Living in the Benelux

The countries of Belgium, Luxembourg and the Netherlands make up the economic union known as the Benelux

BELGIUM

SANDWICHED BETWEEN FRANCE, GERMANY and the Netherlands is the small, densely populated country of Belgium. The south consists of the Ardennes uplands, while the north is mainly flat and agricultural, and is where Brussels and the large city of Antwerp merge into a vast urban area. Belgium has a mild, wet climate with cool summers and winters. It's politically stable, although demands for further autonomy from the Wallonia (French) and Flanders (Flemish) people often cause political friction. The economy is also stable and GDP growth picked up in 2004, but high unemployment is a problem. Belgium has an average crime rate, although this rises considerably in the main cities.

Healthcare facilities are among the best in the world. Foreign employees who make contributions to the social security fund qualify for subsidised treatment – visits to doctors are reimbursed by around 75 per cent and hospital treatment has a daily fee. Private medical care is also excellent but expensive, so insurance is essential.

State education is of a high standard, free for residents and compulsory for children aged from 6 to 18 (from 16, part-time education is an option). Brussels is home to several prestigious international and European schools. Further-education standards are high – the country has eight universities.

The Belgians are proud of their cuisine and "homegrown" dishes include the internationally famous mussels, other seafood and chips (Belgium claims to have invented them), not to mention the delicious chocolate and beer.

LUXEMBOURG

EUROPE'S SMALLEST, BUT RICHEST, COUNTRY lies between southern Belgium, France and western Germany. It has wooded hills in the north and flat agricultural plains in the south, where the capital, Luxembourg City, is situated. Luxembourg has a temperate climate with mild winters and warm summers. It is a stable country both politically and economically, unemployment is among the EU's lowest and the country enjoys a very high standard of living with a very low crime rate.

"The Netherlands is politically stable, with a strong economy, making it one of Europe's most prosperous countries"

Healthcare facilities are excellent: state healthcare provisions are included under social security contributions, which are compulsory for all employees, and most treatment is reimbursed. Private healthcare is also available, but you'll need private insurance to cover the expense.

State education standards are very high and education is compulsory from ages 4 to 15. The capital has three international schools and three higher-education institutes but no universities.

BELOW: **The stunning Bourscheid Castle in the Luxembourg Ardennes region**

© DUTCH TOURIST BOARD

ABOVE: Amsterdam's canals look stunning when they are lit up at night

Food and drink are taken very seriously in Luxembourg, which boasts one of the world's highest concentrations of Michelin stars. Traditional cuisine consists mainly of country food, such as thick soups and game, and modern dishes are strongly influenced by France and Germany.

THE NETHERLANDS

THIS SMALL, BUT VERY DENSELY POPULATED country has borders with Belgium, Germany and the North Sea, and generally consists of flat agricultural land, mostly reclaimed from the sea. Most of the population lives in the urban area known as The Randstat, which stretches from Amsterdam to the huge port of Rotterdam further south. The climate is very changeable, with high rainfall and cold winters.

The Netherlands is politically stable with a traditionally strong economy, making it one of Europe's most prosperous countries. It also enjoys low unemployment and inflation, but the country did suffer a recession in 2003. There's generally a low incidence of crime, although racism is on the increase, bringing the ideal of Dutch tolerance into question.

Healthcare facilities are very good, both in the private and public sectors, although the self-employed and employees whose income exceeds €30,700 (£21,200) a month aren't eligible for state healthcare and must have private insurance.

Dutch education is one of the best in Europe and is compulsory for children from 5 to 18 (part-time from 16). State schools are free for all residents, but you have to pay for extras. Two-thirds of the school population attend private schools. There are several international schools in The Hague and Amsterdam, and Dutch universities are internationally renowned.

The Netherlands, one of the world's biggest food exporters, specialises in traditional cuisine such as nourishing "winter warmers" based around beans and meat, and foreign dishes, including the acclaimed Indonesian Rice Table, all washed down with excellent Dutch beer.

Importing pets into the Benelux

All dogs and cats require microchip identification, an up-to-date rabies vaccination and an EU pet's passport, issued by Local Veterinary Inspectors (LVI) in the UK and by registered vets elsewhere. Dogs must be registered with a local vet in Belgium or the local authorities in the Netherlands. ●

TRAVEL FILE

BELGIUM
Belgium is well served by daily flights to Brussels (Zaventem, which is 12km from the city). Travel from London, Bristol, Manchester, Southampton or Birmingham with **British Airways** (www.ba.com; 0870 850 9850) or use **SN Brussels Airlines** (www.flysn.com, 0870 735 2345) from London, Birmingham, Bristol, Manchester or Newcastle. **Ryanair** (www.ryanair.com; 0871 246 0000) flies from Dublin and Glasgow to Brussels Charleroi, which is 50km from Brussels. **VLM** (Flemish Airways, www.vlm-airlines.com, 0207 476 6677) flies regularly from London City Airport to Antwerp.

The **Eurostar** (www.eurostar.co.uk; 0870 518 6186) travels to Brussels, and is one way to get a car to Belgium. The drive from Calais to Brussels takes about two hours.

An overnight trip on a car ferry from Hull to Zeebrugge is available from **P&O Ferries** (www.poferries.com; 0870 598 0333). Alternatively, a Seacat from Dover to Calais is available from **Hoverspeed** (www.hoverspeed.co.uk, 0870 240 8070).

LUXEMBOURG
Luxembourg's airport has flights to most European capitals. **Luxair** (www.luxair.lu, 0800 3899 443) operates from London's City and Heathrow airports, Dublin and Manchester. **British Airways** flies from Gatwick and **VLM** from London City Airport.

Luxembourg has good rail connections with the rest of Europe, including the **Eurostar** service from London.

Public transport services are excellent. The trains (www.cfl.lu) and buses connect most of the country with the capital. Roads are good but busy, and traffic jams are unavoidable in the capital. To compensate, petrol is among the cheapest in the EU. EU licence holders must register their licence with the traffic authorities after a year, and non-EU licence holders must exchange their licence for a Luxembourg one.

THE NETHERLANDS
Amsterdam's Schiphol Airport has links with most major cities. Daily flights from several UK airports are run by **KLM** (www.klm.com, 08705 074 074), **British Airways** and **Easyjet** (www.easyjet.com, 0871 244 2366). **Ryanair** flies from London Stansted and Dublin to Eindhoven.

The country can be easily reached by road or rail from neighbouring countries, and ferry services run from Harwich to the Hook of Holland (**Stenaline**: www.stenaline.co.uk, 08705 707 070), Newcastle to Amsterdam (**DFDS Seaways**: www.dfdsseaways.co.uk, 08705 333 111) and Hull to Rotterdam (**P&O Ferries**).

A comprehensive network of trains (www.ns.nl), buses and trams links the main cities. Holders of EU driving licences can drive in the Netherlands for up to ten years, but other nationalities need to exchange their licence for a Dutch one and possibly take a driving test.

THE BENELUX

Who moves there?

A high standard of living, combined with excellent salaries, makes the prosperous Benelux countries an attractive option

"Between them, Belgium and the Netherlands are home to all the main EU institutions"

IN COMMON WITH MOST EU COUNTRIES, THE Benelux has large foreign populations – eight per cent in Belgium, nearly ten per cent in the Netherlands and a massive 40 per cent in Luxembourg. Although there are large numbers of migrants from countries outside the EU (for example from Surinam to the Netherlands and Morocco to Belgium), the Benelux is home to large populations of EU migrants, which in Luxembourg's case constitute the majority of foreigners. However, unlike Germany or Spain, the Benelux has relatively few UK residents: Belgium's EU foreign population consists mainly of other Benelux nationals, French and Italians. UK nationals (around 26,000) account for less than three per cent of foreigners. Luxembourg's 148,700 EU foreign residents are mainly from the other Benelux countries, France and Germany

with just 4,600 UK nationals living and working there. Figures for UK nationals working in the Netherlands are higher (around 76,000), but still constitute only about five per cent of foreigners. Immigration to the Benelux countries from the UK has remained steady over the last few years.

Who moves there?

Given that the main reason for relocation is employment, most expats are professionals, often recent graduates, although the largest group of UK nationals in Belgium is within the 30–54 age group. Most relocators to the Benelux do so in order to gain work experience in an international environment – between them Belgium and Luxembourg are home to all the main EU institutions, providing employment for thousands of expats, and few jobs can be more international than working for an entity representing 25 countries! A substantial number of expats are employed in the European headquarters of NATO in Brussels, in multinational companies that have their headquarters in the Netherlands or Brussels, and in Luxembourg, one of the world's financial capitals.

Why move there?

Reasons for moving to the Benelux are usually connected with employment, and all three countries offer high standards of living and excellent salaries. Luxembourg tops the EU salary ranks, the Netherlands comes sixth and Belgium ninth. Luxembourg and the Netherlands have very low crime rates.

The Benelux countries are easy to get to, and popping back to the UK for a weekend is straightforward. Transport infrastructure within the countries is excellent, which makes commuting to and from work relatively easy. The central location of the countries is also an attraction, and most other EU capitals are only a two-hour flight away, or less.

The Benelux countries have very cosmopolitan societies and are used to welcoming foreigners, so it's relatively easy to make friends and socialise. English is widely spoken, particularly in the Netherlands and Brussels, although you need to speak local languages for most jobs. ●

LEFT: Knuedler Square, Luxembourg City, where the statue of Luxembourg's liberal ruler, William II, sits

Working in the Benelux

From the financial sector to the EU institutions, the Benelux countries offer a range of job opportunities, particularly for those with language skills

■ ECONOMY

Despite their small size, the Benelux countries are among the world's most prosperous, and Luxembourg frequently tops the world's richest country rankings.

Belgium's successful economy is based mainly on its strong import and export markets and very high productivity. Growth during 2004 was 2.7 per cent, although predictions for 2005 and 2006 are lower.

The tiny country of Luxembourg owes its wealth to its heavy industry (mainly steel and coal), although these industries are in decline and the financial and services sectors are largely responsible for the country's consistent growth.

The Netherlands entered recession in 2003, and although figures for 2004 were better, growth is expected to remain low during 2005 and 2006. However, the Netherlands generally has a stable economy supported largely by its huge export market and ability to attract foreign investment.

■ LABOUR MARKET

Opportunities for employment are good in Belgium, where there is a range of opportunities in the EU and NATO organisations. Unemployment is eight per cent (2004), although there are huge regional variations. Luxembourg has a buoyant labour market and there's a constant demand for foreigners. Reports suggest it's taking several months to find a job in the Netherlands, and salaries have remained static. During 2004, unemployment rose to 4.7 per cent, although this is low compared with the EU average (8.8 per cent in 2004), and one of the lowest rates in Europe for the under 25s.

■ JOB OPPORTUNITIES AND KEY INDUSTRIES

The Benelux offers a range of job opportunities for expats, particularly graduates and linguists. EU institutions have plenty of vacancies in translation and administration work. The financial

ABOVE: Amsterdam enjoys an exciting social scene

sector is booming in all three countries, and jobs are available in banking, auditing and investment funds as well as the related insurance sector. Luxembourg has perhaps the best opportunities, and ten per cent of its workforce is in finance.

Graduate starting salaries range from €19–23,000 (£13–16,000) in Belgium, €23–35,000 (£16–24,000) in the Netherlands and €42–60,000 (£29–41,000) in Luxembourg. Key industries are: **Belgium**: tourism (Flanders), IT, financial management and services; **Luxembourg**: finance, steel, aluminium and services; **the Netherlands**: chemicals, engineering, finance, food processing and technology.

■ FINDING A JOB

The best route is through specialist recruitment agencies and job centres and by visiting companies in person with your CV. Networking is key in the Netherlands, where personal recommendation is often your best bet. Self-employment is possible, but red tape can be complicated, especially in Belgium.

■ LANGUAGE REQUIREMENTS

English is widely spoken, but a knowledge of the local language(s) is essential and fluency in at least French or German is a must for job-seekers – your language skills will be tested at interview.

■ BUSINESS ETIQUETTE

Punctuality is important and, except in the Netherlands, business is conducted formally. English will probably be spoken in the Netherlands, but don't count on it elsewhere. ●

VISAS AND PERMITS

● EU NATIONALS

No visa or work permit is needed. Stays longer than three months require a residence permit. In Belgium and Luxembourg you must apply for this at the local town hall within three months of arrival. In the Netherlands, apply at the local Civil Affairs Department (GBA) within three to five days of arrival.

● NON-EU NATIONALS

Both a visa and work permit are necessary for stays over three months. These must be obtained before arrival in the country. Non-EU nationals (except those from Australia, Canada, New Zealand and the USA) who plan to relocate to the Netherlands also need a temporary residence permit (MW) before arrival.

■ USEFUL WEBSITES

Belgium:
www.vacature.com; www.jobat.be
Luxembourg:
www.luxjob.lu
Netherlands:
www.cwinet.nl; www.werk.nl; www.rwi.nl

THE BENELUX

© DUTCH TOURIST BOARD

Finding a home

Although city rental prices are high, the property market is buoyant in all three countries, and you can always commute from France or Germany

R ENTED ACCOMMODATION IS THE BEST SHORT-TERM OPTION, but it isn't always easy to find. It is usually unfurnished – apartments in towns and cities, and houses in rural areas.

Renting
Belgium and Luxembourg have a good supply of rental property, but the Netherlands, where property ownership is low, has a huge shortfall of around 100,000 properties. High-quality furnished apartments are difficult to find and unfurnished means empty, with no kitchen appliances or fittings. Rental accommodation can be found via estate agents (the best option in the Netherlands), local newspapers or word of mouth. Expect to pay a deposit (three

© LUXEMBOURG TOURIST BOARD

months' rent in Belgium, two months' in the Netherlands one month's in Luxembourg) and sign a contract and an inventory. You should be careful of binding three-year leases in Belgium.

Rentals in the main cities – and everywhere in Luxembourg – are pricey. Many people rent somewhere in France (Thionville is popular) or Germany (eg Trier).

Buying
The property market is healthy – Luxembourg and the Netherlands both had some of the highest price rises in the EU over the four years from 1999 to 2003, although the Dutch market is currently less buoyant and prices have risen by less than two per cent in 2003 and 2004. Belgium is one of the few countries in the EU where prices continued to rise in 2004. The Benelux is generally a buyer's market, but Luxembourg properties sell quickly.

Look for property in estate agents and local papers, and word of mouth works well in Luxembourg. Prices in the main towns and capitals are high, although cheaper than in London. Purchase procedure is straightforward and you generally sign a pre-contract, pay around ten per cent deposit and complete before a notary at least one month later. Beware binding agreements in Belgium where the pre-contract virtually makes you the owner of the property, so include conditional clauses if necessary.

Mortgages are available and interest rates are low (variable rates start at around 3.5 per cent and fixed rates at around 4.5 per cent). Loans typically constitute 80 per cent of the property's value over a period of 20 to 30 years. Set-up fees and expenses can be high.

Restrictions on foreign buyers
Foreigners can buy property with no restrictions.

Property taxes
Belgium: allow for a massive 17 per cent of the price, which includes registration tax at 12.5 per cent (ten per cent in Flanders). Property tax based on the rateable value is payable at national (1.25 to 2.5 per cent), regional and local levels.

Luxembourg: budget for at least seven per cent of the price including six per cent property registration tax and one per cent transcription tax. Annual property taxes range from 0.7 to 1.5 per cent of the rateable value and you may be liable for annual net wealth tax (0.5 per cent).

Netherlands: purchase costs account for 10 to 12 per cent of the price including six per cent transfer tax. Annual property taxes vary but average around 0.5 per cent of rateable value. ●

LEFT: **Luxembourg City is a World Heritage site**

TAXES

● **BELGIUM**
Income tax: 0 per cent (on income under €5,570) to 50 per cent (on income over €29,740). **National insurance:** around 13 per cent of gross monthly salary. **Capital gains tax:** None.

● **LUXEMBOURG**
Income tax: 0 to 38 per cent. **National insurance:** around 10 per cent of gross monthly salary. **Capital gains tax:** income tax rates apply; main residences are exempt.

● **THE NETHERLANDS**
Income tax: 36.35 to 52 per cent (tax credits are available). **National insurance:** high – amounts depend on your age and income level. **Capital gains tax:** flat rate of 25 per cent.

AVERAGE RENTAL/SALE PRICES

Hotspot	2-bed apartment rentals	2-bed apartment sales	4-bed house sales
Brussels	€1,340 (£924)	€267K (£184K)	€530K (£366K)
Luxembourg City	€1,230 (£848)	€288K (£199K)	€506K (£349K)
Amsterdam	€1,250 (£862)	€229K (£158K)	€357K (£246K)

THE BENELUX

Employment hotspots

Enjoy a multicultural lifestyle in the three capital cities of the Benelux – Brussels, Luxembourg City and Amsterdam

1 Brussels

A city with a notable history, Brussels is the home of NATO and the EU, which has brought a significant multilingual expat community to the city. It is one of the greenest capital cities in Europe, with a well-preserved 17th-century centre, top-flight architecture and good cuisine.

There is a range of job opportunities here. As well as the EU and NATO, there are many international trade and finance companies, and lots of possibilities for work in the service sector. Brussels has a huge number of banks, a stock exchange, many insurance companies and publishing houses. A range of conferences and trade fairs are held in the city, and tourism is growing.

There has been a property price boom in Brussels. The current economic climate is good and interest rates are low, which has sparked more interest in property. Buying a property is expensive, with 21 per cent VAT payable on new housing, and 10–12 per cent stamp duty.

KEY FACTS
- **Population:** 140,000
- **Airport:** Brussels Airport, Tel: 00 32 2 753 7753
- **Medical:** University Clinic St Luc, Tel: 00 32 2 764 1085
- **Schools:** The British International School of Brussels, Tel: 00 32 2 736 8981
- **Rentals:** Strong long and short-term rentals market ■ The market is geared to deal with foreigners
- **Pros:** Very good standard of living
- Excellent food and bars
- Large number of jobs for foreign workers, and many postings with UK

companies and the UK government
- **Cons:** High cost of living
- Property is expensive.

2 Luxembourg City

A role model for international finance, Luxembourg City is the headquarters of the European Court of Justice and European Investment Bank. It is surrounded by magnificent historical fortifications and beautiful scenery. The city has diverse cultures and languages, and an excellent quality of life.

Luxembourg is reliant on immigrant and cross-border workers and work is easy to find, but you must be able to speak French or German. Jobs in banking and insurance are plentiful, and ICT and tourism provide a number of positions. The city is home to the satellite operator SES and the electronic service providers AOL, Amazon and Apple ITunes.

Luxembourg City has some of the highest house prices in Europe. The rate of home ownership is 65 per cent, but it can be difficult to find property.

KEY FACTS
- **Population:** 81,800
- **Airport:** Findel, Tel: 00 35 22 464 2001
- **Medical:** Centre Hospitalier de

Luxembourg, Tel 00 35 24 4111
- **Schools:** International School of Luxembourg, Tel: 00 35 226 0440
- St George's International School, Tel: 00 35 24 23224
- **Rentals:** Rental property is affordable, if difficult to find
- **Pros:** French, German and the official language Lëtzebuergesch are all spoken ■ Spectacular scenery
- **Cons:** Property is expensive.

3 Amsterdam

Gabled houses, cobbled streets, humpback bridges and a network of tree-lined canals all contribute to the atmosphere of Amsterdam. Recent prosperity has not changed the easygoing and liberal attitudes of the residents, who are welcoming towards visitors. The prime position, stable economy and relaxed attitudes are what attracts many expats to the city.

The city is becoming an international business centre. It has easy access to the major European markets, and IBM, Sony and Canon have their European headquarters here. There are job opportunities in banking, electronics, digital media, agriculture, publishing and tourism. The city also has a diamond cutting and polishing industry, as well as huge fashion and flower sectors.

Amsterdam has an acute shortage of housing and prices are high. There are a number of new residential neighbourhoods springing up around the city.

KEY FACTS
- **Population:** 735,328
- **Airport:** Amsterdam Airport Schiphol, Tel: 00 31 20 601 4530
- **Medical:** Sint Lucas Ziekenhuis, Tel: 020 510 8911 ■ Slotervaart Ziekenhuis, Tel: 00 31 20 512 9333
- **Schools:** International School of Amsterdam, Tel: 00 31 20 347 1111
- British School in the Netherlands, Tel: 00 31 71 560 2251
- **Rentals:** Prices can be high
- Property is in demand
- **Pros:** Filled with theatres, museums and galleries ■ Bikes and trams provide eco-friendly transport
- **Cons:** Renowned for its "coffee shops" and red light district, areas where you should be alert for crime.

OTHER HOTSPOTS
- **Rotterdam:** The principal trading city of the Netherlands and the largest port in the world, Rotterdam provides many jobs. The housing market is stable and property prices are rising.
- **Antwerp:** A commercial and financial city, centre of the diamond industry and one of the world's busiest ports, Antwerp has a selection of job opportunities. Housing is reasonably priced. ●

THE BENELUX

RIGHT: **The town of Ehnen, located in the Moselle Valley**

Property price guide

Property in the Benelux countries may be expensive, but homes are comfortable, chic and spacious

PROPERTIES FOR RENT

From single room apartments to spacious family homes

€765 PER MONTH

STUDIO LUXEMBOURG, L.

£530 PER MONTH
- Fully furnished ✔
- Pool ✘
- Parking ✘   **CODE** ICR

€950 PER MONTH

2-BED ESCH SUR ALZETTE, L.

£655 PER MONTH
- Fully furnished ✔
- Pool ✘
- Parking ✔   **CODE** ICR

€975 PER MONTH

2-BED ROTTERDAM, NL.

£670 PER MONTH
- Fully furnished ✘
- Pool ✘
- Parking ✔   **CODE** HOL

€1,200 PER MONTH

2-BED ANTWERP, B.

£830 PER MONTH
- Fully furnished ✔
- Pool ✘
- Parking ✔   **CODE** ZKI

APARTMENTS FOR SALE

Attractive and traditional-style city-centre apartments with all mod cons

€139,000

2-BED MAASMECHELEN, B.

£95,900
- Fully furnished ✘
- Pool ✘
- Parking ✔   **CODE** ZKI

€140,000

2-BED BERCHEM, B.

£96,600
- Part furnished ✔
- Pool ✘
- Parking ✔   **CODE** ZKI

€174,500

1-BED AMSTERDAM, NL.

£120,300
- Fully furnished ✘
- Pool ✘
- Parking ✔   **CODE** MAK

€179,000

2-BED WORMERVEER, NL.

£123,400
- Fully furnished ✘
- Pool ✘
- Parking ✔   **CODE** MAK

HOUSES FOR SALE

Benelux houses are large and spacious, and excellent for family and friends

€250,000

4-BED TIENEN, B.

£172,400
- Fully furnished ✘
- Pool ✘
- Parking ✔   **CODE** ZKI

€294,000

3-BED AMSTERDAM, NL.

£202,800
- Fully furnished ✘
- Pool ✘
- Parking ✔   **CODE** MAK

€330,000

5-BED BERTEM, B.

£227,600
- Fully furnished ✘
- Pool ✘
- Parking ✔   **CODE** ZKI

€415,000

3-BED BELLEGEM, B.

£286,200
- Fully furnished ✘
- Pool ✘
- Parking ✔   **CODE** ZKI

THE BENELUX

For the more discerning buyer, the upper end of the Benelux market can offer traditional homes and apartments – an ideal investment

PROPERTIES FOR RENT

€**1,250** PER MONTH

3-BED MECHELEN, B.

£860 PER MONTH
- Part furnished ✔
- Pool ✘
- Parking ✔ **CODE** ZKI

€**1,400** PER MONTH

1-BED AMSTERDAM, NL.

£965 PER MONTH
- Fully furnished ✔
- Pool ✘
- Parking ✔ **CODE** HOL

€**1,575** PER MONTH

2-BED AMSTERDAM, NL.

£1,085 PER MONTH
- Fully furnished ✔
- Pool ✘
- Parking ✔ **CODE** HOL

€**1,850** PER MONTH

1-BED AMSTERDAM, NL.

£1,275 PER MONTH
- Fully furnished ✔
- Pool ✘
- Parking ✔ **CODE** HOL

APARTMENTS FOR SALE

€**218,000**

2-BED LUXEMBOURG, L.

£150,300
- Part furnished ✔
- Pool ✘
- Parking ✘ **CODE** ICR

€**320,000**

2-BED LUXEMBOURG, L.

£220,700
- Part furnished ✔
- Pool ✘
- Parking ✔ **CODE** ICR

€**425,000**

3-BED AMSTERDAM, NL.

£293,100
- Fully furnished ✘
- Pool ✘
- Parking ✔ **CODE** MAK

€**1,195,000**

5-BED AMSTERDAM, NL.

£824,138
- Fully furnished ✘
- Pool ✘
- Parking ✔ **CODE** MAK

HOUSES FOR SALE

€**529,000**

5-BED AMSTELVEEN, NL.

£364,800
- Fully furnished ✘
- Pool ✘
- Parking ✔ **CODE** MAK

€**575,000**

5-BED BERCHEM, B.

£396,600
- Fully furnished ✘
- Pool ✘
- Parking ✔ **CODE** ZKI

€**750,000**

4-BED LUXEMBOURG, L.

£517,200
- Fully furnished ✘
- Pool ✘
- Parking ✔ **CODE** ICR

€**950,000**

6-BED ROELFARENDSVEEN, NL.

£655,200
- Fully furnished ✘
- Pool ✘
- Parking ✔ **CODE** MAK

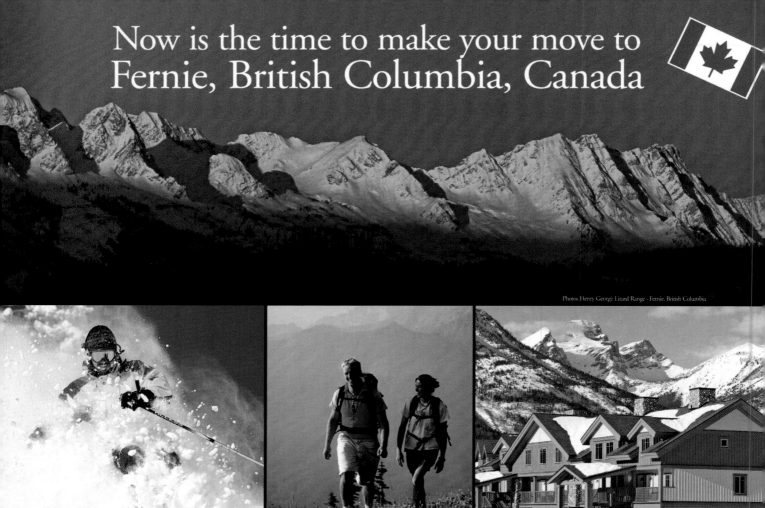

Now is the time to make your move to Fernie, British Columbia, Canada

Photos Henry Georgi: Lizard Range - Fernie, British Columbia

Have you heard about what is happening in Canada, and in particular, in the western most province, British Columbia?

More than ever before, the Rocky Mountains of British Columbia are playing host to an international host of investors, adventurers and vacationers. The areas mountains, lakes and valleys provide a beautiful landscape to experience a distinctive four season climate - perfect conditions for a four season resort. And so the dream begins...

People are coming here from all over the world, especially the UK and Australia, to set up business, invest in their future and live the Canadian lifestyle. The beautiful scenery, open spaces, resort homes and the friendly people is what draws people here - the publically funded health care, free public education and employment opportunities, is what keeps people here.

Fernie B.C. is a small mining town of 5000 residents that triples in the winter months because of the world-class skiing terrain and powder conditions. The spring, summer and fall plays host to golfing, hiking and mountain biking. People are employed in private businesses, resort operations, tourism, hospitality and many trades.

Make your dream come true by investing in your own 143 - 207 metre Timber-framed Chalet starting from L190,000 UKP. Check out www.pinnacle-ridge.com or call toll free 0.800.032.8836 for more information.

PINNACLE RIDGE
ALPINE RESORT
FERNIE, BC CANADA

0.800.032.8836
www.pinnacle-ridge.com

AHC Developments Ltd. Building Resort Homes with a Difference

Canada

Stunning scenery and a sense of space

FACT BOX

- **Population** 32,507,874
- **Population growth rate** 0.92%
- **Economic growth rate** 1.7%
- **Inflation rate** 2.8%
- **Capital** Ottawa
- **Hotspots** Toronto, Vancouver, Montreal
- **Average house price** (4-bed) $714,500
- **Average rental price** (2-bed) $1,810

Living in Canada

Outstanding natural beauty, vibrant cities and a high standard of living make Canada an attractive country to live in

FACT FILE

AREA	9,100,000km²
POPULATION	32,500,000
CAPITAL	Ottawa
LIFE EXPECTANCY	80 years
LITERACY	97%
GOVERNMENT	Confederation
GDP PER CAPITA	US$29,800
UNEMPLOYMENT RATE	7.0%
CURRENCY	Canadian dollar (CAN$)
EXCHANGE RATE	CAN$1 = £0.43;
	£1 = CAN$2.33
LANGUAGES	English, French

COST OF LIVING

PETROL (1L)	CAN$0.90
WINE (75CL)	CAN$8.00
MEAL (3-COURSE)	CAN$25.00
BEER (33CL BOTTLE)	CAN$1.50
LOAF OF BREAD (600G)	CAN$1.65
MILK (1L)	CAN$4.00

BELOW: **Newfoundland is a region of fjords, gorges, mountains and forests**

WITH A TOTAL LAND AREA MORE THAN 40 times that of the UK, Canada is the second largest country in the world. Because of its size, Canada's climate varies greatly from place to place. The north is within the Arctic Circle and is almost entirely ice-bound, yet the southernmost point is on the same latitude as sunny California. Canada's distinct seasons attract large numbers of tourists who come for the beautiful autumn scenes, the outdoor pursuits and wildlife in the summer, and of course the skiing in the winter. With ten provinces and three territories covering mountains, lakes, coast and prairie lands, Canada has something for everyone.

Politics and economy

The Canadian parliament is made up of the Senate and the House of Commons for which there are elections every five years. The government is run by a prime minister who is the leader of the majority party. The British monarch is head of state. The major issue in Canada is the relationship between the English- and French-speaking areas, which could result in a split in the federation.

Canada has high living standards and low interest rates. Unemployment is slightly higher than in the UK, but it has been falling steadily for more than a decade. In terms of industry, the service sector has been growing in importance and now accounts for around three out of every four jobs. International trade, especially with the USA, plays a large role.

Although crime rates rose in 2003 for the first time in a decade, it was mostly counterfeiting and minor offences, such as disturbing the peace, that caused the rise. Violent crime did not increase and the number of murder and drug crimes fell.

"Canada has high living standards and low interest rates, and unemployment figures have been falling steadily since 1994"

Education

In Canada, individual provinces or states run their own education, and there is no national ministry. However, the Council of Ministers of Education Canada (CMEC) acts as a forum for coordinating education nationally.

Primary and secondary education is free and is compulsory from the age of 5 to 7 until 16 to 18. The school year runs from September to June.

As well as publicly run schools, there are private schools and colleges. These must meet government standards but do not have to follow the curriculum. Home schooling is possible in all provinces.

There are 90 universities in Canada, 64 of which teach in English, 20 in French and six in a combination of both. Tuition fees must be paid at all colleges and universities except in Quebec, where residents may attend free. UK students must obtain a visa to study in Canada.

Healthcare

Canada has a publicly funded system for necessary healthcare, known as Medicare. It is provided on a needs rather than ability-to-pay basis.

In most provinces, there are some restrictions on what Medicare will cover, for example dental care, ambulances, prescription drugs and spectacles.

To have access to Canadian healthcare you will need a health insurance card, which is available from doctors and hospitals as well as immigration services. In some provinces, there is a waiting period during which time you will need to get short-term private medical insurance.

Preventative healthcare, such as immunisation, is key in Canada. Before becoming a permanent resident you will need to have a medical examination and may have to have another one when you arrive.

Food and drink

Canada has a multicultural society, which is reflected in its food and drink. Although there are no particular national dishes, there is an abundance of delicious seafood, including salmon, crab and scallops, along the coastal regions. Maple syrup is probably Canada's best known fare, and pancakes, steak, stew and clam chowder (a kind of thick seafood soup) are all popular foods.

ABOVE: **There are two million lakes in Canada, which cover 7.6 per cent of the Canadian landmass**

Expat communities

There are countless Internet sites that offer general information and specific advice and often include forums where you can chat to other expats.

Pets

Pets are allowed into the country but you will need a certificate to show that they have had a

ABOVE: **Some handiwork of the Inuit people, who make up 85 per cent of the population of Nunarut**

rabies injection within the previous 36 months. The Pet Travel Scheme (PET) could allow you to avoid quarantine. Seeing-eye dogs are allowed access without restriction both to the country itself and to shops, restaurants and other businesses.

Retirement and pensions

There are two main types of pension in Canada. The Old Age Security (OAS) pension is available to Canadian citizens and permanent residents. To get the full pension you must have been in the country for 40 years after the age of 18.

The Canadian and Quebec Pension Plans are a form of insurance to which you must contribute while working. The amount paid depends on the amount you have contributed. It is available at the age of 65 or at a reduced amount from 60 and can be claimed by anyone who has paid both contributions and income tax.

The Consolidated Arrangements on Social Security came into force in 1995. This means that certain periods of residence in Canada can be treated as if they were periods of contribution to the National Insurance scheme in the UK when determining whether that person is eligible for benefits. The Convention on Social Security came into force in 1998 and means that if you work temporarily in Canada you don't lose out under the UK pension scheme. ●

TRAVEL FILE

AIR The national airline is **Air Canada** (www.aircanada.com, 0871 220 1111). **Alitalia** (www.alitalia.com, 0870 544 8259) provides consistently low-cost flights and **British Airways** (www.britishairways.com, 0870 850 9850) also operates a range of flights. It is sometimes possible to get a cheap deal by flying via the USA. Seasonal price fluctuation is similar to that in the UK because Canadian holidays are the same; however, winter is just as popular as summer due to skiing. Although Canada has 13 international airports, Toronto is the main gateway, with daily flights from London, Glasgow and Manchester. There are also major airports at Montreal, Vancouver and Ottawa. Flight times are 6 hours 30 minutes to Montreal, 7 hours 15 minutes to Toronto and 9 hours 20 minutes to Vancouver. Within Canada, flying is still a good way of crossing the vast country. **Air Canada** links most major cities but there are other smaller airlines, such as **Air Transat** (www.airtransat.com), **West-Jet** (www.westjet.com) or the cheap airline **Tango** (www.flytango.com).

ROAD Driving in Canada may be tricky at first. Not only do they drive on the right-hand side of the road, but speed limits and distances are signposted in metric. Speed limits are usually 100km/h on highways and 50km/h in residential areas and cities. In winter, it is important to remember to buy snow tyres or chains to help you through the heavy snows. You can drive in Canada with an international driver's licence, but if you become a resident you will need to apply for a local driving licence, usually within 90 days of settling. Drivers' licences are issued by provincial governments. You must be 21 to rent a car.

GETTING AROUND Canada has extensive train and bus networks. Trains link all big cities and are a great way to see the country. Contact **VIA Rail** (www.viarail.ca). Buses are a cheaper option. The main company is **Greyhound** (www.greyhound.ca).

CLIMATE

	OTTAWA			LONDON	
-4	Dec	7	66	Dec	81
4	Nov	10	76	Nov	78
12	Oct	14	74	Oct	70
20	Sept	19	81	Sept	65
25	Aug	21	66	Aug	62
27	July	22	86	July	59
24	June	20	89	June	58
19	May	17	64	May	57
11	April	13	69	April	56
1	March	10	71	March	64
-6	Feb	7	56	Feb	72
-6	Jan	6	74	Jan	77

Average monthly temperature °C   Average monthly rainfall mm

Relocating to Canada

We did it!

Names: Louise & Rob Dyer

Job: Employed by Nestlé

Where: Toronto suburbs

Eight years ago, Louise Dyer and her husband Rob moved to Canada when he was offered a new job there

LOUISE AND ROB ARE NOW PERMANENT residents in Canada and their children have decided to return there once they finish their university degrees in the UK. Louise tells us how she went about readjusting to life in a foreign country.

Q: Why did you buy a home in Canada?
A: My husband Rob originally worked in York, but he was relocated first to Switzerland and then to Sweden. In 1997, he was offered a position in Toronto, Canada. After visiting and researching the area, we decided we would like to move there.

Q: How did you choose the area?
A: We chose an area just outside Toronto primarily for the good schools. We also liked the fact that, at that time, it was a fairly rural area with excellent walking trails, horse riding and golf courses nearby.

Q: What did you do about accommodation when you first moved to Canada?
A: To begin with we rented a place because Rob's job contract was only short-term. But after 15 months, our landlord wanted to sell the property and we decided we would buy our own home here. We had become very settled in the area and property prices were half the price of those in the UK. We decided it would be sensible to invest our money in a property rather than lose it through renting.

Q: How did you purchase your home?
A: When we bought our property, Rob was resident in Canada on a work permit, I was here on a visitor's permit and we had no Canadian credit history. On this basis, we had to fund 25 per cent of the purchase price ourselves. A Canadian bank gave us a mortgage for 75 per cent. There is no mortgage tax relief in Canada, but the mortgage rates are fairly low.

Q: Can you describe your home to us?
A: It is a 25-year-old detached, brick-built house on a quiet crescent. It has five bedrooms, two bathrooms, an eat-in kitchen, three reception rooms and an attached double garage. We have an open garden to the front and an enclosed garden with a heated swimming pool and decked barbecue area to the rear. As with many Canadian homes, there is also a huge basement. We have plenty of room for ourselves and any guests, and all for half the price we would have paid in the UK.

Left: Traditional-style, older homes like Rob and Louise's are in great demand

CANADA

ABOVE: It gets very hot in the summer and it's great to have a place to enjoy the sun

RIGHT: Canadian homes generally come with a pool

Q: Has it been a good investment?
A: So far, we do feel our property has been a good investment. Canada has a very intensive immigration policy so the population in large city suburbs such as this is increasing rapidly, and the property market is buoyant. There is a lot of new housing development in Canada, but the demand is for old, established properties like ours. So while it does cost us quite a lot in terms of maintenance and improvement, we believe the investment in our house is worth it in the long run.

"Canada's intensive immigration policy has resulted in an amazing ethnic diversity, particularly around the large cities, so there is a real United Nations feel to the place"

Q: How did you find the move and did you settle in easily?
A: I think you get back what you put into a situation. When we first arrived, people were much more reserved than I had anticipated, but we arrived in late November and the cold winters meant we did not see our neighbours much! Generally, people are friendly and welcoming. I find the easiest way to make friends is to buy or borrow a dog – people will stop and chat for hours if you have a dog! There are plenty of clubs and organisations that help you to meet new people.

Q: What is the way of life like in Canada?
A: Everything is on a grand scale – the country itself, the houses, cars, 16-lane motorways, even the appliances. Canada's intensive immigration policy has resulted in an amazing ethnic diversity, particularly around the large cities, so there is a real United Nations feel to the place. This brings a closer understanding, tolerance and respect for others. There are lots of different cultural festivals and an amazing variety of cuisine.

Q: What are the downsides to living in Canada?
A: One of the major downsides of living here is we are a long way away from our extended family. Although air travel, telephones and email make it easy to keep in touch, it is not the same as having your whole family close at hand. Canadian taxes are high, but because I have lived in Sweden they seem reasonable to me! Other problems, such as overburdened healthcare, youth crime and gridlock on the roads, can be found wherever you live, and it is very easy to blame your adopted country. In the end, wherever you live you have good and bad days, and we just enjoy the good days.

Q: What are your plans for the future?
A: We have no major plans. Rob and I have learnt never to plan too far ahead because you can never be sure what life has in store for you. Our children are attending university in the UK, but they intend to return to Canada and settle here when they have graduated. We were granted Canadian citizenship in 2001, and Rob has just been given another new position within the organisation where he works. This means we can go on living here for the time being. Consequently, our Canadian adventure continues, and we are very happy living here. We may return to the UK later, but have no plans for this at the moment. ●

Top tips

It will take time to get used to being far away from family and friends, but it is essential to persevere. Canada is like any other developed country; it has its downsides but it is a great place to live.

● Be prepared for a certain amount of isolation that comes with the winter months. It's very cold and you may not see your neighbours for a while.

● Get or borrow a dog! People will want to stop and chat to you when you take it out.

● Get involved in clubs and organisations. It's a great way to meet new people.

ABOVE: Enjoying a Canadian Christmas

Who moves there?

A real land of opportunity, especially for young professionals, Canada has a long tradition of attracting immigrants

"It has been said that Canada represents the best of the USA and the UK"

EVERY YEAR MORE THAN 90,000 FOREIGN workers enter Canada temporarily to help Canadian employers address skill shortages. Currently, 606,000 British people are living in Canada and only one per cent are unemployed.

Who moves there?

Canada has a long history of attracting immigrants, and as a result is a thriving multicultural society. The largest proportion – 2.3 million – are from Europe. Asia is the next biggest contributor with just under 2 million. The number of people migrating to Canada from the UK has been falling steadily over the years – from 160,000 in the 1960s down to just 42,500 in the 1990s. On the other hand, the number of immigrants from Asia has been steadily rising, and in the 1990s accounted for more than half of total immigrants.

People come to Canada in one of three ways – as economic immigrants, family immigrants or refugees. Most are of working age, and a high proportion have university degrees. Immigrants have tended to settle in large urban areas. Toronto, Vancouver and Montreal account for 73 per cent of new arrivals. The location of family and friends is an important factor. However, job prospects influence just under 20 per cent of immigrants, with lifestyle, education prospects and housing prices holding very little sway.

The largest number of jobs are in the services sector, followed by the goods-producing sector. The largest number of foreign workers in Canada are employed in health and retail, with just over 24 per cent in each, and three million of the 5.5 million settle and work in Ontario.

Why move there?

It has been said that Canada represents the best of the USA and the UK, bringing together vast areas of outstanding natural beauty and varying terrain and climate with a stable political framework, and good health and education systems.

Nature-lovers will love the prairie lands and the mountains, the ocean and the lakes. There is a huge range of outdoor activities to pursue, including skiing, hiking, kayaking and even dog-sledding. But Canada is not just about the great outdoors. From historic sites to performing arts, there is plenty to keep culture vultures busy.

The slower pace of life makes Canada an ideal place to which to retire, with an excellent public health system and low crime rates to boot. The tax position is also favourable, because assets outside Canada can remain tax-free for the first five years, and there is no death or inheritance tax.

Although Canada has the most educated workforce in the world, many of its own workers are emigrating to the USA, leaving countless opportunities for young professionals to fill the gap. With an ageing workforce and a skills shortage among Canadians there is likely to be a continued demand for foreign workers. With unemployment rates at seven per cent and GDP growth 0.2 per cent, Canada is in a healthy economic state and predictions are for growth to continue. ●

LEFT: Quebec is three times the size of France, and home to 95 per cent of Canada's French Canadians

Working in Canada

Despite a highly educated workforce, Canada needs immigrants across its industries, from the expanding service sector to skilled trades

■ ECONOMY

Canada is an affluent society similar to the USA in its economic system and patterns of production. It enjoys a high trade surplus, and international trade remains key. Overall, Canada boasts strong economic prospects and a high standard of living. The main change in the Canadian economy has been a shift in focus to knowledge-based service industries.

■ LABOUR MARKET

Due to the "brain drain" of Canadian skilled workers to the USA and the ageing population, Canada relies heavily on immigrants. Unemployment rates have been falling steadily for more than a decade. There are three times as many employees in the service sector as there are in goods-producing industries and the same ratio of private to public sector workers.

■ JOB OPPORTUNITIES AND KEY INDUSTRIES

There are many areas where skilled trades people such as electricians and welders are lacking, especially in rural communities. Canada's key industries include transportation equipment, chemicals, processed and unprocessed minerals, food products, wood and paper products, fish products, petroleum and natural gas.

■ FINDING A JOB

Many people search for jobs on the Internet, and "job banks" are popular. Job listings can also be found in national and local newspapers. Temping agencies are a good way to find a temporary job, and some of these operate both in the UK and Canada.

■ LANGUAGE REQUIREMENTS

Canada is bilingual so it is essential that you speak either English or French to work or study there. Which language is more important depends on the province. Quebec is mostly French-speaking, while Ontario is mostly English. ●

© CANADIAN TOURISM COMMISSION

CANADA

ABOVE: Vancouver is situated next to the Pacific with a mountain backdrop

VISAS AND PERMITS

As a UK citizen, you can visit Canada unrestricted for up to six months. You do not need a temporary residency permit, but you will need health insurance because Medicare does not cover every illness and ailment.

● STUDY PERMIT

Around 130,000 students a year come to Canada to study. If you are doing a course of less than six months in duration, you do not need a permit. If you wish to extend your study period once you are there, you will have to leave the country to obtain one, so it is worth getting one anyway. To apply for a study permit you will need a letter of acceptance from an educational institute, proof that you can support yourself and no criminal record. You may also have to have a medical examination.

● WORK PERMITS

For almost all jobs, you must obtain a work permit. A job offer is an essential part of your application and it is normally necessary for Human Resources Development Canada (HRDC) to confirm that it is ok for a foreign national to fill the post. You may also need a Social Insurance Number (SIN).

● IMMIGRATION POINTS SYSTEM

If you wish to become a permanent resident, you will need to meet the criteria on the immigration points system. You must gain a minimum of 67 points from a range of factors including age, education, skills and other factors such as partner's skills or relations in Canada. You must also have skills that fall into one of three types – A, B or O – which usually require a higher education qualification. Practical training also counts, for example a qualified plumber would have level B skills, whereas a general labourer would have only level D. A matrix of professions and their skill levels can be found at www.hrdc-drhc.gc.ca.

You can apply for these permits at the Canadian High Commission in London or download them at the Citizens and Immigration Canada (CIC) website www.cic.gc.ca.

■ USEFUL WEBSITES

www.canada.gc.ca Main Canadian government website
www.travelcanada.ca The Canadian Tourism Commission
www.cic.gc.ca Citizenship and Immigration Canada
www.canadajobsearch.com Canada Job Search
www.canada.org.uk Canadian High Commission Immigration Division
www.aucc.ca Association of Universities and Colleges of Canada
www.sdc.gc.ca Social Development Canada

Finding a home

Affordable, spacious housing is the norm in Canada, and property prices, even in the cities, compare favourably with those in the UK

CANADA

AROUND 73 PER CENT OF CANADA'S five million immigrants settle in Toronto, Montreal or Vancouver. Ontario, Quebec and British Columbia are also popular hotspots, and this inflates prices there. The cheapest housing is in the Prairie Provinces.

The housing market has been one of the fastest-growing sectors of the economy in recent years due to falling mortgage rates. New housing reached a 15-year high in 2003, which increased available rental accommodation. The 2001 census showed that almost 70 per cent of Canadians live in affordable, uncrowded housing in good repair. Fifty-seven per cent live in detached houses with apartments being the next most popular form of property. However, the supply of affordable housing for immigrants in Toronto, Vancouver and Montreal remains a challenge.

ABOVE: **Much of Canada's housing is situated on the waterfront**

Renting

You will probably spend between 35 and 50 per cent of your income on housing, including telephone and utilities. Renting a property can cost from $350 (£150) a month for a room, to $2,000 (£860) for a luxury apartment or a large house, and there are huge variations across the country. The laws relating to renting also differ. In most jurisdictions you will have to pay a deposit, usually equal to a month's rent, and landlords will want to check your credit history, so take some details with you from the UK.

Buying

The best times to buy property in Canada are spring and summer, when people tend to move. You can buy a house and secure a mortgage, but it is easier if you are a resident. Non-residents will need a deposit of between 25 and 35 per cent, but residents need only 10 per cent. Mortgage rates vary, from 3.9 per cent to 7.8 per cent depending on the lender and the term. If you want to buy somewhere to live, you will have to show that you are applying for permanent resident status.

If you build your own home, it is essential to have a good realtor and lawyer and to agree everything in writing from the outset. Canadian houses are often timber frame rather than bricks and mortar because of the availability of timber.

Finding a property

There are many ways to search for property, such as the Internet, bulletin boards and local papers. Citizenship and Immigration Canada (CIC) maintains a list of organisations that can help you find local housing, and publishes The Newcomer's Guide to Canadian Housing. Download the guide at www.cmhc-schl.gc.ca.●

TAX

Canadian taxes include income tax, employment insurance, contributions to the Canada pension plan, provincial sales tax and goods and service tax.

● **INCOME TAX**

Income tax is collected on a withholding method by retaining a portion of your salary each month. As well as income tax, you will have money deducted for the Canada pension plan and employer's insurance. You may also be taxed on benefits provided by your employer, such as dental care. Federal income tax rates for 2005 are as follows:

16% on the first $35,595 of taxable income
22% on the next $35,595 of taxable income
26% on the next $44,549 of taxable income
29% on taxable income over $115,739

Provincial tax is calculated in the same way as federal tax but at slightly different rates, depending on the province.

For more information on taxes, contact the Canada Revenue Agency (CRA) at www.ccra-adrc.gc.ca, or find useful hints and tips at www.taxtips.ca.

AVERAGE RENTAL/SALE PRICES

Hotspot	2-bed apartment rentals	2-bed apartment sales	4-bed house sales
Toronto	$1,920 (£825)	$308K (£132K)	$844K (£362K)
Montreal	$1,910 (£820)	$359K (£154K)	$628K (£269K)
Vancouver	$1,600 (£687)	$279K (£120K)	$672K (£288K)

Employment hotspots

The three vibrant cities of Toronto, Montreal and Vancouver all offer a great environment in which to work and live

1 Toronto

Located at the edge of Lake Ontario, Toronto has a liberal and outgoing attitude. With an immigrant population of over one million, it is a hugely cosmopolitan city. It boasts a varied landscape, a safe centre and dramatic architecture.

Toronto is the financial, communication and business hub of the nation. It is the busiest Canadian port on the Great Lakes and international trade plays a big role. The economy is varied and there are many investment opportunities. Most jobs are in banking and finance, manufacturing, tourism and communications.

Over the past ten years, property prices have risen by 42 per cent. With low interest rates and inflation, and the Canadian dollar doing well, property is a good investment. A recent freeze on construction means that land prices, and therefore prices of new houses, will rise.

KEY FACTS
- **Population:** 2.4 million
- **Airport:** Toronto-Pearson International Airport, Tel: 00 1 416 776 3000
- **Medical:** Toronto General Hospital, Tel: 00 1 416 340 4800
- **Schools:** The Great Lakes College of Toronto, Tel: 00 1 416 763 4121
- **Rentals:** Large number of new condos being built ■ 30% of new units are bought by investors for rental income ■ Vacancy rates are expected to rise to 5% in 2005
- **Pros:** High quality of life ■ One-sixth of Canada's jobs are here ■ Good public transport ■ Lots of nightlife and culture ■ Plenty of central housing
- **Cons:** Large number of homeless people ■ Downtown Toronto is plagued by skunks and raccoons.

2 Montreal

Situated on an island connected to the mainland by bridges, Montreal is a friendly and romantic city with a very European atmosphere. Sixty-six per cent of the population speak French, but many other nationalities are represented, with five per cent of the population being British and seven per cent Italian.

A vibrant centre of industry, commerce, culture, finance and world affairs, it has a diverse selection of job opportunities, and unemployment has shrunk recently to only six per cent. The city has an important manufacturing sector. Other industries include hi-tech, transportation, pharmaceuticals tourism, media and multimedia. This is an important rail city, and the port offers the shortest route between Europe and North America.

Montreal is undergoing a building boom, and a healthy economy is expected to continue to support growth in the housing market in 2005.

KEY FACTS
- **Population:** 3.4 million
- **Airport:** Montreal Dorval International Airport, Tel: 00 1 514 633 3221
- **Medical:** Royal Victoria Hospital, Tel: 00 1 514 934 1934
- **Schools:** Lower Canada College, Tel: 00 1 514 482 9916
- **Rentals:** A shortage of apartments in 2003 pushed up rents but prices are now stabilising ■ Downtown apartments are popular with people who work in the centre of the city
- **Pros:** Crime rates hit an all-time low in 2000, and have not risen ■ Subway, or Métro, is modern and swift ■ Streets are clean and safe ■ Property is a good investment ■ Unemployment is low
- **Cons:** Certain aspects are expensive ■ Traffic congestion can be a problem.

3 Vancouver

Nestled between the sea and the mountains, Vancouver is one of Canada's most scenic cities. A progressive city known for its liberal politics and recognition of alternative lifestyles, it is a centre for the arts, business, fashion, sports and politics.

Vancouver is the busiest port on the west coast of North America and one of the nation's largest industrial centres. It offers a range of job opportunities and the leading industries include hi-tech, film production, tourism, forest products and financial services. Vancouver has also emerged as a centre for biotechnology and software development. It is hoped that, as the host city of the 2010 winter Olympic Games, the city will attract more visitors and investment in the coming years.

Vancouver has a variety of housing, including high-rise apartment buildings, single family homes, condos and low-rise apartments. Interest rates are low, the economy is strong and the property market is active but stable, making this an ideal time to invest. Prices are expected to rise steadily for the foreseeable future.

KEY FACTS
- **Population:** 2.1 million
- **Airport:** Vancouver International Airport, Tel: 00 1 604 276 6500
- **Medical:** Vancouver General Hospital, Tel: 00 1 604 875 4111
- **Schools:** Vancouver International School, Tel: 00 1 604 460 8477
- **Rentals:** Properties are widely available ■ The most expensive areas are those close to commercial centres ■ Most rentals are long-term ■ Short-term rentals to business people can be profitable
- **Pros:** A safe city ■ Property prices are reasonable ■ Has an impressive infrastructure ■ Many job opportunities
- **Cons:** Very wet in winter ■ Theft and beggars can be a problem. ●

ABOVE: Toronto is home to 2.4 million residents

Property price guide

Canada offers modern city properties, although traditional Canadian-style homes are in high demand

APARTMENTS FOR RENT

Canadian rental properties are newly built with mod cons

$1,350 PER MONTH

1-BED MISSISSAUGA

£580 PER MONTH
- Fully furnished ✔
- Pool ✔
- Parking ✔   CODE RLP

$1,900 PER MONTH

2-BED MONTREAL

£820 PER MONTH
- Fully furnished ✘
- Pool ✘
- Parking ✔   CODE MON

$1,950 PER MONTH

3-BED TORONTO

£840 PER MONTH
- Fully furnished ✘
- Pool ✘
- Parking ✔   CODE BOS

$2,200 PER MONTH

3-BED MONTREAL

£950 PER MONTH
- Fully furnished ✔
- Pool ✘
- Parking ✘   CODE MON

APARTMENTS FOR SALE

Mainly found in the city centre, cosy boltholes for professionals

$239,900

1-BED VANCOUVER

£103,000
- Fully furnished ✘
- Pool ✘
- Parking ✔   CODE DUN

$271,900

1-BED TORONTO

£117,000
- Fully furnished ✘
- Pool ✘
- Parking ✔   CODE BOS

$279,900

2-BED VANCOUVER

£120,000
- Fully furnished ✘
- Pool ✘
- Parking ✔   CODE DUN

$399,000

2-BED TORONTO

£171,500
- Fully furnished ✘
- Pool ✘
- Parking ✔   CODE BOS

HOUSES FOR SALE

Canadian homes are built in a traditional style and enjoy a garden

$289,900

3-BED TORONTO

£125,000
- Fully furnished ✘
- Pool ✘
- Parking ✔   CODE BOS

$389,900

2-BED VANCOUVER

£168,000
- Fully furnished ✘
- Pool ✘
- Parking ✔   CODE DUN

$639,000

3-BED TORONTO

£275,000
- Fully furnished ✘
- Pool ✘
- Parking ✘   CODE BOS

$1,280,000

5-BED VANCOUVER

£550,500
- Fully furnished ✘
- Pool ✘
- Parking ✔   CODE DUN

52

China & Hong Kong

A blend of communist modernity and ancient civilisation

FACT BOX

CHINA
- ■ **Population** 1,298,847,624
- ■ **Capital** Beijing
- ■ **Economic growth rate** 9.1%
- ■ **GDP per capita** US$5,000

HONG KONG
- ■ **Population** 6,855,125
- ■ **Capital** Victoria
- ■ **Economic growth rate** 3.3%
- ■ **GDP per capita** US$28,800

FACT FILE

CHINA

AREA	9,596,960km²
POPULATION	1,298,847,624
CAPITAL	Beijing
LIFE EXPECTANCY	72 years
LITERACY	91%
GOVERNMENT	Communist
GDP PER CAPITA	US$5,000
UNEMPLOYMENT RATE	4.2%
CURRENCY	Yuan (CNY)
EXCHANGE RATE	1CNY = £0.06; £1 = CNY15.45
LANGUAGES	Mandarin, Cantonese, Shanghaiese, Fuzhou, Hokkein-Taiwanese, Xiang, Gan

HONG KONG

AREA	1,092km²
POPULATION	6,855,125
CAPITAL	Victoria
LIFE EXPECTANCY	81 years
LITERACY	93.5%
GOVERNMENT	Limited democracy
GDP PER CAPITA	US$28,800
UNEMPLOYMENT RATE	7%
CURRENCY	Hong Kong Dollar (HKD)
EXCHANGE RATE	HKD1 = £0.07; £1 = HKD14.66
LANGUAGES	Cantonese, English

CHINA & HONG KONG

Living in China

As the world's fastest growing country, China is a huge and varied country and soon-to-be superpower

WITH A GROWTH RATE IN 2003 OF nine per cent – four times the world's average – China is a developing power and has a population five times that of the USA. It is gradually opening its doors to the West, and the government is trying to make foreign investment and integration easier. On first arrival in cities such as Shanghai, a Western-style metropolis, the differences between East and West don't seem so glaring. Look a little closer or travel further inland, however, and you will uncover a different world.

The former British colony of Hong Kong is a cultural and economic hotspot and has long been popular with foreigners. The low rates of tax, along with great shops, restaurants and cinemas, continue to attract both investment and relocators.

Politics and economy

Established in 1949, The People's Republic of China (PRC) is governed by The National People's Congress (NPC). The largest political party is the Chinese Communist Party (CCP). Hong Kong is technically part of China, but is now run by a special administrative government. It has the freest economy in the area, and is the highest per capita holder of foreign currency.

Hong Kong has the second largest stock market in Asia, and the world's largest container port and cargo airport.

Climate

Spread over a vast area, China is subject to marked variations in weather. Generally, the south and south east have less extreme temperatures, and seasonal changes are not too sudden. Summer can be as hot as 38°C, with typhoons and rainfall of more than 400mm. Winters are short and mild, with the temperature averaging 10°C. The weather in the north and west is more extreme. In winter, the temperature in Beijing averages –10°C or less. In the far north, it can hit –40°C. Sandstorms can also cause problems and, in summer, temperatures may soar to 40°C. Rainfall is scarce.

Hong Kong has a sub-tropical climate. The weather is normally fine, and exceptionally hot.

"There are currently about 440,000 foreigners working and living in China – the largest expat population resides in Shanghai"

The months of November and December are the most comfortable, although humidity, fog and drizzle can be problems all year round. September often experiences tropical cyclones.

Education

Nine-year compulsory education was implemented in 1986 in China, and trying to uphold this universally is one of the government's main projects. Foreign children can attend state schools, but the culture shock is massive. Lessons

BELOW: The infamous Tiananmen Square in Beijing

© CHINESE TOURIST BOARD

© CHINESE TOURIST BOARD

ABOVE: Beijing is a modern and forward-thinking city, very open to Western influences

CLIMATE

3	Dec	7		3	Dec	81
9	Nov	10		11	Nov	78
20	Oct	14		16	Oct	70
26	Sept	19		58	Sept	65
30	Aug	21		141	Aug	62
31	July	22		243	July	59
31	June	20		78	June	58
27	May	17		35	May	57
21	April	13		17	April	56
11	March	10		8	March	64
4	Feb	7		5	Feb	72
1	Jan	6		4	Jan	77

BEIJING / LONDON

Average monthly temperature °C

BEIJING / LONDON

Average monthly rainfall mm

TRAVEL FILE

Air China (www.air-china.co.uk; 020 7630 0919) is China's state carrier, and operates direct flights to Beijing five days a week from Heathrow. **British Airways** (www.ba.com; 0870 850 9850) fly to Beijing, while **KLM** (www.klm.com; 0870 243 0541) offer flights via Amsterdam to several destinations. **Singapore Airlines** (www.singaporeair.com; 0870 6088886) offer flights from London and Manchester via SIngapore, and **Finnair** (www.finnair.com; 0870 241 4411) fly via Helsinki. Direct flights from Heathrow to Hong Kong International are offered by **Cathay Pacific** (www.cathaypacific.com; 0208 834 8888), **British Airways** and **Virgin Atlantic** (www.virginatlantic.com; 0870 380 2007). Indirect flights are offered by **Lufthansa** (www.lufthansa.com; 0870 8377 747) from Manchester, Birmingham and London via Germany. Other airlines include **Qantas** (www.qantas.co.uk; 08457 747 767) and **Japan Airlines** (www.jal-europe.com; 08457 747 700).

GETTING AROUND
ROAD Driving in China is not recommended due to the high number of accidents. If you must drive, comprehensive insurance is advisable and a local licence is a legal requirement. UK and International driving licences are accepted for up to 12 months in Hong Kong, but you have to be a resident before you are entitled to drive in China. It is worth noting that many roads outside the cities are in poor condition. Taxis are a common way for westerners to get around, but keep an eye on fare costs. **AIR** Flying is the fastest way to travel, but some Chinese airlines have poor safety records. The main internal passenger carriers are **Air China** (www.airchina.com.cn/en), **China Eastern** (www.ce-air.com/en), **China Southern** (www.cs-air.com/en), and **China Northern** (www.cna.com.cn). **RAIL** The best way to travel around China is by rail. Trains are comfortable, efficient, and cheap. The **Mass Transit Railway** network (www.mtr.com.hk/en) in Hong Kong is clean, modern and efficient.

---

are conducted in Mandarin and the national anthem is sung every day. Consequently, most children from foreign families attend international schools. These can be found only in large and affluent cities like Beijing, Shanghai and Shenzhen, and fees are expensive. Children in Hong Kong attend nine years of compulsory education. Schools are separated into English and non-English, and the system is similar to that in the UK. International schools remain the most popular option for British residents.

Healthcare

The state healthcare system in major cities like Shanghai is better than in Europe. Charges are a fraction of those in the West. In developing cities or rural areas, facilities are more primitive. Contributions are paid by employers and employees to government medical insurance, but you are also encouraged to have private health insurance. There are lots of private hospitals, too.

Hospitals are of a high standard in Hong Kong. All healthcare must be paid for and, although charges are low, private insurance is advisable. Demand is huge, so you may have a long wait for non-urgent treatment.

Food and drink

Food is an important part of Chinese culture, with cookery divided into four schools: Northern, Eastern, Western and Southern. The Southern school refers mainly to the *Guangdong* style, in which food is often stir-fried or steamed, with the emphasis on freshness. Northern China, such as Beijing, Inner Mongolia and Shangdong, serves a chunkier and oilier diet, and mutton is common. In the East, including Shanghai, there is a lot of fresh water fish and shrimps. Food tends to be fried, stir-fried or stewed. Shanghai cuisine has a range of flavours, and can be found all over the country. Western cuisine is probably the most vegetarian friendly. Wherever you go, rice is a staple ingredient, and pork, poultry, legumes and soybeans are common. Green tea is the most popular drink, but beer is also common. Chopsticks are used in most restaurants, but forks and spoons may be provided if necessary.

As a former British territory, Hong Kong offers a range of cuisines. Seafood is a particular highlight. Street snacks are popular, and local specialities include fish balls and sharkfin. There are a number of pubs and bars.

Expat communities

There are currently about 440,000 foreigners working and living in China. The largest expat population (70,000) resides in Shanghai, with people from 102 countries and regions. Since expatriate work permits were first issued in1996, some 59,384 people have found employment here.

There are about 34,000 British expats in Hong Kong and there is a strong Western feel to the area.

Pets

You can bring only cats and dogs into China. A family may own only one dog, and you are required to register it with local police.

Pets that are moved to Hong Kong require vaccinations and a permit from the agriculture, fisheries and conservation department. ●

We did it!

Names: Juliette and Royce Lowe

Job: Juliette is a psychotherapist, but she and her husband spent two and a half years teaching English to children in the Shanxi Province of North Central China

Teaching English

Juliette and Royce decided to spend two and a half years in China teaching English – it was a moving experience

EMPLOYED ON A TWO-YEAR CONTRACT WITH THE Voluntary Service Overseas to teach English, Royce and Juliette also spent a lot of time travelling in China and Tibet. They taught English to children aged four and upwards, became intimately acquainted with the culture and learned that the Chinese are loving, generous and hospitable. Juliette tells us about her experiences and the hard-working nature of the Chinese students she taught.

Q: Tell us about VSO and your employment in China

A: Royce and I were employed with the Voluntary Service Overseas (VSO) to teach English to Chinese trainee teachers. Our students would go on to teach English in Chinese middle schools. VSO looked after us extremely well. They cleared all the immigration and visa issues and set up contracts with a local teacher training college in Shanxi Province. Fully furnished accommodation was provided by the college and all bills were paid. We received a salary from the college which, in Western terms, was very little but more than adequate because living costs were so cheap. We even saved half our salary for travelling and, each year, the college gave us a travel grant equivalent to a month's salary and an additional grant from VSO. During the long academic holidays we travelled extensively around China.

Q: Tell us more about your teaching

A: I also taught English songs to tiny tots in the kindergarten one afternoon a week, and every Saturday morning Royce and I taught English to Chinese children. At the end of our contract with VSO, we explored more of China and then went to Tibet. I had a job in Kathmandu, Nepal, with an organisation called Art Refuge, working with Tibetan refugee children. I provided art activities in the mornings and games in the afternoon. All of the children had escaped from China (where there is persecution of Tibetans) and travelled over the Himalayas to make their way to Dharamsala in India, where their spiritual leader the Dalai Lama lives. We also travelled to Dharamsala, where I continued to work with the Tibetan children I'd met in Kathmandu. My husband taught English to Tibetan monks and nuns, and to Thai, Japanese, Korean and Mongolian students.

ABOVE: Even poor farming families welcomed Juliette and her husband into their homes

RIGHT: Juliette and Royce spent time in Lhasa, Tibet, teaching English

RIGHT: Chinese children were keen to learn and to find out about Western culture

Q: What did you learn in China?
A: Many young Chinese people aspire to travel and study in the West, and the Chinese students we met were respectful, keen and fascinated by learning. We had to be careful about discussing religion and politics, but found that students were interested in the Western world's view of China and the politics of other countries. In classes, we spoke freely about the way the students' families had suffered during the Cultural Revolution. Our students were under great pressure to succeed academically because their families sacrificed a lot to pay for their education.

Q: How does the work ethic for students in China compare with that in the UK?
A: Children get to school before 7am, have a two hour break for lunch then return to school and don't get home until 9pm. At weekends, they have music lessons, extra tutorials and English lessons. The rationale for this level of pressure to study is that, with a population of 1.3 billion, unless you are excellent in your field, you won't achieve anything.

Q: What are the Chinese people like?
A: The Chinese people have no sense of boundaries or personal space, perhaps influenced by their "collectivist" culture. They tend to cram together in a way that horrifies most British people, and there is no organised queuing system. The Chinese are also loving, generous, and hospitable people. They have a saying that "the guest is God", and we were certainly entertained, even by poor farming families, as if we were "gods". It is a food-oriented culture, and Chinese food is wonderful. Even families with no running water and no indoor lavatory would concoct us delicious and expansive meals and welcome us warmly.

Q: What is it like being an English person in China?
A: In the big cities, such as Beijing and Shanghai, people don't take much notice of Westerners, but in more rural areas people will stare. You will also find that the Chinese like to practise their English on you. Although there seems to be total freedom to come and go in China, there are Public Security Bureaus in every area, and people in uniforms are fairly austere. It is important to have all your documentation in order in case you are apprehended. On the whole, however, we were surprised how free and comfortable we felt. Public demonstrations are illegal in China, and it can be dangerous to get involved. At such times, you sense that the apparent freedom is an illusion.

"Our students were under great pressure to succeed academically because their families sacrificed a lot to pay for their education"

Q: Did you get the sense that China as a nation is moving forward?
A: People in China are obsessed with material things and getting rich – a "communist capitalist ideology". There is a rush to knock down all the traditional buildings and put up skyscrapers. All young people want a car, and this is worrying because of the level of pollution that already exists in the country. The air is thick with pollution, like Britain in the 1950s. I had a cold every month for a year because of the pollution, although we did live just 45 minutes from Taiyuan, one of the world's most polluted cities.

Q: What are your plans for the future?
A: Our plan now is to live in France in a small house we've just bought, to teach English to French children and to do some trading in Kashmiri shawls and Tibetan jewellery. Ultimately, I hope to set up a Creative Therapy Retreat business in France because my real training and skills are as a psychotherapist. We have also taken on the sponsorship of a six-year-old Tibetan girl, and I've made a commitment to try to find sponsors for all the children (about 90) that I worked with. ●

Top tips

Juliette's experiences
● The Chinese railway service is efficient and reliable. You have to share a compartment with strangers, male or female, but, if you speak a little Chinese, you can have a wonderful time chatting and sharing food.

● Even the smartest restaurants and hotels are likely to have dirty, smelly squat toilets with no paper and nowhere to wash your hands. You must always carry tissues, baby wipes and hand disinfectant if you want to stay sane. One of my students' homes had an outside toilet and, charmingly, you had to do your business with a big black pig peering over a little wall at you!

● Markets are some of the most interesting places in China. In Xian, we saw snakes, huge bullfrogs, terrapins, rabbits and eels. We know that dogs are eaten in China, but we never saw them in markets. Chinese people love their food, and they are brilliant at preparing it. Markets in any country are fascinating, but those in China were even more so.

Working in China & Hong Kong

There are many openings for experienced workers with specific skills throughout China and Hong Kong

■ ECONOMY AND LABOUR MARKET

Since China joined the World Trade Organisation in 2001, foreign investment has increased by more than 20 per cent. Shanghai is the main force behind the economy. In rural areas, township and village enterprises (TVEs) have become a driving force for national economic development. A number of Specific Economic Zones – including Shenzhen, Zhuhai, Shantou, Xiamen and Hainan – have also been set up to encourage foreign investment. Service industries have been developing rapidly in the last two decades, but the Chinese economy is currently supported by secondary industries – hi-tech and manufacturing – and agriculture. The unemployment rate is 4.2 per cent and the cost of living is low.

Described as the world's most open and freest economy, Hong Kong is the largest venture capital centre in Asia, and the second largest source of outward direct foreign investment in Asia. The economy is a major hub connecting China and the international markets. Tourism, banking, finance and cargo service are major contributors to the economy. The Hong Kong dollar is tied to the US dollar. Consequently, the US economy has a large impact on Hong Kong's financial markets. Unemployment is 7 per cent.

■ JOB OPPORTUNITIES

Throughout China, there are many shortages in IT, management and engineering, and the government is keen to attract foreign, university-educated professionals. Hi-tech industries are developing rapidly and recruiting highly skilled staff. Manufacturing and social services account for the greatest influx of foreign experts, followed by commerce, education, media, arts, scientific research and general technical services. To teach English, you need a university degree. China also offers a prime opportunity for entrepreneurs because the authorities are very supportive of new businesses, and offer all sorts of perks.

In Hong Kong, skilled employees are in demand in IT, finance, banking and the import and export industries. Imports and exports

– particularly to China, Japan, the USA and the UK – contribute 20 per cent of Hong Kong's GDP. Finance and insurance contribute 10 per cent. Telecommunications, in which Hong Kong has the second largest market in Asia, has become an important industry, and tourism is also an area of major development. A degree is desirable for most jobs. Those seeking temporary employment should look for positions in childcare, seasonal retail work or domestic help. There are plenty of positions in schools for those with TEFL qualifications.

■ FINDING A JOB

The most convenient resource for jobs in China is the Internet. Many online newspapers and websites post recruitment adverts, and there are a variety of online recruitment agencies that advertise vacancies. You can also write directly to the company of your choice. For teaching jobs, approach Chinese embassies abroad because they recruit English teachers for regions throughout the country. The British Council also arranges for university students to work as teaching assistants in China for a year.

If you are starting your search for employment in Hong Kong from the UK, there are several newspapers – including the *Guardian*, the *Economist* and *Overseas Jobs Express* – which advertise positions there. There are also a large number of employment agencies in both the UK and Hong Kong, such as Gemini Personnel (www.gemini.com.hk) and Expats Direct Limited (www.expatsdirect.com). If you are already in Hong Kong, try the *South China Morning Post* (www.classifiedpost.com), the *Ming Pao* Chinese newspaper and specialist recruitment publications such as *Career Times* and *Recruit*. It is common practice to send a formally styled letter of application, or CV, which highlights your achievements, experience and qualifications.

■ LANGUAGE REQUIREMENTS

Despite attempts over the last 2,000 years to introduce a single dialect, there are still many different dialects in China. This can make it difficult for foreigners to master fluency across the nation. The official spoken language is Mandarin and, realistically, anyone seeking to work in China should be familiar with it.

English and Chinese are the official languages of Hong Kong, and Cantonese is the most spoken dialect. Since China opened to international trade, it has become more important for Hong Kong residents to speak Mandarin, in order to do business on the mainland. Your job prospects in Hong Kong will be much improved if you can speak Cantonese and English. Fluency in Mandarin as well will make you very much in demand.

© CHINESE TOURIST BOARD

LEFT: Ice sculptures at the Harbin Ice and Snow Festival

■ BUSINESS ETIQUETTE

The Chinese take business hierarchy seriously. People in higher positions tend to be experienced and older, and they usually keep their distance from subordinates. Those in authority expect to be addressed by their surname, and employees are not encouraged to criticise those more senior to them. Business partners do not comment on the performance of their companies in social situations, especially when their employees are present. If a colleague invites you for dinner or sends you an expensive gift, it is expected that you should reciprocate. When eating in a restaurant, you should ask your guests what they like to eat before suggesting anything from the menu.

In Hong Kong, business cards should be exchanged when you first meet a business associate. Exchanges can be done quickly, although it is important to treat the cards with respect. Wait to be introduced to people before introducing yourself. The most important person on a Hong Kong business team generally sits in the middle of the negotiating table. Do not seat yourself – you should wait to be seated. You will typically be placed opposite your perceived peer. Avoid discussing politics, your personal opinions or potentially offensive topics. Opening conversations should be short. Hong Kong Chinese are impressed by status and rank, so it may be beneficial to give the appearance of wealth and position. Formal business attire is the standard. The pace of business can be very fast, and people from Hong Kong are quick to assure you that they can take care of things. Values like risk-taking and efficiency are particularly important. ●

© CHINESE TOURIST BOARD

ABOVE: Forty-four per cent of the Chinese workforce are employed in agricultural industries

CHINA & HONG KONG

VISAS AND WORK PERMITS

CHINA

● F-VISA BUSINESS

This type of visa is necessary for research purposes, to give lectures, scientific, technological and cultural advice and for people on exchange programs. Students making a short trip to China (for a period up to six months) should apply for an F-visa. You can secure a multiple entry Business visa for six or 12 months.

● Z-VISA EMPLOYMENT

If you have received an offer for a place in a university or college for longer than six months, you need an Employment visa. This is for people looking to enrol in advanced studies or internships. As well as your visa application, you must also submit a foreign student application form and a letter from the university or college.

● D-VISA
PERMANENT RESIDENCE

This visa applies only to those who have been granted permission to live full time in China. The government confirmation for residency must be submitted with the visa application. It is not hard to obtain residency in China. Generally, if you have a valid reason or family in China and can prove you have been a good citizen in your country of birth, you are granted access. Obtaining residence for business purposes has been harder, but the government is currently revising their policy for foreign investors and property owners without relatives in China.

● WORK PERMITS

In order to work in China, it is compulsory to have an employment contract sorted out before a work permit is granted. You need to then apply for a Z-visa, which is given to anyone who has been offered a job by a company. This is not a formal work permit, however, and you then need to contact the local government office to secure permission to stay longer than 30 days. Residency is generally granted for two to five years, and you must be employed for the duration of this time.

HONG KONG

If you hold a valid UK passport, there is no need to secure a visa to visit Hong Kong unless you are planning to stay for longer than 180 days (90 days if you live anywhere else within the EU). You are not, however, allowed to work during this period. Visas for employment as a professional or imported worker are only granted to those who can bring knowledge into Hong Kong that the country does not already possess, either through the workforce or the city itself. You can also apply for a visa as a Capital Investment Entrant. This refers exclusively to investments in real estate or specific financial assets. You may also apply for a student visa, which will allow you to stay in Hong Kong for the duration of your studies. In order to become a Hong Kong citizen, you have to have lived in the country for seven years.

Finding a home

Anyone buying property now should expect to see enormous capital growth and appreciation over the next 20 years

CHINA & HONG KONG

IN FEBRUARY 2004, THE CHINESE government announced their intention to grant full private land ownership to foreign buyers, as opposed to a 70 year lease of a property. This was a historic step and, since then, the government have actually introduced tax incentives to encourage foreigners to invest in property in China.

Hong Kong property prices hit a peak in 1997, soon after which the property market crashed, bottoming out in 2003. Prices in 2004 rose again by 30 per cent, but they are still 50 per cent below 1997 levels. A large number of current transactions are new-build properties. Owners often have difficulty re-selling properties, particularly those more than ten years old – most residents consider a property this old to be completely past it!

Renting

Most people in China rent through estate agents, who may or may not charge commission. The minimum let is usually six months. Agents may demand between one and three months' rent upfront if you ask for a short-term lease. Before signing a contract, find out whether the property is mortgaged or part-owned by more than one entity. If the latter, you need to seek permission from them all. The landlord will then register you as the tenant with the local police. Only then should you sign the lease.

People in Hong Kong also tend to rent through estate agents. A multiple listings system is practised, so a responsible agent can cover the whole market. Most rental properties here are unfurnished, but a growing number of luxury serviced apartments are becoming available. Many of these are in high-rise buildings due to the severe lack of space in Hong Kong. The majority of residential tenancy agreements last for two years. Shorter contracts can sometimes be negotiated, but many landlords are reluctant. If the property is mortgaged, you will need to obtain the mortgage holder's consent to let. A deposit of two to three months' rent will be payable.

ABOVE: The Central Axis of Beijing, which runs from the Forbidden City to the Bell Tower

Buying

Property on the market in China must have a title document or real estate ownership certificate, or any transaction is void. When you have chosen a property, a sale agreement will be drawn up. Within 30 days of this, an application for registration of the sale should be logged with the local government office and a new title deed must be issued. Fees usually amount to about 4.5 per cent of the cost of the property. As a foreigner, you will need a tax clearance document. If you are buying a new property, developers are allowed to sell it before completion. Ensure that they have a pre-launch certificate, or you could lose your property.

Hong Kong property is expensive. Prices are based on the area of the property in square metres, which usually includes common areas, balconies and terraces. There is no official title registration system, so you will need a lawyer. A ten per cent deposit is payable, and the agent's fee will be about one per cent of the property price.

Restrictions on foreign buyers

Foreign investors are encouraged in China, and there are no restrictions here or in Hong Kong.

Property tax

China's property tax is currently 1.2 per cent of the property's estimated worth, levied on between 70 and 90 per cent of its value.

In Hong Kong, tax is levied at a flat rate of 16 per cent of the total rental income on properties that are let out. ●

AVERAGE RENTAL/SALE PRICES

Hotspot	2-bed apartment rentals	2-bed apartment sales	4-bed house sales
Shanghai	CNY21K (£1K)	CNY772K (£49K)	CNY3M (£169K)
Beijing	CNY20K (£1K)	CNY490K (£31K)	CNY2M (£134K)
Hong Kong	HK$36K (£2K)	HK$8M (£546K)	HK$43M (£3M)

Employment hotspots

For a real change of culture, try one of China's dynamic hotspots, all actively encouraging foreign investment

1 Shanghai

Shanghai is evolving at an astonishing pace. Since 1990, it has taken major steps to become a showcase for China's global ambition, exhibiting a palpable energy and economic strength. Known as "the dragon head", Shanghai is China's top commercial centre and has a booming property market.

Shanghai rivals Hong Kong as the major centre for foreign trade and investment. It is an ideal location for expats to find employment. As the leading port in the country, it handles a quarter of China's exports and imports. Its pillar industries are steel, telecommunications, automobiles, petrochemicals, electronic appliances and textiles. Key developing sectors are finance, commerce, real estate, tourism and information. Shanghai is home to one per cent of China's population, but contributes more than ten per cent of its industrial output and five per cent of its GDP.

Property prices in Shanghai are continuing to rise steeply, and authorities have imposed a 5.5 per cent capital gains tax to cool the market. About five per cent of all property is sold to non-Chinese nationals. Gu Bei is a favourite with foreigners due to the desirable properties and international schools.

KEY FACTS
- **Population:** 7.5 million
- **Airport:** Shanghai-Pudong International, Tel: 00 86 216 884 2000
- **Medical:** Shanghai East International Medical Centre, Tel: 00 86 215 879 9999
- **Schools:** British International School Shanghai, Tel: 00 86 215 812 7455

- **Rentals:** On average, a two-bedroom apartment will cost CNY20,600 (£1,312) per month
- Most units charge a monthly management fee
- **Pros:** Shanghai has some of the best services in China ■ It owes much of its economic success to excellent transport links ■ The Bund area has evolved into a centre for international finance and trade ■ The city is becoming established as a trendsetter for fashion, design and culture
- **Cons:** Shanghai has one of the highest population densities in the world ■ House prices are some of the highest in the country.

2 Beijing

The proud capital of modern China, Beijing is a fast-growing, international metropolis and a melting pot of cultures. While courting foreign business, Beijing maintains a grip on its rich cultural heritage and a close look reveals stunning traditional features.

The international companies in Beijing provide plentiful employment opportunities for expats. The authorities are particularly keen to develop the IT, biotech and pharmaceutical industries. Other major employment sectors include publishing, electronics, textiles, chemicals and automobile production. The service sector is currently experiencing the most rapid growth.

Property in Beijing is growing steadily in value, and construction is taking place on an unprecedented scale. Old buildings are disappearing to be replaced with key national projects and impressive modern buildings in preparation for the Olympics in 2008. The most popular district of Beijing with expats is Chaoyung.

KEY FACTS
- **Population:** 13.8 million
- **Airport:** Beijing Capital airport, Tel: 00 86 106 456 3220
- **Medical:** Beijing Shunyi Hospital, Tel: 00 86 106 942 3220
- **Schools:** Yew Chung International School, Tel: 00 86 108 553 3731
- **Rentals:** Prices are falling slightly as supply of new properties increases
- **Pros:** Beijing is trying to introduce more green areas to combat pollution ■ Beijing is the transport hub of China ■ The Olympic games are bringing investment to the area
- **Cons:** Beijing still suffers from pollution ■ It is one of the most crowded cities in the world.

3 Hong Kong

One of the most vibrant and invigorating cities in Asia, Hong Kong is both a paragon of the virtues of capitalism and a part of the largest communist country in the world. The city moves at a whirlwind pace, has a real buzz about it and is popular with expats.

Hong Kong is a trading centre, and the mainstays of the employment market are banking and financial services, advertising, publishing, light manufacturing and property. The service sector is becoming ever more important, with Hong Kong attracting 14 million visitors a year.

Property in Hong Kong is expensive but, in recent years, the market has been slack. Developers are now starting to snap up land for development again, and new properties are a sound investment.

KEY FACTS
- **Population:** 6.81 million
- **Airports:** Hong Kong International, Tel: 00 85 221 887 111
- **Medical:** Queen Mary Hospital, Tel: 00 85 228 553 838
- **Schools:** Hong Kong International School, Tel: 00 85 228 125 000
- **Rentals:** There are few one-person apartments; it is common for people to share ■ Rental prices are very high
- **Pros:** English is widely spoken, and most street signs are bilingual ■ The public transport network is excellent
- **Cons:** Hong Kong suffers from pollution ■ The number of people in the city is rising. ●

© CHINESE TOURIST BOARD

ABOVE: The Summer Palace in Beijing, begun in 1750

CHINA & HONG KONG

Property price guide

Homes in cities are generally apartments due to chronic space shortages, but houses and villas are available at a premium, especially in rural areas

RENTAL HOMES

Rental properties are the most popular choice among Chinese

CNY6,280 PER MONTH

2-BED BEIJING

£400 PER MONTH
- Fully furnished ✔
- Pool ✘
- Parking ✔   CODE PAC

CNY10,750 PER MONTH

4-BED SHANGHAI

£685 PER MONTH
- Fully furnished ✔
- Pool ✘
- Parking ✔   CODE PAC

CNY16,485 PER MONTH

3-BED BEIJING

£1,050 PER MONTH
- Fully furnished ✔
- Pool ✔
- Parking ✔   CODE PAC

CNY24,800 PER MONTH

2-BED BEIJING

£1,550 PER MONTH
- Fully furnished ✔
- Pool ✘
- Parking ✔   CODE PAC

HOMES FOR SALE

Be prepared for a slightly smaller apartment than those found in Western countries

CNY1,334,500

2-BED SHANGHAI

£85,000
- Fully furnished ✔
- Pool ✘
- Parking ✔   CODE SHV

CNY1,413,000

2-BED SHANGHAI

£90,000
- Fully furnished ✔
- Pool ✘
- Parking ✔   CODE SHV

CNY1,884,000

2-BED SHANGHAI

£120,000
- Fully furnished ✔
- Pool ✘
- Parking ✔   CODE SHV

CNY2,367,560

4-BED SHANGHAI

£150,800
- Fully furnished ✔
- Pool ✘
- Parking ✔   CODE PAC

CHINA & HONG KONG

TAXES

CHINA

If you work for a foreign company and are in China for fewer than 90 days, you pay no income tax. From 90 days to a year, you pay tax on income earned in China. After a year, you pay tax on income from China and abroad. Urban Real Estate Tax is levied to ensure the best use is made of urban land. It ranges from CNY0.3 (£0.02) to CNY10 (£0.60) per m2.

Income tax rates are as follows:

Monthly income	Rate
first CNY5,000	5%
next CNY1,500	10%
next CNY3,000	15%
next CNY15,000	20%
next CNY20,000	25%
next CNY20,000	30%
next CNY20,000	35%
next CNY20,000	40%
remainder	45%

HONG KONG

Income tax in Hong Kong is fairly simple. It is charged at 16 per cent after deductions or according to a sliding scale, whichever is cheaper. The tax is based on the previous year's income. Many residents do not pay any income tax, however, as their incomes don't reach the first rung on the tax liability ladder. The current tax-free allowances are HK$108,000 (£7,600) for a single person, or HK$216,000 (£15,100) for a married couple.

The sliding scale is as follows:

HK$0 – HK$35,000	2%
HK$35,001 – HK$70,000	8%
HK$70,001 – HK$105,000	14%
HK$105,001 plus	20%

Residents pay no capital gains tax.

Location, location, location. *currency*

Fluctuating exchange rates could put your dreams out of reach

Whether you are emigrating to a new life in France or simply buying a second home, we can save you time, stress and money when you buy currency.

Call our consultants now or visit our comprehensive website www.hifx.co.uk/abroad.

01753 859159

 **HIFX** PLC

info@hifx.co.uk

59–60 Thames Street Windsor Berkshire SL4 1TX

Dubai

Brilliant business opportunities and a luxurious lifestyle

© DUBAI TOURISM

FACT BOX

- **Population** 1.1 million
- **Population growth rate** 1.57%
- **Economic growth rate** 6%
- **Inflation rate** 2.5%
- **Capital** n/a
- **Hotspot** Dubai
- **Average house price** (4-bed) Dh2,480,000
- **Average rental price** (2-bed) Dh8,400

Living in Dubai

Once a huddle of buildings clustered around a salt inlet, Dubai is one of the world's fastest growing economies

FACT FILE

AREA	3,885km²
POPULATION	1.1 million
CAPITAL	n/a
LIFE EXPECTANCY	75 years
LITERACY	78%
GOVERNMENT	Monarchy
GDP PER CAPITA	US$23,300
UNEMPLOYMENT RATE	0%
CURRENCY	Emirati Dirham (Dh)
EXCHANGE RATE	Dh1=£0.14; £1=Dh6.96
LANGUAGES	Arab, English, Persian, Hindi, Urdu

COST OF LIVING

PETROL (1L)	Dh1.4
WINE (75CL)	Dh90
MEAL (3-COURSE)	Dh110
BOTTLE OF BEER (330ML)	Dh18
LOAF OF BREAD (650G)	Dh2.2
MILK (1L)	Dh3.5

CLIMATE

DUBAI				DUBAI		LONDON	
26	Dec	7		16	Dec	81	
31	Nov	10		3	Nov	78	
35	Oct	14		1	Oct	70	
39	Sept	19		0	Sept	65	
41	Aug	21		0	Aug	62	
41	July	22		1	July	59	
39	June	20		0	June	58	
37	May	17		0	May	57	
33	April	13		8	April	56	
28	March	10		25	March	64	
25	Feb	7		30	Feb	72	
24	Jan	6		18	Jan	77	

Average monthly temperature °C

Average monthly rainfall mm

IN THE PAST 30 YEARS, DUBAI HAS BECOME synonymous with great city living. Once, camels laden with goods and gerry-can-trussed Landrovers filled the narrow, sandy streets. But now, Porsches and Landcruisers swish between five-star resorts. Every kind of entertainment and convenience is on your doorstep, and year-round sunshine and white sand beaches draw people from all over the world. Dubai is the world's fastest growing commercial and leisure centre, offering a very high quality of life and the chance to be part of the city's stunning commercial success.

Politics and economy

Dubai is one of the United Arab Emirates' seven separate domains. It has managed to maintain its independence from the Federal Government, and power currently rests with the city's ruling family the Al-Maktoums. The current ruler is Sheikh Maktoum bin Rashid al-Maktoum, who is also Vice President and Prime Minister of the UAE. His brother, Sheikh Mohammed, is the

BELOW: The stunning Jumeirah mosque

© DUBAI TOURISM

"Dubai has a sub-tropical climate – blue skies and high temperatures can be expected all year round"

Crown Prince of Dubai. There are no political parties or elections in Dubai and, although the UAE has a federal government, each emirate is presided over by a ruler with absolute sovereignty.

Stability and growth are assured in Dubai. The economy has grown by an annual average of 8.6 per cent during the last eight years, and this is expected to continue for the next five years. Dubai's wealth was initially founded on limited oil deposits but, when it was realised that these would run out, Dubai's founder, Sheikh Rashid, decided that diversification was the key to success. Despite opposition, he built the Jebel Ali port and Free Zone to help develop regional transshipment routes and increase foreign investment. It was a roaring success.

Climate

Dubai has a sub-tropical and arid climate, and sunny blue skies and high temperatures can be expected throughout most of the year. Rainfall is infrequent and irregular, occurring mainly from November to March. Temperatures range from a low of about 10°C in winter, to a high of 48°C in summer. During the winter, there are occasional sand storms when the sand is whipped up off the desert. The wind is known as the *Shamal*. The most pleasant time to visit is in the cooler winter months because summer humidity can approach 100 per cent. This can be less of a problem than it might appear because all hotels and public buildings are air-conditioned.

Education

Dubai has a modern network of 85 private schools offering education to the curriculum requirements of the UK as well as the USA, Italy and Japan. The American School of Dubai is a prime example of the quality of education in the country. It caters for children of all ages, and is well-located, safe, and has excellent facilities and staff. Many families

© DUBAI TOURISM

LEFT: Modern architecture blends with the old

DUBAI

ABOVE: Horse racing is a firm favourite in Dubai, the most famous event being the Dubai World Cup

with young children have a live-in nanny. Wages are lower than in the USA or Europe, and most villas are built with separate maid's quarters. Nannies are vetted and made available by several reputable agencies. Cleaning maids and day care are also readily available, and children can go to nursery from two years of age.

Healthcare
Everybody legally visiting or living in Dubai has free access to emergency medical care. Other medical services were free until recently, and costs for standard medical procedures remain heavily subsidised. All expats living in Dubai are provided with an official medical card, and many have private medical cover – often provided by companies as part of their employment package. There are several top-class private hospitals such as Welcare and American Hospital, which are internationally recognised.

Food and drink
There are more than 450 licensed restaurants in Dubai, and the quality of the current array blows the mind. There are quite literally thousands of different places to choose from – Lebanese eateries compete with Chinese take-aways and brilliant Indian curry houses. A wander through the Bur Dubai or Deira areas reveals a cornucopia of different foods and dining themes. There is something to suit every taste while eating out in Dubai, at any time of day or night. The most common Middle Eastern food you will see is Lebanese, although Syrian and Persian food can also be found. Bear in mind that Muslims don't

eat pork and, although Dubai is a city of religious tolerance, you need a special dispensation to bring pork into the city. Alcohol is available but very expensive, and it can only be served in restaurants and bars that are attached to hotels.

Expat population
There are at least 50,000 Britons living in Dubai, and the number is growing by the day. This comes as no surprise because twenty new companies open in the region each week. The UAE's population topped four million in 2003, with the vast bulk of this influx coming, not from population growth, but expatriates. Dubai has an official population of about 1.1 million (2002), but it is probably larger if you include people working for extended lengths of time without official status. Expats make up approximately 94 per cent of the UAE population, and at least 70 per cent of these are from the subcontinent.

Pets
You can take your pets with you to Dubai, and the process is reasonably simple. Permission is required in the form of a permit from the UAE Ministry of Agriculture and Fisheries before the pet travels. To obtain the permit, owners need to submit the pet's travel itinerary, copies of veterinary health certificates (showing that the animal is free from disease and vaccinated), the sex and colour of the pet and a completed import permit application form (available from the Ministry at UAE Ministry of Agriculture and Fisheries, PO Box 213, Abu Dhabi, UAE; Tel: 00 971-4-222816). ●

TRAVEL FILE

AIR The national airline of the UAE, **Emirates** (www.emirates.com; 0870 243 2222), flies non-stop to Dubai from Glasgow, London, Manchester and Birmingham, and the trip takes between seven and eight hours. **Gulf Air** (www.gulfairco.com; 0870 777 1717) runs flights via Bahrain, but this nudges the travel time up to ten hours. Other major airlines that offer direct flights to Dubai include: **British Airways** (www.ba.com; 0870 850 9850), **Royal Brunei Airlines** (www.bruneiair.com; 00 673 221 2222) and **Bangladesh Biman** (www.bimanair.com; 0207 629 0252). The cost of travel can be reduced by flying via a European hub with a major airline such as **KLM** (www.klm.com; 0870 243 0541), but this increases travel time by a few hours.

ROAD Holders of UK driving licences can obtain a temporary driving licence, but for extended periods a local licence is recommended. A transfer from a UK licence only requires an eye test, a UK passport and a UAE residency permit. The road network in Dubai and the surrounding area is well-maintained, modern and fairly safe. Driving laws are strictly enforced.

GETTING AROUND City buses are easy to use and inexpensive. Taxis within the city are good value too, and are certainly the most convenient way to travel. Air-conditioned buses are available for travel between towns, but these are fairly limited and taxis are often used instead. Fares should be agreed on prior to travel, because taxis in Dubai tend to be unmetered. Expect to pay extra for an air-conditioned taxi.

I bought in Dubai

I did it!

Name: Richard Sealey

Job: Managing Director

Where: Dubai

Contacts: Oryx Real Estate:
Tel. 00 971 435 15770;
www.oryxrealestate.com
Arabian Ranches:
www.arabianranches.com
Celta Doura: Tel. 00 351 259
957 330; www.celtadoura.com

DUBAI

Renting an apartment in Dubai was proving costly, so Richard Sealey bought a villa to live in and rent out

RICHARD SEALEY WAS LIVING IN LONDON AND regularly commuting to Dubai on business. When in Dubai, he lived in rented serviced accommodation, which saw no return for his money. He decided to buy his own family villa on a new development. He rents this out when he is not using it for himself and his family.

Q: Why did you decide to buy in Dubai?
A: Mostly the fact that my business operates an AV consultancy office out of Dubai, and rather than continue renting a serviced apartment at a premium rate, buying would at least assure me of something in return. The purchase does also represent very good value for money in terms of overall size and build quality.

Q: How long was it before you found the right property?
A: Six months, although we did run into a few problems. Communication from the developer's sales office was pretty poor, and at one point our house was sold to somebody else. This was frustrating at the time, especially as we had set our hearts on a particular plot at the Arabian Ranches. But the problem was resolved and we managed to secure the original plot.

Q: How did you choose the area where you made your purchase?
A: Looking into the long-term development plans for Dubai, it's obvious that the city is slowly moving west along the Sheikh Zayed Road. Most of the "foreign" buying opportunities are west of the city. Numerous developments are scattered in an area of approximately 25 square kilometres, all with easy access to the beach and city facilities.

Q: Would you mind telling us how much you paid for your property?
A: I bought the villa for Dh1.18 million (approximately £180,000).

Q: How did you fund your purchase?
A: I paid the 30 per cent deposit required upfront, with the balance funded over 15 years through one of the three major banks in the United Arab Emirates.

Q: Can you describe your property and what you will be using it for?
A: The property is a three-bedroom detached villa covering 327 square metres, with a total plot size of about 760 square metres. It is located on the Arabian Ranches development. This particular development appeals because of its location, build specification and quality, and recreational facilities, which include an equestrian centre with polo club and a golf course. The Ranches are detached, with double garages set in acres of parkland and, in my view, offer great value for money.

Q: Do you feel that buying a property has been a good investment?
A: It's still early days, but if all goes well with renting out the property, I would expect a return of around 10 to 15 per cent per annum for the next two to three years. I'm in close contact with Oryx Real Estate and Dubai Property Centre. They're more than willing to keep me in the loop about market trends, so I feel like I have enough advice to be able to make good decisions.

Q: Do you intend to learn the language?
A: No I don't. Luckily, I don't have to because English is spoken universally, as it is throughout the United Arab Emirates.

ABOVE: Richard's apartment is located in a secure compound and comes with a pool

RIGHT: The apartment is modern and spacious with well-tended gardens

ABOVE: Richard has furnished his apartment in a subtle Arabian style

"Numerous developments are scattered in an area of approximately 25 square kilometres, all with easy access to the beach and city facilities"

Q: Are the local people friendly and welcoming?
A: Yes, the locals are very relaxed and do not easily get flustered. They are a proud nation, with a positive outlook.

Q: What's the best thing about life in Dubai?
A: For the young, its appeal is most definitely the sun, beaches and nightlife. Dubai does have something for everyone. It is still a relatively small town but very accessible. If you are resident and maintain an active social life, it's easy to become part of the local party crowd, and before you know it your picture appears in *Time Out Dubai* magazine or one of the other tabloids… *Tatler*-style!!

Q: What are the downsides of living in Dubai?
A: Communication can be a problem, particularly when dealing with immigration and employment issues at the government offices. Another problem is nobody tells you about changes to standard utility or telephone charges, but they are still pretty cheap.

Q: What are your plans for the future?
A: I presently live in London and will continue to commute to Dubai for business purposes. My wife travels with me on occasion, when she needs a break from her hectic work schedule. Longer term, we may consider moving out to Dubai permanently for a few years. ●

Top tips
SETTING UP A BUSINESS

Free trade zones (FTZs)
● These are designed to attract foreign investment through allowing 100 per cent foreign ownership of businesses. Outside FTZs, federal law demands that a UAE national owns 51 per cent of the business
● There are currently 15 FTZs in operation, with seven more planned for the future
● They offer exemptions from corporate taxes for a certain period, eg. Jebel Ali free zone offers exemption for 50 years

"Onshore" UAE
● If you are located outside an FTZ, you need a licence issued by the emirate government
● All companies are required to ensure they have 51 per cent ownership by UAE citizens or appoint a local service agent
● You can secure one of the following licences:
1) A professional licence, eg for accountants, lawyers, surveyors
2) A vocational licence, eg for artisans or artists
3) A trade licence, eg to import or export items and goods
4) An industrial licence, eg for manufacturing or services

Taxes
Each emirate has its own laws on corporate taxation. Foreign companies are not subject to corporate tax, except branches of foreign banks and oil and gas companies. Indirect taxes include a ten per cent tax on hotel revenues in Dubai and a tax on the annual rent of residential (five per cent) and commercial (ten per cent) properties in most emirates. There is no personal income tax.

Useful contacts
http://www.uae.gov.ae/
http://www.difc.ae/
www.jafza.co.ae/frame-fzc.htm
www.dubaimediacity.com

Who moves there?

Zero taxation and a high standard of living are major attractions for Dubai's huge foreign workforce

"Dubai is tax-free, the lifestyle is excellent, opportunities for advancement in almost every field are amazing and crime is non-existent"

DUBAI

AT THE END OF 2003, THE UAE HAD A labour force of about 2.2 million, with private sector employment accounting for about 52 per cent of the total. Of this workforce, about 92 per cent were foreign workers, as were 98 per cent of employees in the private sector.

Who moves there?

Traditionally, the British have always had a foothold in Dubai. In the past, businessmen came to the area as part of Britain's political staff, or as merchants and seamen using the port. As Dubai moved towards independence in 1971 (the year the United Arab Emirates was formed), British business grew, to the extent that thousands of Dubai companies are British-backed, and still more are run by Britons. The UK expats are by far the largest group of immigrants, but Russians are showing a lot of interest, as are other Europeans – predominantly the French, Swiss, Dutch and German. Germany is potentially a huge market because the Germans already know the place well through their tourist links. Approximately 90 per cent of the Dubai population are people who have relocated there, with 70 per cent of the workforce coming from the subcontinent. The rest are Arabs and Europeans – most notably British.

The city now plays host to 150 nationalities, including large communities of Europeans, South Africans and Australians. Each new wave of migrants brings a new level of business acumen.

Why move there?

Dubai shows an amazing capacity for economic growth and expansion. The economy is currently growing at a rate of ten per cent per annum. The diversification of Dubai's economy is a major reason for this growth, and the flourishing tourist sector and the retail, wholesale and transport sectors have made the economy buoyant. The business climate is optimistic, and expansion is forecast to continue at ten per cent.

Wholesale and retail trade is the largest sector in terms of employment, accounting for 20 per cent of the total workforce, followed by construction at 17 per cent and manufacturing at 14 per cent.

Dubai is fast becoming a major attraction for young British professionals, and with the official unemployment rate still at zero per cent, foreigners can easily secure jobs or become self employed. Immigrants come for the beaches, bistros and bars as much as for the business. Dubai is tax-free, the lifestyle is excellent, opportunities for advancement in almost every field are amazing and crime is non-existent. For most Westerners, the ridiculously high standard of living is the real bonus. The freehold property market has added to the stunning array of housing options, and the development of world-class tourist facilities means the lifestyle for expats is sumptuous.

Business practice in Dubai is now the most sophisticated in the entire region. Dubai is growing fast, and the market offers fantastic opportunities for skilled workers. The sponsorship system has also changed. Where you once had to have a local UAE national as a partner to do business, the introduction of free zones like Dubai Internet city, Dubai Media City and Jebel Ali Free Zone allows 100 per cent foreign ownership. Indeed, new World Trade Organisation regulations coming into force in a couple of years will abolish the necessity for local sponsorship outright.

Any difficulties found in setting up in Dubai are minimal when compared with most markets in the West. Regulation is limited, taxation is non-existent, and the number of serious movers and shakers is small. Business relationships can be set up fast, and you can meet everyone of importance, and of any nationality, within a year. ●

BELOW: Camels have been transporting goods for thousands of years and they are known as the "ships of the desert"

© DUBAI TOURISM

Working in Dubai

Jobs are plentiful but business in Dubai is all about networking, so be prepared to be pro-active

■ LABOUR MARKET

Essentially, Dubai is a society made up of a foreign labour force. With the economy designed as a free-trade zone to encourage foreign investment, it is totally geared towards supporting a foreign labour market.

■ JOB OPPORTUNITIES AND KEY INDUSTRIES

Dubai earns 30 per cent of its revenue through tourism, and there are a large number of jobs associated with that industry. Tourism, along with retail, new media, ICT, property, financial services and broadcasting, is currently fuelling Dubai's massive economic growth. Job opportunities of all types are plentiful, and the potential for entrepreneurship is huge. Nearly every field has the opportunity for development and growth.

ABOVE: **Dubai is a thriving metropolis, turning over £1.86bn a year**

■ FINDING A JOB

As with the majority of jobs overseas, most are advertised on the Internet, and there are a number of sites that list jobs in the UAE. Many international companies advertise in the UK's national press, and recruitment agencies also play a major role in finding work for people looking to relocate to Dubai.

■ LANGUAGE REQUIREMENTS

Doing business in Dubai has none of the problems associated with other countries in the area. Arabic is the official language, and any of 150 languages are spoken on the streets, but everyone speaks English. From chauffeurs to the heads of corporations, English is the lingua franca of Dubai business.

■ BUSINESS ETIQUETTE

Business meetings in Dubai tend to be very relaxed, and most are conducted at home, or during an evening out. Meetings generally begin with leisurely chit-chat, and you should expect to be addressed by your surname throughout. Personal connections (*wasta* in Arabic) are important, and once you are integrated into the business community doors will begin to open for you. Make sure that you carry a stack of business cards with you wherever you go (they are extremely important), and never arrange appointments for Fridays because this is Dubai's day of prayer and rest. Avoid making calls between 2pm and 5pm on weekdays, when many Arabs take a siesta. During Ramadan, many companies also operate shorter working days, with normal life resuming after the evening meal. In terms of dress, it is illegal for foreigners to wear traditional Muslim clothing, and conservative business suits are standard for male visitors. ●

VISAS AND PERMITS

Work permits, and the residency visas that go with them, are generally applied for by the company employing the individual, whether they are hired locally or abroad.

There is a set government procedure for permit and visa applications, and the process is normally taken care of by company staff hired for the purpose. In the majority of cases, the company bears the cost of providing work permits. Britons get 60-day visit visas automatically at the airport, making it possible to work normally (though illegally) and simply fly out on a "visa run" every 60 days – returning the same day to receive another 60-day stamp in their passports. The problem is that, without a work permit and residency visa, you cannot open a bank account, register for electricity and water for a home, take on a car for local use, and so on. Married women, however, can be "sponsored" by their husbands for both work and residency.

● **ENTREPRENEURS**

It is possible to set up companies of any size in a variety of free zones, such as Dubai Internet City and Dubai Media City. This automatically entitles company owners and investors to work permits and residency visas, no matter how small the investment.

■ USEFUL WEBSITES

www.theemiratesnetwork.com Site listing job vacancies in the UAE
www.jobsindubai.com A leading and reliable provider of skilled and unskilled workers to the Dubai job market.

DUBAI

Finding a home

Property prices in Dubai are far cheaper than those in central London, and half those in Singapore

ALMOST EVERYONE WOULD LIKE A SECOND HOME IN THE SUN. With limited and restrictive investment choices in Europe, the current surge of British buying in Dubai is likely to accelerate as people realise the great appreciation potential. With an estimated shortfall of 40,000 units within the next five years, supply will dry up as demand continues, and this makes property an excellent investment opportunity. Coupled with this, Dubai has sun, sand and a great lifestyle. There are also the obvious benefits of living in a tax-free environment, which is extended to the property market – there are no government property taxes.

Renting

Buildings being developed by Dubai's rental companies are, for the most part, yet to be completed. This means that rental agencies in the area are running at 100 per cent occupancy in almost all of their existing residential developments. Private freehold owners are therefore reaping the benefits.

The huge influx of Western professionals and regional businessmen in recent months means that rents have risen 10 to 15 per cent across mid-level housing.

The majority of rental property in Dubai comes as unfurnished apartments. Renting is a straightforward process, and many multinational companies have long-term leases on property for their staff. Your contract will generally be for one year, and make sure you secure a sponsor, i.e. a local, in case of disputes. Expect to pay something in advance, possibly a cheque post-dated six months ahead. Many employers will pay for your accommodation and deduct the amount from your pay.

Buying

It is also possible to own your home outright. Foreigners are allowed to take out a mortgage but they are required to obtain life insurance in order to do so. Freehold guarantees given by developers Nakheel, Emaar and Estithmaar are endorsed by the Dubai government. Thousands of foreign home-buyers and investors have flocked to buy freehold property in the most lucrative property market on Earth as a result. Average villa property prices in Dubai are five times cheaper per square metre than London's Docklands area, ten times cheaper than Central London and half the cost of Singapore.

Restrictions on foreign buyers

Foreigners can buy in any of the zoned developments that make up the vast majority of "new Dubai". All property rights are based in contract until such time as the government creates a full, federal property-ownership law. This law is in the making, but until it arrives, property rights remain contractual – between buyer and developer. It should be noted, however, that most developers are actually government owned, which gives a greater level of security. When foreign nationals were first allowed to buy, three years ago, initial purchasers were cautious. This was partly because the concept was so new and partly because investors were used to a stronger regulatory environment elsewhere. Uncertainty has been replaced by enthusiasm to invest due to the quality of return and the stabilising of the rental market. There may still be a huge number of investors watching and waiting. But if they have genuine interest, they cannot afford to wait for too long. ●

ABOVE: **The world–renowned Royal Meridian hotel in Dubai**

AVERAGE RENTAL/SALE PRICES

Hotspot	2-bed apartment rentals	2-bed apartment sales	4-bed house sales
Dubai City	Dh8,400 (£1,207)	Dh1.16m (£167K)	Dh2.5m (£356K)

TAXES

● **INCOME TAX**

There is no direct income tax levied on foreigners in Dubai.

● **PROPERTY TAX**

There is no government property tax in Dubai. Developers often charge a transfer fee (between one and three per cent) on the sale of a property. This is because the properties are purchased as freehold, but the lot upon which they stand is under the control of the developer until land registration occurs. The fee is an administrative charge, to ensure that contract and ownership documentation are transferred into the new purchaser's name.

Employment hotspot

The epitome of luxury, Dubai offers expats the mystique of Arabia combined with technological wonders

1 Dubai

Dubai is a multicultural, vibrant and futuristic city, combining the glamour of the Jumeirah district with the traditional buildings of the Bastakia quarter and the *dhow* wharfside. Offering every luxury going, the lifestyle is fantastic and the business opportunities unique. Dubai is a city of religious and political leniency, with alcoholic sale and consumption allowed and relaxed rules regarding dress and behaviour. The UAE is also the most politically secure country in the Middle East.

The central hub of Dubai is focused around Deira and Bur Dubai. Deira is home to Dubai's modern skyline, but still hosts traditional *souks* (markets). In Bur Dubai, the juxtaposition between old and new is at its most striking, with the *dhow* wharfage. Traditional boats laden with cargo stand against the backdrop of modern architectural wonders. Jumeirah is Dubai's glamorous district. It is the area of beach resorts, the famous Burj Al Arab hotel and the Palm Jebel Ali development. An affluent residential district is also located here. Dubai is continually modernising, and a wealth of new developments are underway.

Dubai's economy and currency are stable, with inflation rates remaining low and the city enjoying a GDP growth of ten per cent annually. Dubai is a member of the World Trade Organisation, and is the world's third most important exports centre.

Jobs are plentiful. It is also possible to set yourself up as a freelancer or establish your own business in the free zone.

The largest employment sector is services, particularly tourism. Only ten per cent of the city's GDP comes from oil, compared with 30 per cent through tourism. Media, finance, ICT and property are the next biggest employment sectors. Dubai's media industry is booming and offers many job opportunities for British media workers. The ICT industry is also flourishing since the opening in 2002 of the Media and Ecommerce free zone. Since then, 650 companies have been registered and 50 per cent of the world's computers and their component parts have originated in Dubai.

Wages are slightly higher than in the UK, and because there is no income tax, your net pay each month is much more than it would have been back home. It needs to be, because the cost of living is high.

Since 2002, about 5,000 apartments have been built, ranging from Dh292,000 (£42,000) to Dh5,600,000 (£800,000). Property development is likely to continue apace. The most well-known development is the

Palm Jumeirah, but there are a number of others.

If you are looking for apartments outside developments, the more exclusive areas are Jumeirah, Umm Seqiem and the Sata Parkland area, while cheaper options can be found in Satwa and Garhaud. The primarily Arabic areas of Rashidiya, Mirdif and Al Quoz are also receiving a lot of expat interest. The more expensive property options come with luxurious lifestyle packages such as a gym, pool, parking and regular maid service. Expect to pay an average of Dh8,400 (£1,207) per month for a two-bedroom rental apartment, and about Dh1,160,000 (£166,667) to buy a two-bedroom apartment. A four-bedroom house will set you back roughly Dh2,480,000 (£356,322).

KEY FACTS
■ **Population:** 1.1 million
■ **Airports:** Dubai Airport, Tel: 00 971 421 62525
■ **Medical:** Al Mousa Medical Centre, Tel: 00 971 345 0745
■ **Schools:** American School of Dubai, Tel: 00 971 434 40824

ABOVE: Dubai has a thriving, but expensive, nightlife

■ The Apple International School, Tel: 00 971 434 44441/434 20363
■ **Rentals:** With tourism increasing by over 30 per cent since 2002, this is a red-hot investment ■ There are a number of higher profile developments where you can purchase an apartment for rental purposes ■ Rentals for a two-bedroom apartment average Dh8,400 (£1,207)
■ **Pros:** Easy to find a job ■ The lifestyle is luxurious and second to none ■ Job prospects are enormous, with plenty of great opportunities ■ Three championship golf courses and the option to pursue a wealth of sports, culture and social activities ■ A safe city with excellent healthcare and educational facilities ■ Economic prospects are excellent, with ten per cent GDP growth per annum and a diversified economy
■ **Cons:** You do need to have a lot of staying power to be successful ■ Business is all about who you know, and making good contacts is essential ■ The lifestyle is expensive and living costs are very high ■ You have to be prepared to do things the Dubai way and adapt to a different lifestyle and working hours. ●

DUBAI

Property price guide

Property in Dubai reflects the sophistication and luxury of the city itself; prices may be expensive but you certainly get your money's worth

APARTMENTS FOR RENT

Rental properties tend to come with a year's lease

DH7,500 PER MONTH
2-BED DUBAI
£1,075 PER MONTH
● Fully furnished ✗
● Pool ✔
● Parking ✔　　CODE PRF

DH11,665 PER MONTH
5-BED DUBAI
£1,675 PER MONTH
● Fully furnished ✗
● Pool ✔
● Parking ✔　　CODE PRF

DH13,335 PER MONTH
3-BED DUBAI MARINA
£1,915 PER MONTH
● Fully furnished ✗
● Pool ✔
● Parking ✔　　CODE PRF

DH41,665 PER MONTH
3-BED EMIRATES HILLS
£6,000 PER MONTH
● Fully furnished ✗
● Pool ✔
● Parking ✔　　CODE PRF

APARTMENTS FOR SALE

Stylish apartments with stunning views, in world-famous developments

DH775,434
2-BED RAS AL KHAIMAH
£110,000
● Part furnished ✔
● Pool ✔
● Parking ✔　　CODE PRF

DH1,000,218
2-BED LAKEPOINT
£144,000
● Fully furnished ✗
● Pool ✔
● Parking ✔　　CODE PRF

DH1,635,600
2-BED AL FATTAN MARINA
£235,000
● Fully furnished ✔
● Pool ✔
● Parking ✔　　CODE PRF

DH11,203,052
5-BED MARINA SCAPE
£1,600,000
● Fully furnished ✗
● Pool ✔
● Parking ✔　　CODE ORY

HOUSES FOR SALE

Elegant and spacious homes, ideal for family and friends alike

DH978,731
2-BED THE SPRINGS
£140,000
● Fully furnished ✗
● Pool ✔
● Parking ✔　　CODE ORY

DH1,185,791
3-BED ARABIAN RANCHES
£169,000
● Fully furnished ✗
● Pool ✔
● Parking ✔　　CODE ORY

DH3,104,602
4-BED RAS AL KHAIMAH
£441,000
● Part furnished ✔
● Pool ✔
● Parking ✔　　CODE PRF

DH8,200,738
5-BED JUMEIRAH
£1,172,000
● Fully furnished ✗
● Pool ✔
● Parking ✔　　CODE ORY

DUBAI

Destination France?

FranceSolutions® !

Your piece of France with peace of mind

Register now for full details of FranceSolutions®,
the new service from Barclays France if you live,
work or own a property in France, or are thinking
of doing any of these!
For more information call 0800 917 0157*
or visit Destination France at www.barclays.fr

France

A country abundant in culture, cuisine and champagne

© FELIX STENSSON, ALAMY

FACT BOX

- ■ **Population** 60,424,213
- ■ **Population growth rate** 0.39%
- ■ **Economic growth rate** 2.3%
- ■ **Inflation rate** 2.1%
- ■ **Capital** Paris
- ■ **Hotspots** Paris, Côte d'Azur, Dordogne
- ■ **Average house price** (4-bed) €653,000
- ■ **Average rental price** (2-bed) €1,217

Living in France

Excellent education and healthcare coupled with a great climate – a place for all the family

FACT FILE

AREA	547,030km²
POPULATION	60,424,213
CAPITAL	Paris
LIFE EXPECTANCY	79 years
LITERACY	99%
GOVERNMENT	Republic
GDP PER CAPITA	US$27,600
UNEMPLOYMENT RATE	9.7%
CURRENCY	Euro (€)
EXCHANGE RATE	€1.45 = £1; £1 = €0.69
LANGUAGES	French

COST OF LIVING

PETROL (1L)	€1.19
WINE (0.75L)	€13
MEAL (3 COURSES)	€25
BEER (0.5L)	€0.66
LOAF OF BREAD (650G)	€0.90
MILK (1L)	€0.78

CLIMATE

PARIS		LONDON		PARIS		LONDON
7	Dec	7		50	Dec	81
11	Nov	10		50	Nov	78
16	Oct	14		55	Oct	70
20	Sept	19		52	Sept	65
25	Aug	21		62	Aug	62
25	July	22		58	July	59
23	June	20		52	June	58
16	May	17		60	May	57
15	April	13		50	April	56
10	March	10		32	March	64
7	Feb	7		42	Feb	72
7	Jan	6		55	Jan	77

Average monthly temperature °C

Average monthly rainfall mm

FRANCE IS A LAND OF DIVERSITY, FROM THE craggy outcrops of the Brittany coastline to the sunshine and sand of the Côte d'Azur. It is Europe's largest country and one of the most popular tourist and second-home destinations in the world.

Politics and economy

France has a strong tradition of republicanism, which began with the French Revolution in 1789. The current president is Jacques Chirac, whose Republican government was re-elected in 2002. The government has taken a strong stand against the intrusion of Americanism into France and has promoted and protected the use of the French language. Within France itself, however, there are a number of cultural groups, most notably Breton and Catalan, who speak their own language. France is the world's fourth largest industrial power. It has a GDP of €1.5 trillion, experiences an annual growth rate of 2.3 per cent and has an inflation rate of two per cent. The economy is dominated by the service sector and the government, which employs one in four workers. Home to some of the world's largest corporations, such as Danone and Citroën, France does a large amount of exporting within the EU and to America.

Climate

There are considerable variations of climate within France. The north and northwest of the country experience changeable weather that comes in over the Atlantic and is rather similar to that of the UK. Southern France has a Mediterranean climate and is warmer than the north, particularly during the summer. Central and eastern France have a more continental climate, which bears some resemblance to that found in western Germany and Switzerland.

Education

Any child of non-French origin who is living in France has the right to join the excellent French education system. He or she may attend a local state school, a private school or one of the many bilingual schools – both state-run and private – depending on which school best suits their needs. Between the ages of three and five, children can join an *école maternelle* (nursery school). All six to 16-year-olds must first attend an *école primaire* (primary school), then a *collège* (secondary school). The last two years of compulsory education are spent at a *lycée*, where students can choose either to study for a *baccalauréat* (roughly equivalent to A levels) or for vocational qualifications.

BELOW: The French markets are world-renowned and brimming with fresh produce

ABOVE: La Roque-Gageac is squeezed between the cliffs and the Dordogne River

© EMMA GYPPS

The French state education system has an outstanding reputation, but if children arrive in the country with a poor command of the French language, they may be better off attending a bilingual school.

"It is Europe's largest country and one of the most popular tourist and second-home destinations in the world"

Healthcare

In 2000, the World Health Organisation voted the French healthcare system the best in the world. If you are an EU national and only visit France for short periods, you will qualify for free emergency medical treatment in France if you present a valid E111 form. If you are in France for more than three months but don't work there, you may be entitled to the same treatment and benefits as French nationals. But this entitlement will only cover you for so long, after which time it is wise to make voluntary contributions to the state health insurance scheme.

If you are employed in France, your employers should register you with the social security and pay contributions to the state health insurance scheme. This will cover most of your healthcare costs. The same applies if you are self-employed and paying contributions to the *caisse*. If you are planning to retire in France and receive a state pension from another EU country, that country will usually pay your healthcare. Unless you fall into the low income bracket or have a serious illness, the full cost of treatment is not usually met by the state. It is normal to pay for treatment and be reimbursed, in full or part, by the *caisse*.

ABOVE: The Musée d'Orsay is just one of Paris's many popular attractions

Food and drink

The French love their food and drink, and the country has a host of Michelin-starred restaurants, famous chefs and unique traditional fare. Some of the most noteworthy dishes are *bouillabaisse* and *cassoulet*, and food ranges from the rich cream and apples of Normandy to the herbs and vegetables of Provence. French wines are famous worldwide, as are cognac and champagne. France is also a haven for cheese-lovers with more than 340 different types being produced.

Expat communities

There are a number of strong expat communities in France, with 130,000 British people currently in permanent residency. The Dordogne is known as "Dordogneshire" because of the high ratio of British to French living there. There are also large numbers of British buyers in Brittany, to the extent that locals are complaining of a shortage of property. If you are seeking to escape the British buyers, however, there are numerous areas such as the Limousin or Burgundy that remain traditionally French in nature.

Pets

Cats and dogs must be microchipped and vaccinated against rabies in order to qualify for a British pet passport. You will also have to sign a declaration stating that your pet hasn't been in a country that does not qualify for the Pet Travel Scheme within the last six months. Pets not meeting these requirements must spend six months in quarantine. For re-entry to the UK, you must have your pet checked for ticks and tapeworms by a vet one to two days before travelling. If you wish to take an exotic pet to France, check with the French authorities. ●

TRAVEL FILE

AIR There are a number of carriers that fly from UK airports to various destinations in France. Most notable are **Air France** (www.airfrance.co.uk; 08453 591000), which flies from Birmingham, Bristol, Edinburgh, Cardiff, Leeds, Manchester, Newcastle, Southampton and all London airports. **BMI** (www.flybmi.com; 08706 070555) flies to Paris from Aberdeen, Durham, Leeds, Heathrow, Nottingham and Manchester, while **Flybe** (www.flybe.com; 08717 000535) goes from Southampton, Exeter, Bristol and Birmingham to Brest, Cherbourg, Paris, Rennes, La Rochelle, Limoges, Bordeaux, Bergerac, Toulouse, Perpignan, Chambéry and Geneva. **British Airways** (www.britishairways.co.uk; 08708 509850) flies to Bordeaux, Lyon, Marseille, Montpellier, Nantes, Nice, Paris and Toulouse from airports throughout the UK. **Ryanair** (www.ryanair.com; 08712 460000) flies from London, Liverpool, Dublin and Glasgow to 15 destinations throughout France, and **Easyjet** (www.easyjet.co.uk; 08717 500100) flies from Belfast, Newcastle, Liverpool, London, Luton and Bristol to Nice, Toulouse, Paris, Marseille, Lyon and Grenoble.

TRAIN You can travel from London Waterloo to Paris with **Eurostar** (www.eurostar.co.uk; 08705 186186). From there, the **TGV** (www.tgv.com; 0033 892 35 35 35) serves stations throughout France.

SEA You can travel to Caen, Cherbourg, Calais, Dieppe, Dunkirk, Le Havre, Roscoff or St-Malo with **Brittany Ferries** (www.brittanyferries.co.uk; 08703 665333), **Condor Ferries** (www.condorferries.co.uk; 08453 452000), **Hoverspeed** (www.hoverspeed.co.uk; 08702 408070), **Norfolkline** (www.norfolkline.com; 08708 701020), **P&O** (www.poferries.com; 08706 000600), **SeaFrance** (www.seafrance.com; 08705 711711) and **Transmanche Ferries** (www.transmancheferries.com; 08009 171201).

ROAD Eurolines (www.eurolines.com; 0870 514 3219) travels from bus stations all over the UK to destinations throughout France. It is also possible to take your car via ferry or **Eurostar**. France has excellent motorways, which directly serve all of the major towns and cities in the country.

GETTING AROUND France has a quick, affordable and reliable train network. Contact **TGV** (www.tgv.com; 0033 892 35 35 35) or **SNCF** (www.sncf.com; 0033 8 9036 1010) for details. **SNCF** also runs buses to areas not served by rail. Flights within France can be arranged through **Air France** and smaller airlines such as **Air Littoral** (www.airlittoral.com) and **Air Lib** (www.airliberte.fr).

We did it!

Names: Marcus and Laura Nightingale

Jobs: Ex-TV producer/journalist and qualified forester; graphic designer

Where: Moved from the Chilterns to Auvergne in October 2003

Contacts: 00 33 470 06 51 32; mnightingale@wanadoo.fr

FRANCE

Buying a business

Marcus and Laura Nightingale gave up their careers in the UK and bought a farm in France

EIGHTEEN MONTHS AGO, MARCUS NIGHTINGALE left his job in television to turn an Auvergne farm into a *gîte* business. Having worked as a freelance TV producer and journalist, he and his partner and graphic designer, Laura, decided to move to France, despite the fact that Laura was five months pregnant. The couple and new arrival, Barnaby, intended to start a completely new life running their *gîte* once they had finished the renovation work. We find out how they're getting on.

Q: What made you decide to leave your successful careers and move to France?
A: For years we'd been planning to move abroad and have both always enjoyed France, particularly the food and wine! We wanted to get out of the rat race, because our jobs involved working under great pressure. Laura is a keen artist, and for years I have been putting off the novel that is supposedly within all of us!

Q: Where were you living in the UK?
A: We lived in the small Buckinghamshire village of Monks Risborough. We had a chocolate-box cottage in the Chilterns with a beautiful garden, for which Laura must take the credit. We also grew our own vegetables, which is something we intend to continue doing in France.

Q: Where are you living now?
A: We live on a smallish farm between the medieval village of Hérisson and the small town of Vallon-en-Sully. Clermont-Ferrand airport is about an hour away. We arrived in France at the start of October but didn't take possession of the property until the end of the month. So we had to spend a few awful days and nights living in a caravan in a neighbour's garden, surrounded by cows, dogs and chickens.

Q: How did you find your home?
A: Laura spent several weeks on the Internet planning a two-week trip to visit properties. We arranged appointments and managed to stick to a fairly rigid timetable, and by the end of two weeks, we'd agreed to buy Les Chauvissards.

Q: What kind of property is it?
A: We've got the main house with two bedrooms on the ground floor, a large open-plan kitchen-lounge-dining room, an office, a new bathroom and the old bathroom, which is halfway to becoming a conservatory with wonderful views of the Troncais forest. Upstairs is currently accessible only via an external stone staircase and inside is one very large room built of oak beams supporting a tiled roof. We'll turn this into four bedrooms and a bathroom. The house has a workshop to the side with a cave underneath.

Then we have two large barns, one of which has a *gîte* at one end. The rest of the barn requires reconnection to the electricity and water supplies, as well as a couple of staircases and the room divisions. The second barn needs a lot more restoration. There's also a small, one-bedroom cottage that needs electrics and some renovation. We have 4.3 hectares of pasture including an overgrown vineyard and a large pond.

Q: How much did you pay for the property?
A: Back in July 2003, when we first saw it, the property was priced at

RIGHT: The Nightingales have so far paid about £8,000 for renovations

BELOW: Marcus and Laura have been hard at work restoring and refurbishing outbuildings

ABOVE: The farm has 4.3 hectares of land

LEFT: Marcus and Laura have created stunning gardens

"For years we'd been planning to move abroad and have both always enjoyed France, particularly the food and wine"

€185,000, which is just under £130,000. The property is now worth €244,107 (£168,350) and that's without taking into account the renovation work we've already done.

Q: How far have you got with the renovations?
A: We've done a fair amount of work on the main house, fitting a new bathroom on the ground floor, starting to convert the old bathroom into a conservatory, doing the electrics and dealing with the dreaded septic tank. Readers should be aware that regulation septic tanks are officially required in all properties from 2005 and can be a costly process. A 7,000-litre tank (medium-size) including fitting and connection, which can actually be a major job, will cost in the region of €7,250 to €8,700 (£5,000 to £6,000).

Q: What else needs to be done?
A: There's a wealth of things to be done before we can open our doors to paying guests. Among other things, we need to source a good supply of quality oak for the wood burner and fit a decent-size water heater. The previous tank had a capacity of only 150 litres and constantly ran out of hot water during a shower, which is no fun when the outside temperature is -7°C!

Q: How much do you think the renovations have cost so far?
A: I estimate that we have spent about €11,600 (£8,000) so far. We had to invest in things like chainsaws, strimmers and other power tools to cope with the land, which all adds up. The rest has been spent on materials for renovations. I have done most of the work, although we did decide to pay a local English builder to help with some bits.

Q: Are you on track to open the gîte business?
A: We were hoping to open in March but had trouble gaining the *permis de construire* (building permission). We filled in a huge application form with the help of a translator and sent it to the local *mairie* with architect's drawings; this took three months. The drawings were rejected because the total floor area came to more than 170 square metres. So they had to be created by a local architect and re-submitted. The architect's fees were nearly €3,000 (£2,070) and the time wasted cost us three months in living costs! We've had to be aware of paying tax, too. The more land you own, the more tax you pay because there is an additional land tax.

Q: What are your long-term plans?
A: To earn a modest income – me through freelance writing and forestry (I hope to get some work in the Forêt de Troncais), and Laura through design and art – while raising a family in what can only be described as an area of amazing natural beauty. In five years' time, we hope to be here having achieved all our goals, with a successful business and one or more happy, healthy children. ●

RIGHT: Marcus with his son Barnaby, who was born in France

Top tips

If you're looking to go into business:

● Make sure that you have a rudimentary grasp of the French language – you may struggle to fit in and get things done if you do not.

● When planning your budget, always look on the pessimistic side. It is an expensive and long-winded process setting up a business in France.

● Check that you have sufficient qualifications. People with vocational training or practical experience, for example hairdressers, can register for work with their current qualifications. However, people like lawyers and estate agents must have the equivalent French qualification.

● Be prepared for the French bureaucracy and red tape!

FRANCE

Who moves there?

France is a hotspot for property buyers, eager to take advantage of the climate, food, wine and beautiful properties

© THIERRY DANIEL

FRANCE

LEFT: The Eiffel Tower attracts 5.5 million visitors a year

"Whatever your intentions are, it is essential that you speak the language"

WITH 3,260,000 FOREIGN RESIDENTS, France is regularly voted as one of the favourite places for permanent relocation by the British, of whom there 150,000 living full time in the country. But as second-home buyers get younger, many question whether it is feasible to expect to find work in France.

Who moves there?

The demographic breakdown of those buying in France is now much wider than it was a couple of years ago. It is no longer just those in the 55-plus age bracket who are buying there, perhaps with a view to retiring. France is increasingly becoming the country of choice for younger couples and families. People are also looking to the French property market for investment. The last year has seen a huge rise in the number of investment purchases, with 50 per cent of new build property buyers buying for this reason alone.

France is currently experiencing a 5.6 per cent growth in the number of foreigners going there to live. Italians and Portuguese represent one of the largest groups of immigrants, closely followed by Moroccans and Algerians. The age of immigrants has also risen. The largest age bracket for foreigners is 30 to 45-year-olds, with a 15 per cent increase in the number of foreign immigrants over the age of 40. It is worth noting that unemployment levels in France are fairly high, with the immigrant unemployment rate presently standing at 20 per cent.

Why move there?

The attraction of a better climate, cheaper living and the French way of life means that the number of relocators and buyers of French property has doubled over the past three years, with twice the number of people buying a house in France last year than in 2002. In line with this, some estate agents have seen interest increase by up to 120 per cent over this period.

With email and the Internet playing a huge part in business communications, and transport links between France and the UK being frequent and affordable, it is now possible to live full time in France while continuing with work commitments in the UK. In addition, France has among the best education and healthcare systems in the world, so it is little wonder that parents are choosing to raise their family here.

Rental income is also excellent. By making the most of the government-sponsored leaseback scheme, investors receive a guaranteed rental income while expecting good capital appreciation for holiday-home purchases. Buyers of new build property are motivated by hassle-free holiday properties that can make them money to cover costs when they are not using them themselves. With more and more developments being offered across France, the new build market is likely to feature strongly in the plans of UK buyers of French property. A survey conducted at the start of 2004 revealed that 73 per cent of UK buyers of French property were looking to move to France permanently in the next five years.

The largest sector for foreign employment is construction, with 17.3 per cent employed in this industry. In 1999, 1,592,000 foreigners were employed in France, and 46 per cent of them were manual workers. Out of the total number of French workers, one in four is employed by the government and most work in services. With 75 million visitors a year, most of those employed in the service industry work in tourist-related fields. Only four per cent of the workforce are employed in agriculture.

Most British buyers are seeking either to retire to France, let out their home or become part of the *gîte* industry. Whatever your intentions are, it is essential that you speak the language. ●

Working in France

With the world's largest tourist market, it is no wonder that the majority of French are employed within the services sector

■ ECONOMY

France's economy is reliant upon tourism, and with 75 million visitors every year, the majority of the workforce are employed in the services market. Services account for 73 per cent of GDP, with industry coming in second with 24.4 per cent. Unemployment currently stands at nine per cent overall, but 25 per cent of young people are unemployed. The largest export industries include Citroën cars, Danone yoghurt products and TGV high-speed trains, but machinery, agricultural products and chemicals are also important.

■ JOB OPPORTUNITIES

It is possible to secure a job as an EU national in France, despite the high unemployment rates. There are programmes designed to recruit foreign workers in fields where there is a lack of home-grown workers. With limited shortfalls in the labour market, however, the French are virtually self-sufficient. It is vital to check that any qualifications you hold are recognised by French employers before applying for work. Finding a job in rural areas is virtually impossible, and can be difficult in cities if you lack experience or have no grasp of the language. Expansion by many French companies abroad means that employers are looking for foreign workers to support expansion plans, but these openings are few. Most foreigners are self-employed in the tourism industry.

ABOVE: The Dordogne River attracts thousands of activity holiday fanatics yearly

FRANCE

■ FINDING A JOB

Looking for a job in France is much the same as in the UK. You can send speculative letters to companies of interest or apply for vacancies published in the press or online. There are also numerous temporary employment agencies, recruitment centres and vocational guidance centres to help you. If you are already in France, you could try the *Agence National Pour l'Emploi* (ANPE). If you are job-hunting from Britain, try the Recruitment and Employment Federation or the European Employment Services.

■ LANGUAGE REQUIREMENTS

The French government is protective of the French language, and French is strongly promoted in the work place and schools. If you plan to work in government or business, it is particularly important to have a working knowledge of French.

■ BUSINESS ETIQUETTE

France has a hierarchical management system, which means there is often very little contact between workers and managers. Loyalty and experience are highly valued by French employers, so it can be difficult for a newcomer to walk straight into a senior management position. Business relations and dress are formal, and hand-shaking obligatory. The French attitude towards work is healthy, and it is virtually unheard of to take work home or work at the weekend. ●

VISAS AND PERMITS

If you are an EU national, you no longer have to apply for a resident's permit (*titre* or *carte de séjour*) after living or working in France for more than three months. You will need another form of ID from your country of origin that includes proof of your home address. If you are a UK resident, your passport and a recent utility bill with your address on are acceptable.

● RESIDENT'S PERMIT

Many French officials are not yet familiar with how to apply the new law, and in some instances, for the time being at least, it may be easier to obtain a resident's permit. If, for example, you apply for a job or set up a business, you may still be asked for a *carte de séjour* because this permit has traditionally served as an ID card and as proof of the right to work.

● SOCIAL SECURITY

Anyone who is working in France, either as an employee of a French company or self-employed, will need to be registered with – and pay contributions to – the social security organisations (*caisses*) that cover their particular occupation.

■ USEFUL WEBSITES

www.parisfranceguide.com The official anglophone site for France, with a comprehensive feature on finding a job in France
www.anpe.fr Website of the *Agence National Pour l'Emploi*
www.rec.uk.com Website of the Recruitment and Employment Federation
www.ukworksearch.com A huge searchable database of job vacancies in a range of sectors for the UK and Europe, including France

Finding a home

For the many foreign buyers who still desire to purchase a little piece of France, the country continues to offer an excellent investment

SINCE 2002, THE NUMBER OF BUYERS ENTERING THE French market has doubled annually, and prices are rising. According to the European Union, house prices across France rose by 12 per cent last year, with the Languedoc Roussillon seeing a massive rise of 28 per cent.

Renting

France has excellent long- and short-term rental opportunities. If you are looking for a home to rent when you first move to the country, there is usually plenty of availability – although prices vary. It isn't difficult to find a short-term rental property in which to stay until you find a permanent home, but in many areas this might be a bed and breakfast or holiday cottage, which can be really expensive, especially during peak season.

As much as 45 per cent of the French population rent a property. Rentals are strictly controlled by French law and designed to protect the renter. A rental contract (*contrat de location*) generally lasts for three years, but a tenant can terminate the contract at any point provided they give three months' notice. Rent can be increased only once a year, and this must be in line with the increasing cost of construction and maintenance.

Buying

France offers an excellent investment, with an increasing number of new build developments as well as traditional homes. The best places to look for property are through *agents immobiliers* (estate agents), *notaires* (public notaries) and specialist magazines and websites. You will sign a preliminary contract, committing the buyer and the seller to the deal, and pay a ten per cent deposit. The sale is completed with the signing of the final deed. The whole process usually takes two to three months. You can secure a mortgage through a French bank or the French branch of an English one.

Restrictions on foreign buyers

There are no restrictions on foreign buyers purchasing in France.

Property taxes

There are two types of local tax. The *taxe foncière* is a property ownership tax paid by the owner, whether resident in France or not. The *taxe d'habitation* is a residential tax always paid by the occupier, whether they are the owner, tenant or free occupant. Both are paid on the first of January annually. Retired residents may be exempt, as may owners of new houses. ●

© LISA MCGEE

ABOVE: The Côte d'Azur's stunning coastline attracts many buyers

AVERAGE RENTAL/SALE PRICES

Hotspot	2-bed apartment rentals	2-bed apartment sales	4-bed house sales
Paris	€1,600 (£1,103)	€579K (£399K)	€1,050K (£724K)
Nice	€1,200 (£828)	€242K (£168K)	€655K (£455K)
Dordogne	€850 (£586)	€122K (£85K)	€254K (£176K)

TAXES

● INCOME TAX
Income tax, or *impôt sur le revenu des personnes physiques* (IRPP), is levied on earned income:

Up to €4,262	0%		
€4,263 to €8,382	6.83%	€23,889 to €38,868	37.38%
€8,383 to €14,753	19.14%	€38,869 to €47,932	42.62%
14,754 to €23,888	28.26%	Over €47,932	48.09%

A tax named the *impôt sur les revenus de capitaux* is payable on property and investment income, and interest paid on bank accounts. The *contribution sur les revenus locatifs* is levied on gross rental income.

● WEALTH TAX
A wealth tax called the *impôt de solidarité sur la fortune* is levied on net assets held in France valued above a certain threshold, and can include property, a car and bank balances.

● CAPITAL GAINS TAX
There is no tax on gains made from the sale of a principal home, but capital gains tax, the *impôt sur les plus-values*, is levied on the profits of the sale of other property.

● INHERITANCE TAX
In theory, inheritance tax is paid on the global assets of a French tax resident. The beneficiaries pay inheritance taxes depending on how closely they are related to the deceased. Inheritance tax is payable on any French property owned by a non-resident.

FRANCE

Employment hotspots

With an economy heavily reliant on tourism, France has many job openings for those with a working knowledge of French

1 Paris

Glamorous and cosmopolitan, Paris is one of the world's great cities, both culturally and architecturally. It is a haven for artists and writers, and the streets are lined with cafés, bars and restaurants.

A quarter of France's manufacturing industry is situated in Paris – chemicals, pharmaceuticals, computer software and electrical equipment. More than 8,000 foreign companies are based here and La Défense business centre is home to ELF, Esso and IBM. Sixty-five per cent of jobs are in the business sector, and 138,600 are employed in tourism. Disneyland, to the east of the city, is a major employer. Paris is also a centre of art and publishing.

Property prices are high, but you will get a better deal in areas such as Montmatre and Montparnasse. Prices start at €579,000 (£400,000) for a two-bedroom apartment and €1,050,000 (£725,000) for a four-bedroom house.

KEY FACTS
■ **Population:** 2.15 million
■ **Airport:** Paris Charles de Gaulle, Tel: 00 33 148 62 12 12
■ **Medical:** Clinique Internationale du Parc Monceau, Tel: 00 33 1 48 88 25 25
■ **Schools:** British School of Paris, Tel: 00 33 134 80 45 90 ■ Lycée International of Saint-Germain-en-Laye (American School), Tel: 00 33 134 51 74 85
■ **Rentals:** There is excellent rental potential for long and short-term lets
■ **Pros:** Public transport is excellent ■ There are job opportunities for foreigners who speak French
■ **Cons:** Property prices are high ■ The cost of living is also very high.

ABOVE: Many buyers are attracted by the traditional French lifestyle

2 Côte d'Azur

Provence and the Côte d'Azur are beautiful and varied, with sophisticated resorts, fields of lavender, gorges, rivers and unspoiled villages. Cannes is most famous for its film festival, and Grasse is perfume capital of the world. The French Riviera has many beaches, golf courses and casinos, which attract tourists and celebrities alike.

The economy in Cannes, St Tropez and Nice is based on tourism, which has encouraged a thriving property market. Tourism accounts for 16 per cent of the region's jobs, and the Côte d'Azur also boasts Europe's silicon valley at Sophia Antipolis, which is home to 1,200 companies.

A two-bedroom apartment in Nice will set you back €242,000 (£167,000). A four-bedroom house costs about €654,800 (£452,000).

KEY FACTS
■ **Population:** 4,506,151
■ **Airport:** Toulon/Hyères Aéroport, Tel: 00 33 4 9400 8383
■ St Tropez Aéroport du Golfe, Tel: 00 33 4 9449 5729
■ **Medical:** Centre Hospitalier Universitaire de Nice, Tel: 0033 4 9203 7777
■ Centre Hospitalier du Pays d'Aix, Tel: 00 33 4 4233 5650
■ **Schools:** The International School of Nice, Tel: 00 33 4 9321 0400
■ Mougins School, Tel: 00 33 4 9390 1547
■ **Rentals:** The Côte d'Azur is the world's most popular tourist destination ■ You are guaranteed year-round rental income and can charge high prices
■ **Pros:** There is plenty to see and do, from glitz and glamour to relaxing on the beach ■ The weather is fantastic ■ Regular budget flights
■ **Cons:** Property and the cost of living are sky-high ■ The area can get very busy.

3 Dordogne

Bergerac and Périgueux are situated in the historic Dordogne, in the Aquitaine region of France. They are within easy reach of superb châteaux, fortified towns and gentle countryside. Bergerac is the main market centre for the surrounding maize and tobacco farms and vineyards. Périgueux, the old capital of Dordogne, boasts one of the largest clusters of Roman ruins outside Rome.

A huge 70 per cent of Aquitaine's workers are in the service industry, many of whom are government and tourism workers. Other key local industries include chemicals, agriculture and manufacturing.

Cheap flights into Bergerac have helped to sustain the appreciation in property prices, which have risen annually by about 15 per cent over the past few years. The average cost of a four-bedroom home is about €253,833 (£175,000), while a two-bedroom apartment will set you back about €122,000 (£84,000).

KEY FACTS
■ **Population:** 212,494
■ **Airport:** Bergerac-Rouman Aéroport, Tel: 00 33 553 22 25 25
■ Limoges Airport, Tel: 00 33 555 43 30 30
■ **Medical:** Centre Hospitalier, Tel: 00 33 553 45 25 25
■ **Schools:** Bordeaux's international school is 95 kilometres from Bergerac, Tel: 00 33 557 87 02 11
■ **Rentals:** One of France's most popular holiday areas ■ Generates a huge year-round rental income
■ **Pros:** Warm climate ■ Low-cost flights to the region
■ **Cons:** This area is becoming overcrowded and is heavily colonised by British buyers. ●

FRANCE

Property price guide

France is renowned for its bargain properties and renovation projects, but affordable modern properties are also available

PROPERTIES FOR RENT

Attractive holiday apartments, ideal for short-term rents with the family

€1,044 PER WEEK

3-BED, TARN-ET-GARONNE

£720 PER WEEK
- Fully furnished ✔
- Pool ✔
- Parking ✔   **CODE** KIN

€1,327 PER WEEK

3-BED, LOT ET GARONNE

£915 PER WEEK
- Fully furnished ✔
- Pool ✔
- Parking ✔   **CODE** KIN

€1,360 PER WEEK

2-BED, TARN ET GARONNE

£940 PER WEEK
- Fully furnished ✔
- Pool ✔
- Parking ✔   **CODE** KIN

€2,429 PER WEEK

5-BED, LOT

£1,675 PER WEEK
- Fully furnished ✔
- Pool ✔
- Parking ✔   **CODE** KIN

APARTMENTS FOR SALE

Whether for city living or holiday lets, a variety of apartments are available

€161,000

1-BED CALVADOS

£111,100
- Fully furnished ✔
- Pool ✔
- Parking ✔   **CODE** LAT

€250,000

1-BED VAR

£172,500
- Fully furnished ✘
- Pool ✔
- Parking ✔   **CODE** LAT

€1,200,000

2-BED PARIS

£828,000
- Fully furnished ✘
- Pool ✘
- Parking ✘   **CODE** SIF

€1,200,000

3-BED PARIS

£828,000
- Fully furnished ✘
- Pool ✘
- Parking ✘   **CODE** SIF

HOUSES FOR SALE

From small country cottages to lavish mansions, there is something for all

€302,043

3-BED COTES D'ARMOR

£208,400
- Fully furnished ✘
- Pool ✔
- Parking ✔   **CODE** LAT

€513,000

5-BED HAUTE GARONNE

£354,000
- Fully furnished ✘
- Pool ✘
- Parking ✔   **CODE** SIF

€580,000

4-BED DORDOGNE

£400,200
- Fully furnished ✘
- Pool ✔
- Parking ✔   **CODE** LAT

€1,130,000

3-BED CANNES

£780,000
- Fully furnished ✘
- Pool ✔
- Parking ✔   **CODE** SIF

FRANCE

All our properties can be found on our website:
www.latitudes.co.uk

LATITUDES
FRENCH PROPERTY AGENTS

Aude: New development of furnished Provencal style 1, 2 & 3 bed houses with garden, parking, balcony & electric heating. Pool & tennis court. Leaseback – lots of personal use. Ref: Port M Prices from: 84,752 euros

Nr Le Touquet, Pas de Calais: Well situated new development of 1 & 2 bed houses & apartments, views over the Baie de Canche. Garden or balcony/ terrace, parking, heating. Ref: Amarel Prices from: 97,000 euros

Savoie: Leaseback ski development of 1, 2, 3 & 4 bed apartments with balcony & mountain views. Heated communal pool & sauna. Guaranteed return, personal use possible. Ref: Belleco Prices from: 117,088 euros

Cotes d'Armor, Brittany: New development of 1, 2 & 3 bed apartments with views over the port & bay, 500m from the beach. Parquet floors, heating & balcony/ garden. Ref: Hautes Prices from: 126,555 euros

Burgundy: Colombage farmhouse with garden, outbuildings & views. Offers reception/kitchen with fireplace, 2 bedrooms, bathroom, study, convertible attic. Ref: 3152GV Price: 150,000 euros

Herault: Villa with pool, garage & large garden. Offers equipped kitchen, reception with fireplace, 3 bedrooms, bathroom, heating. 15 mins from the beach. Ref: 341000E Price: 341,000 euros

Calvados, Normandy: 18C colombage property with 2 gites (1x2 bed, 1x1 bed), pond & pool in 5 acres. Offers 2 receptions, fitted kitchen, 5 bedrooms, 4 bathrooms, heating. Ref: 2800SOC Price: 545,000 euros

Dordogne: 15C chateau + several gites, stables, out-buildings & superb views in 180 acres. Offers 4 receptions, equipped kitchen, 19 bedrooms, 5 bathrooms, original features. Ref: 3149/1BER Price: 1,500,000 euros

Cote d'Azur: Spacious villa with sea views & pool in half an acre. Offers equipped kitchen, reception, 5 bedrooms & bathrooms, terraces, garage. 15 mins from the sea. Ref: 134CAZ Price: 2,750,000 euros

Established in 1989, Latitudes specialise in the sale of French property, both resale and new 'off-plan' properties.

With the benefit of our long experience we can help and advise you throughout every aspect of your purchase from arranging viewing itineraries to bi-lingual assistance with your contracts.

- Latitudes have properties in most areas of France to suit all budgets

- Our website offers over 6000 properties, and is updated daily

- We work with over 250 registered French agencies and developers in France and as such can give you a good overview of the property market

- We make absolutely no charge to our purchasers

Tel: 020 8951 5155 Fax: 020 8951 5156 Email: sales@latitudes.co.uk Web: www.latitudes.co.uk ⊞ FOPDAC

Germany

A major world economy in the heart of Europe

FACT BOX

- ■ **Population** 82,424,609
- ■ **Population growth rate** 0.02%
- ■ **Economic growth rate** -0.1%
- ■ **Inflation rate** 1.1%
- ■ **Capital** Berlin
- ■ **Hotspots** Frankfurt, Munich, Berlin, Cologne, Stuttgart, Hamburg
- ■ **Average house price** (4-bed) €481,000
- ■ **Average rental price** (2-bed) €1,352

Living in Germany

From the Baltic ports to the Bavarian Alps, Germany is a country of contrasts and opportunities

FACT FILE

AREA	357,021km²
POPULATION	82,424,609
CAPITAL	Berlin
LIFE EXPECTANCY	78.54 years
LITERACY	99%
GOVERNMENT	Federal republic
GDP PER CAPITA	US$27,600
UNEMPLOYMENT RATE	12.1%
CURRENCY	Euro (€)
EXCHANGE RATE	€1 = £0.70; £1 = €1.44
LANGUAGES	German

COST OF LIVING

PETROL (1L)	€1.19
WINE (0.75L)	€3.50
MEAL (3-COURSE)	€25
BEER (33CL)	€1.40
LOAF OF BREAD	€1.90
MILK (1L)	€0.55

© GERMAN TOURIST BOARD

ABOVE: The spectacular Bavarian Alps

CLIMATE

BERLIN		LONDON	BERLIN		LONDON
3	Dec	7	43	Dec	81
7	Nov	10	46	Nov	78
13	Oct	14	49	Oct	70
20	Sept	19	48	Sept	65
23	Aug	21	69	Aug	62
24	July	22	73	July	59
22	June	20	65	June	58
19	May	17	49	May	57
13	April	13	42	April	56
7	March	10	33	March	64
3	Feb	7	40	Feb	72
2	Jan	6	46	Jan	77

Average monthly temperature °C

Average monthly rainfall mm

SITUATED IN THE HEART OF EUROPE, Germany boasts a varied terrain, with lowlands in the north and the Bavarian Alps in the south. Its most spectacular features include the river Rhine, Lake Konstanz, and the 2,962-metre high Zugspitze on the Austrian border. The most densely populated areas of the country are Greater Berlin, the Ruhr region and Frankfurt-am-Main and its surrounding area.

Germany's recent history has been dominated by the reunification of East and West Germany. This involved major lifestyle changes for those from the East, and in the past few years, *Ostalgie*, nostalgia for ideas and products from the East, has surfaced.

Germans are generally liberal, forward-thinking and pro-Europe. Current issues in Germany include multiculturalism and the environment.

Politics and economy

Germany is a federal republic with a democratic government, currently a coalition between the SDP (social democrats) and Alliance90/Green Party. It has the largest economy in the Eurozone, and despite recent economic problems GDP has grown at its fastest rate for four years. The most important industries are services, IT, biotech, environmental and renewable energy technology, chemicals, telecommunications and car-manufacturing. Current political concerns include the high level of unemployment, which, at over 12 per cent, is at its highest since the 1930s, and the increasing support for the neo-Nazi party, especially in the economically depressed states of former East Germany.

Crime rates in Germany are lower than in the UK, at 76.02 crimes per 1,000 people, but with higher numbers of gun-related crimes. The most prevalent crime is theft, particularly of cars.

Climate

Germany has a temperate climate. The mean temperature for the country is 9°C, and there are no sustained periods of cold or heat. Northwestern and coastal Germany have a maritime climate characterised by warm summers and mild, cloudy winters. Further inland, the climate is continental, marked by greater variations in temperature, with warmer summers and colder winters. The Alpine regions endure lower temperatures, due to higher altitudes and greater precipitation. Upper Bavaria also experiences a warm Alpine wind from the south called a Föhn.

Healthcare

Germany has a very high-quality healthcare system. There is an EU-wide agreement that guarantees free medical treatment for those with an E111 form. Those wishing to live in the country must register for a local health insurance scheme and obtain a health insurance card (*Krankenversicherungskarte*). About 85 per cent of the population is insured under the *Gesetzliche Krankenkasse* (GKV), which is similar to the NHS. If you are an employee and earn less than €3,825 (£2,638) per month you are obliged to enroll, and monthly contributions of around 14 per cent of your gross income will be deducted from your salary and matched by your employer. If you earn more than this you can opt to be privately insured.

If you need to see a doctor, the first port of call is usually a GP, and Germans are free to visit any. However, about half of all specialists practise outside the hospital system, so if a specialist is needed, Germans would not waste time seeing a GP. There are a large number of independent clinics with the most sophisticated equipment, and waiting is largely unknown. A patient may walk in or ring for an appointment, which will invariably be booked for the same day.

Education

Germany is a country that values education and vocational training highly (9.1 per cent of the budget was spent on it in 2002). The entire school system is under the supervision of the state and is completely free. Education is compulsory until the age of 18; pupils must complete a nine-year course before doing two years' part-time vocational

ABOVE: St Nicholas Church in Potsdam

training or going on to a full-time vocational or academic course. Children enter *Grundschule* (primary school) at the age of six. They then go on to one of four types of school: a *Hauptschule*, where they study for a basic secondary certificate, a *Realschule*, to study for an intermediate secondary certificate, a *Gymnasium* or grammar school, where they can complete the *Abitur* (equivalent to A levels) and go on to university, or a *Gesamtschule* (comprehensive school), which combines the three forms of schooling.

> *"Germany is a very international and cosmopolitan country, and you will find that there are plenty of expat societies"*

Food and drink

There is much more to the German diet than the stereotypical Sauerkraut! The main staples of the diet are bread, of which there are 200 different types, sausage, of which there are an amazing 1,500 varieties, and potatoes, which take every form imaginable.

Few countries can match Germany for beer – it is home to 5,000 varieties, from the light Pilsener in the north to the black beer famous in the east. The classic grape Riesling also thrives in Germany,

and there are 13 wine-growing regions. Schnapps, a warming spirit, is served here in a two-centilitre measure called a *Stamper*.

Cities and towns have a selection of international restaurants. Vegetarian food is widely available, although vegans may experience some problems finding suitable food.

Expat communities

Germany is a very international and cosmopolitan country, and there are plenty of expat societies. Berlin, Hamburg and Munich are particular hotspots for expats, with conversation groups, guides and scouts, sports clubs, choirs and many other groups. British and Irish pubs are good places to meet fellow foreigners. There are also various publications aimed at expats, such as the *Munich Found* (www.munichfound.de) or *New in the City* (www.new-in-the city.com/munich/en).

Pets

Before your pet dog or cat travels, he or she must be fitted with a microchip or have a readable tattoo; be vaccinated against rabies; be blood tested; be issued with an official PETS certificate or passport; have an up-to-date vaccination card; have the fitness-to-fly section of the passport completed within seven days prior to travel.

For parrots, parakeets and rabbits, a veterinary health certificate issued no longer than ten days prior to entry is required. The veterinary authority of the state must also be contacted for authorisation to import domestic or wild fowl. Guinea pigs, hamsters and fish can be imported without authorisation. ●

TRAVEL FILE

AIR The main gateway into Germany is Frankfurt-am-Main airport, although there are also airports in Berlin, Düsseldorf, Hamburg, Munich and Cologne/Bonn. **British Airways** (www.ba.com; 0870 850 9850) offers frequent flights from Heathrow, Manchester, Birmingham, Edinburgh, Bristol and Gatwick to various locations. **Lufthansa** (www.lufthansa.co.uk; 0208 750 3460 / 00 49 1805 838 005) also has a comprehensive schedule of flights from Heathrow, Birmingham, Manchester, Newcastle and Edinburgh. **Air Berlin** (www.airberlin.com; 0870 738 8880 / 00 49 1805 737 800) flies from Stansted and Manchester. **Easyjet** (www.easyjet.com, 0871 244 2366) operates flights from various UK locations. **Ryanair** (www.ryanair.com; 0871 246 0000) provides flights from London Stansted. **German Wings** (www 23.germanwings.com; 0870 252 1250 / 00 49 1805 955 855) operates from London, Edinburgh and Stansted.

RAIL The country rail network connects all major German cities and many towns, as well as neighbouring countries. Rail services are operated by **Deutsche Bahn** (www.bahn.de; 0870 243 5663 / 00 49 1805 194 195). From the UK, it is possible to catch the **Eurostar** (www. eurostar.com; 0870 518 6186) to Paris or Brussels and connect with the international **Thalys** service (www.thalys.com; 00 33 835 35 36). There are various types of train service. The fastest is the **ICE** or **Intercity Express**, which travels at high speeds between large cities. The **IC (Intercity)** and **EC (Eurocity)** trains offer long distance services, connecting major centres within Germany, and some neighbouring countries. **IR (Inter-regional)** and **RB (Regional)** trains link small towns to the long-distance trains.

ROAD The long-distance coach company **Eurolines** (www.eurolines.co.uk; 0870 514 3219) goes to more than 50 towns and cities in Germany and connects them with destinations all over Europe. **Berlin Linien Bus** (www. berlinlinienbus.de; 00 49 308 619 331) has a comprehensive network linking many towns and cities across the country, as do **Gullivers Reisen** (www.gullivers.de; 00 49 3031 102 110).

SEA It is possible to reach Germany from the UK by ferry, although the journey takes approximately 20 hours. **DFDS Seaways** (www.dfdsseaways.co.uk; 0870 533 3111) runs a service from Harwich on the east coast, to Cuxhaven, near Hamburg.

GETTING AROUND Most cities in Germany enjoy well-linked and reliable public transport services. The commuter rail trains or trams stop at major points throughout a city. These often connect directly with the underground train service. Buses also form a dependable service within cities and towns, and connect with surrounding towns and villages.

Who moves there?

With over 10,000 foreign companies and a skills shortage, Germany has good job prospects for skilled workers

LEFT: Residents in Hanover enjoy a drink in one of the city's many cafés

"The cost of living in Germany is 19 per cent lower than in the UK"

O F THE 96.4 MILLION PEOPLE WHO VISIT Germany every year, 3.2 million are from the UK. With 8.9 per cent of EU immigrants to Germany attributed to the UK, it is estimated that nearly 250,000 British people were registered as living in Germany in 2003, and this figure is rising.

Who moves there?

Although the population of Germany is falling, the number of foreign residents is rising steadily, from 7,334,800 in 2003 to 7,341,820 in 2004. Three German states are home to the majority of expats: North Rhine Westphalia has 1,965,155; Baden-Württemberg has 1,290,258; Bavaria has 1,182,383. The largest age group of immigrants is 21–40, totalling 2,970,552 residents, and there are 1,712,000 foreign students registered at Germany's world-class universities. Although a large proportion of immigrants stay for between only one and four years, the largest number (1,3 million) stay for between 10 and 15 years.

Although families do move to Germany, the most numerous immigrants are young professionals and students. The number of one-person households is rising significantly, due to the number of single people moving there to work. Gap-year opportunities, bar work, seasonal work and jobs teaching English as a foreign language (TEFL) also draw many young people.

Why move there?

There are many reasons why people choose to live and work in Germany. The current shortage of skilled workers means that job prospects for a skilled immigrant are high. More than 10,000 foreign enterprises are located there – a great source for expat employment. Business people place Germany as top within the EU for infrastructure and logistics, research and development and design. There are many job opportunities in the ICT sector, as well as openings for mechanical and chemical engineers, specialists in renewable energy technology and healthcare professionals. Those with publishing experience will also find a wide range of jobs in most major cities.

German employees benefit from excellent working conditions and have about 41 days holiday per year. The cost of living in Germany is 19 per cent lower than in the UK. Germans save an average of 15 per cent of their monthly salary compared to five per cent in the UK. Property is expensive compared with other European countries, but is still good value for money. Homes are more spacious than those in Britain, with the average new home boasting more than 100 square metres of usable floor space compared with a British average of 76.

A good healthcare system, lower crime rates than in the UK and the many different cultural facilities also attract people to Germany. The football World Cup is to be hosted there in 2006, and this is likely to result in an improved infrastructure and an increase in the number of jobs. English is widely spoken, and the country has a similar climate to the UK, making expats feel at home. ●

Working in Germany

From world-leading IT and biotech sectors to mechanical engineering and renewable energy technology, Germany has a wealth of job opportunities

■ LABOUR MARKET

Germany's government is currently facing two major labour market problems: a high rate of unemployment and a lack of skilled workers. Unemployment rates have risen for 12 consecutive months and currently stand at 12.1 per cent, the highest level since the 1930s. To combat these problems, welfare reforms have been introduced, including the creation of "one euro jobs" in public service. These give low wages that top up unemployment benefits. Immigration reforms include unlimited residence for skilled foreign workers and help with integration.

© GERMAN TOURIST BOARD

ABOVE: Regensburg's 12th-century stone bridge is an engineering masterpiece

■ JOB OPPORTUNITIES AND KEY INDUSTRIES

Due to the shortage of skilled workers in certain sectors, and the "brain drain" in the former East German states, the government is recruiting skilled foreign professionals. The IT industry is a particular concern, where 25 per cent of jobs are currently unfilled. Engineers (especially chemical), healthcare professionals, scientists and corporate managers are in demand. The auto industry, paramount to the German economy, is the third largest in the world and employs 1.26 million workers. German IT and biotech industries are world leaders, while current growth areas are mechanical engineering and renewable energy technology. Thriving telecommunications, publishing and chemical industries also provide many jobs.

■ FINDING A JOB

If you have not secured a job before moving to Germany, there are a number of top job sites, such as www.jobpilot.de and www.jobscout24.de, to start your search. There is also a comprehensive database, European Employment Services, known as EURES (www.europa.eu.int/eures), which was created to help EU citizens find jobs in other EU countries. Potential employees with sought–after skills, such as chemical engineers or IT specialists, would be well advised to contact a professional search firm (*Personalberatung*) such as Manpower GmbH or Jobs in Time. The Saturday and Wednesday editions of national newspapers often contain job sections and the Saturday *FAZ* (*Frankfurter Allgemeine Zeitung*) is renowned for its extensive selection. There are more than 800 job centres (*Arbeitsämter*), some with international departments known as *ZAV* or *Zentralstelle für Auslandsvermittlung*, which have comprehensive lists of vacancies.

■ LANGUAGE REQUIREMENTS

English is taught in schools and is widely spoken in the business community, particularly in large international companies, but it is best to know some useful phrases. For work outside TEFL and holiday jobs, a working knowledge of German is necessary.

■ BUSINESS ETIQUETTE

The Germans are formal in their business dealings and place emphasis on punctuality. ●

VISAS AND WORK PERMITS

UK citizens may enter Germany freely and stay for up to three months to look for work or set up a business without registering. They may be required to prove that they have the means to support themselves. If you wish to work or live in Germany for longer, you will need to register with two different organisations.

● RESIDENCE REGISTRATION

Within one week of finding accommodation, it is necessary to register your new address and get a *Meldebescheinigung* (registration certificate) at the *Einwohnermeldeamt* (residence registration office), usually located in the town hall. This rule applies to everyone who moves house in Germany, including German nationals.

● RESIDENCE PERMIT

You must also obtain an *Aufenthaltsgenehmigung* (residence permit). This must be done at the *Ausländeramt* (the foreign nationals authority), where you will need to produce your passport and two photos. This office is also usually located in the town hall. Both offices will be found under *Stadtverwaltung* (local municipal authority) in the telephone directory.

■ USEFUL WEBSITES

www.howtogermany.com
www.german-embassy.org.uk
www.jobscout24.de
www.immobilienscout24.de
www.frankfurtamain.de

Finding a home

Most German housing has been built in the last 60 years, but traditional, good value homes are available in many rural areas

THE GERMAN PROPERTY MARKET IS STABLE BUT SLOW. IT IS unlikely that you will make a fast profit on your investment, although prices will rise over the next few years. Owners have to hold on to their homes for ten years to avoid paying capital gains tax, which has slowed the market. City locations provide the best investment, because demand is pushing up prices, particularly in cities playing host to the World Cup in 2006.

Renting

More than half of Germany's population currently rents. Prices vary, but you can expect to pay more in the large cities. Most apartments are unfurnished, and before you can move in you must pay a deposit of two or three months' rent. Check the contract and inventory carefully. Many tenants are expected to renovate the property when they move out, and specific rules about noise are common. Because of large demand from tenants, buying to let is a viable investment option.

Buying

Property prices are based on floor space rather than the number of rooms. To obtain a mortgage, it is necessary to produce years of bank statements. Mortgage financing is normally arranged for up to 70 per cent of the purchase price, and 80 per cent of mortgages granted are at a fixed rate for at least five years. Interest rates are currently at a low of 5 per cent.

Restrictions on foreign buyers

There are no bars on foreign ownership of property, but banks can be restrictive when it comes to mortgages if you don't live or pay tax in Germany. They may require a larger deposit due to the lack of long-term German financial records, which could be up to around 50 per cent of the purchase price.

Charges

There are several charges when you buy a property: the property transfer tax stands at 3.5 per cent of the purchase price; you pay 1–1.5 per cent to the notary, the agent's fees are in the region of 3.5–6 per cent and the registration fees cost between 0.8–1.2 per cent. There is an annual local property tax, which is calculated on the size of the property and normally amounts to 1 per cent of the rateable value. ●

ABOVE: Property on the River Neckar sells at a premium

INCOME TAX

Anyone who is considered a permanent resident in Germany will have income tax calculated according to their combined income from Germany and overseas.

● To be considered a permanent resident, you must prove a permanent stay in Germany of at least six months within two complete tax years. UK citizens working in Germany for fewer than 183 days in a year will be liable for UK income tax and must declare any German earnings to the Inland Revenue). Those working in Germany for more than 183 days in a tax year are liable for German income tax and must register with the German tax office, the *Finanzamt* (www.finanzamt.de).

● Those working in Germany on a short-term basis (fewer than 183 days in a year) may still be subject to a witholding tax of 25 per cent of any earnings, which could later be reclaimed. The UK has had a double taxation treaty with Germany since 1967, which prevents an individual from paying tax on the same earnings in the two countries simultaneously. The German tax year runs from 1 January to 31 December, and personal income is taxed on a progressive scale – the higher the income, the higher the tax percentage. For the tax year ending 31 December 2004, the tax breakdown was as follows:

Earnings up to €7,664	0%
Earnings between €7,664 and €12,739	16–24%
Earnings between €12,740 and €52,151	24–45%
Earnings in excess of €52,152	45%

A tax reform was introduced in 2000, which planned to lower the income tax rates over four years. It was hoped the cuts would lead to economic growth and create more jobs. The final part of the reform comes into effect in 2005, when the lowest rate of tax will fall to 15 per cent and the highest rate to 42 per cent.

AVERAGE RENTAL/SALE PRICES

Hotspot	2-bed apartment rentals	2-bed apartment sales	4-bed house sales
Munich	€1,715 (£1,183)	€293K (£202K)	€685K (£472K)
Frankfurt	€1,220 (£841)	€280K (£193K)	€412K (£284K)
Berlin	€1,120 (£772)	€163K (£112K)	€345K (£238K)

Employment hotspots

From the capital, Berlin, to the Bavarian city of Munich, Germany's prosperous cities are exciting places in which to live and work

1 Munich

The Bavarian capital and Germany's third largest city, Munich has a cosmopolitan, relaxed feel and has been named the best German city in which to live, located just north of the Alps. The city has an eclectic mix of traditional, Baroque and modern architecture and a good infrastructure, not to mention its Oktoberfest and Bierkeller. Expats are attracted to Munich due to high employment rates.

Known locally as the Silicon Valley of Europe, Munich is a thriving, hi-tech metropolis. Five per cent of the workforce is employed in banking. The biotech industry plays a role in the economy, and 81 per cent of German media companies are here. Major employers include Siemens, BMW, IBM, Microsoft, Apple and Allianz.

Property is a good investment, particularly in central areas and smaller villages just outside the city.

KEY FACTS
■ **Population:** 1.2 million
■ **Airport:** Munich International Airport, Tel: 00 49 899 7500
■ **Medical:** Krankenhaus Martha-Maria, Tel: 00 49 897 2760
■ **Schools:** Munich International School, Tel: 00 49 8151 3660
■ **Rentals:** Shortage of good rental accommodation ■ Prices have risen sharply due to increased demand
■ **Pros:** Surrounded by beautiful countryside ■ A centre for business ■ A large expat population
■ **Cons:** House prices are the highest in the country.

2 Frankfurt-am-Main

Frankfurt is the financial capital of Germany. With 27.6 per cent of residents originally coming from outside Germany, it has

ABOVE: Frankfurt's skyline is dominated by modern architecture

© GERMAN TOURIST BOARD

a real mixture of cultures, languages and lifestyles.

Frankfurt produces a large part of Germany's wealth and there are a variety of job opportunities. Financial openings are plentiful, and there is a selection of PR, marketing and media jobs available. It is also a leading biotech centre. Manufacturing provides many jobs, and tourism is growing.

Although housing costs are reasonably high in comparison to other areas of Germany, property here is likely to rise in price, particularly in Westend, Nordend, Sachsenhausen and Bornheim.

KEY FACTS
■ **Population:** 650,000
■ **Airport:** Frankfurt-am-Main International Airport, Tel: 00 49 696 900
■ **Medical:** Bürgerhospital Frankfurt-am-Main e.V., Tel: 00 49 69 1500 281
■ **Schools:** Frankfurt International School, Tel: 00 49 6171 2020
■ **Rentals:** Many young professionals want to rent ■ Renting is the best option for foreign workers with short-

term contracts ■ During trade fairs, short-term rental prices skyrocket
■ **Pros:** Low unemployment rates ■ A diverse city in terms of industries, people and architecture ■ Excellent shopping district, a prestigious university and many museums
■ **Cons:** House prices are high ■ Highest crime rate in Germany.

3 Berlin

Since the expansion of the EU in 2004, Berlin has become a link between Eastern and Western Europe. Vibrant and progressive, with an unrivalled cultural scene, it is a magnet for creativity and architectural experimentation, a symbol of the modern and a centre for youth culture.

Berlin is the political centre of Germany and a dynamic business location. A large media industry has built up in the area. Other core industries include biotech, advertising and environmental and communications technology. There are also over 2,000 financial consultancies. Despite the current high unemployment, there is an abundance of jobs in

the IT sector and a real shortage of English teachers. Major companies based here include Sony, Coca Cola, Deutsche Bahn and KPMG.

The centre of Berlin has recently experienced a boom, and is now filled with modern hi-tech and hi-spec buildings. There are plans to develop other areas. Property prices in Berlin are lower than in most other major German cities.

KEY FACTS
■ **Population:** 3.4 million
■ **Airport:** Berlin-Tegel Airport, Tel: 00 49 180 50 00 186
■ **Medical:** Charité Universitätsmedizin Berlin, Tel: 00 49 30 45 050
■ **Schools:** Berlin British School, Tel: 00 49 30 30 42 205
■ **Rentals:** Prices have risen steadily in recent years ■ Apartments in Berlin are often surprisingly spacious
■ **Pros:** Numerous museums as well as excellent shopping facilities and entertainment ■ Much of the property is modern and built to a high standard
■ **Cons:** Has been described as a city of cranes, due to the amount of building ■ Some buildings in the east are run down or badly constructed ■ High unemployment.

OTHER HOTSPOTS
■ **Cologne:** An ideal location in which to live and work, with a wide range of jobs. Family homes and apartments are reasonably priced.
■ **Stuttgart:** The city of Stuttgart has a growing financial sector. It has a stable property market, with city centre properties in high demand.
■ **Hamburg:** Hamburg is a wealthy city and its inhabitants have the most living space per person in any major world city. Home to specialised industries such as aviation, medicine and biotechnology. The property market is stable. ●

WITH OUR INTERNATIONAL TRANSFER SERVICE YOUR MONEY WILL FLY AROUND THE WORLD

Sehra, Halifax

Whether you're sending cash to relatives overseas or buying a home in the sun, we can get your money to wherever it has to go, quickly and securely. What's more, the funds can be sent in a wide range of local currencies, as well as in sterling. So, if you're after a full range of international payment services that are quick and easy to use, we'd suggest you fly along to your nearest branch of Halifax.

0845 607 7767

(Lines open 24 hours a day, 7 days a week)

 **HALIFAX** Always giving you extra

Property price guide

Whether you are choosing a city apartment or a large country house, Germany offers excellent value for money

HOMES FOR RENT

Rental homes come in every available style for every budget

€500 PER MONTH

STUDIO FRANKFURT

£345 PER MONTH
- Fully furnished ✔
- Pool ✘
- Parking ✔　　CODE ALL

€1,350 PER MONTH

4-BED HOUSE HOHENBRUNN

£930 PER MONTH
- Fully furnished ✘
- Pool ✘
- Parking ✔　　CODE ALL

€1,750 PER MONTH

3-BED HOUSE BAD SODEN

£1,200 PER MONTH
- Fully furnished ✘
- Pool ✘
- Parking ✔　　CODE ALL

€2,450 PER MONTH

2-BED APARTMENT MUNICH

£1,690 PER MONTH
- Fully furnished ✔
- Pool ✘
- Parking ✔　　CODE ALL

APARTMENTS FOR SALE

City centre apartments in period buildings are commonly found

€159,000

1-BED FRANKFURT

£109,700
- Fully furnished ✘
- Pool ✘
- Parking ✘　　CODE ALL

€165,000

1/2-BED FRANKFURT

£113,800
- Fully furnished ✘
- Pool ✘
- Parking ✘　　CODE ALL

€180,000

1-BED FRANKFURT

£124,200
- Fully furnished ✘
- Pool ✘
- Parking ✘　　CODE ALL

€339,000

2-BED KOENIGSTEIN

£233,900
- Fully furnished ✘
- Pool ✘
- Parking ✔　　CODE ALL

HOUSES FOR SALE

Spacious homes with large gardens are perfect for families

€215,000

2/3-BED HOUSE GRUNDAU

£148,300
- Fully furnished ✘
- Pool ✘
- Parking ✔　　CODE ALL

€255,000

3-BED HOUSE BONN

£175,900
- Fully furnished ✘
- Pool ✘
- Parking ✔　　CODE ALL

€348,750

2-BED BUNGALOW HAMBURG

£240,600
- Fully furnished ✘
- Pool ✘
- Parking ✔　　CODE ALL

€595,000

3/4-BED FRANKFURT

£410,500
- Fully furnished ✘
- Pool ✘
- Parking ✔　　CODE ALL

GERMANY

ON SALE NOW!

Homes Worldwide is the one-stop source for anyone who has ever dreamed of owning a home overseas. Packed with a wealth of real life experience and practical advice from experts in currency, mortgages, law and property, the magazine will guide you to your perfect location, wherever it is in the world.

inspiration & **hard facts** – a winning mix!

Ireland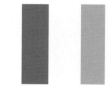

One of the most prosperous nations in Europe

© FÁILTE IRELAND PHOTOGRAPHIC

FACT BOX

- ■ **Population** 3,969,558
- ■ **Population growth rate** 1.16%
- ■ **Economic growth rate** 1.4%
- ■ **Inflation rate** 3.5%
- ■ **Capital** Dublin
- ■ **Hotspot** Dublin
- ■ **Average house price** (4-bed) €413,000
- ■ **Average rental price** (2-bed) €1,080

Living in Ireland

Rated "the best place to live in the world", Ireland boasts a strong economy and an emphasis on traditional values

FACT FILE

AREA	70,280km²
POPULATION	3,969,558
CAPITAL	Dublin
MERCER COST OF LIVING 2004	96.9
LIFE EXPECTANCY	77.4 years
LITERACY	98%
GOVERNMENT	Republic
GDP PER CAPITA	$29,600
UNEMPLOYMENT RATE	4.7%
CURRENCY	Euro (€)
EXCHANGE RATE	€1 = £0.69; £ = €1.48
LANGUAGES	English, Gaelic

TRAVEL FILE

AIR Budget airline **Ryanair** (0871 246 0000; www.ryanair.com) flies to Dublin from many regional airports, as does **Aer Lingus** (0845 084 4444; www.aerlingus.com).

SEA A number of operators run ferries between Holyhead and Dublin, Fishguard and Rosslare, and Swansea and Cork. All can be booked with **Direct Ferries** (0870 458 5120; www.directferries.com).

ROAD The M50 loops around Dublin, from which the national routes spread out to the rest of the country. The M1 connects with Belfast in Northern Ireland. Most road distances are given in kilometres, but speed signs are in miles per hour.

GETTING AROUND The **DART** (Dublin Area Rapid Transit) links the main city areas. The national bus and train network is dilapidated and services are infrequent.

A COUPLE OF DECADES AGO, IRELAND'S citizens emigrated in huge numbers to escape widespread poverty. But since joining the EU, Ireland has become one of the most prosperous nations in Europe.

Although Britain and Ireland have shared a difficult past, relations between the countries are now good. Both governments are committed to a peaceful resolution to the Northern Ireland issue, and the Good Friday agreement was a major step.

Crime is low, especially in rural Ireland, where locking doors is the exception rather than the rule. As in most major cities, however, there is some drug-related crime in Dublin.

Education

Education is free and compulsory from ages six to sixteen. The Leaving Certificate is taken at 16 or 17, after which many students take a year out to consider their options. Universities are free, but there are fees for materials and exams.

Healthcare

Healthcare in Ireland is excellent, but only those on the lowest incomes are entitled to completely free healthcare. Others are entitled to certain free hospital services and can receive subsidised prescription drugs, but they have to pay to visit their GP. Health Insurance is available through the state-run Voluntary Health Insurance board (VHI) and other private health insurance companies, such as BUPA.

Lifestyle

The World in 2005 publication by *The Economist* magazine rated Ireland as the best place to live in the world for quality of life. This is due to the combination of increasing wealth and the importance of traditional values, which are most likely to make people happy.

Ireland is home to that wonderful brew Guinness, and also to some delicious whiskeys. Pubs are the social hub of Irish life. Official licensing hours end at 11pm, but these are routinely flouted, especially in the country.

"Since joining the EU, Ireland has become one of the most prosperous nations in Europe"

In 2004, Ireland banned smoking in all workplaces, including pubs and restaurants. The cuisine is much like the UK's, with meat and potatoes being a mainstay of the diet. Dublin, especially, has many top-class restaurants.

There isn't a large expat community in Ireland, but foreigners are afforded a warm welcome and you should experience little difficulty in integrating into Irish life. ●

BELOW: Dublin is the most popular destination in Ireland for property buyers

CLIMATE

Average monthly temperature °C

DUBLIN		LONDON
8	Dec	7
8	Nov	10
10	Oct	14
13	Sept	19
15	Aug	22
18	July	22
20	June	20
19	May	17
17	April	13
14	March	10
10	Feb	7
8	Jan	6

Average monthly rainfall mm

DUBLIN		LONDON
67	Dec	81
55	Nov	78
51	Oct	70
45	Sept	65
60	Aug	62
57	July	59
70	June	58
74	May	57
72	April	56
70	March	64
67	Feb	72
74	Jan	77

FINDING A HOME

PROPERTY MARKET

The housing market in Ireland, particularly in Dublin, has seen exceptional growth over recent years. As a result, property is only marginally cheaper than it is in the UK.

RENTING

Rented accommodation is advertised in local papers and on websites. You will usually have to pay a deposit of one month's rent. Landlords are obliged to provide tenants with a rent book, which sets out the terms of the tenancy and provides a record of all rental payments.

BUYING

Properties in Ireland tend to be sold either by public auction or by private treaty sales. Stamp duty is the most expensive associated cost, and is on a sliding scale, depending on the value of the property. Legal fees usually amount to between one and 1.5 per cent. Additional fees, such as Land Registration and Land Ownership fees, add another €400 (£275) to €800 (£550). Mortgages are available to foreign buyers of up to 90 per cent of the purchase price.

PROPERTY TAX

Property tax has been abolished; however, there is an annual charge for refuse collection, which varies depending on the location of the property.

© FÁILTE IRELAND PHOTOGRAPHIC

ABOVE: Irish lifestyle appeals to many foreigners

RESTRICTIONS ON FOREIGN BUYERS

There are no restrictions on foreign buyers.

AVERAGE RENTAL/SALE PRICES

Hotspot	2-bed apartment rentals	4-bed house sales
Dublin	€1,080 (£745)	€413K (£285K)

VISAS

British citizens can work without restriction in Ireland, with no need for a working visa. Citizens of other EU nations, and many other countries, may stay in Ireland for up to three months without a visa. If you're an EU citizen, you are entitled to a work permit that allows you to live and work in Ireland. This can be applied for at the Irish Immigration Office in Dublin, or local police station.

Further information: Irish Embassy, 17 Grosvenor Place, London SW1X7HR; Tel: 0207 235 2171

TAX

You're considered resident for taxation purposes if you spend more than 183 days in Ireland during a tax year.

Ireland's tax system is relatively straightforward, with two tax bands: a lower rate of 20 per cent and a higher rate of 42 per cent. The amount you can earn before having to switch to this higher rate depends on your personal circumstances.

For a single person without dependent children, the first €28,000 (about £19,000) is taxed at 20 per cent, the remainder at 42 per cent. This threshold is raised to €32,000 (£22,000) for a single parent qualifying for One-Parent Family tax credit. A married couple with one income pays the 20 per cent rate on the first €37,000 (£25,500), 42 per cent thereafter. When both spouses are earning, the threshold for the first salary remains at €37,000 before going to 42 per cent, but the second income pays 20 per cent on the first €19,000 (£13,000), 42 per cent thereafter.

In addition to income tax, your employer will deduct Pay-Related Social Insurance (PRSI) and a two per cent health contribution.

Various allowances and personal reliefs can be claimed, so a married person with two dependent children earning €50,000 (£34,500) would take home €39,353 (about £27,150) after paying tax and social security.

The tax year runs from January to December. Taxation treaties with the UK (and other countries) mean you won't pay tax twice on income earned in Ireland.

IRELAND

WORKING IN IRELAND

ECONOMY

Membership of the European Union has transformed the Irish economy, which boomed during the 1990s, changing it from one of the poorest countries in Western Europe to the "Celtic Tiger" it is today — so-called because its remarkable growth mirrored that of the "Tiger" economies of Southeast Asia. The economy relies on exports; today, it is the world's biggest per capita exporter.

LABOUR MARKET

Ireland has traditionally had high unemployment, and this reached an all-time high in 2001. The country has seen its nationals leave in droves to find jobs elsewhere. But now unemployment stands at only 4.7 per cent. Ireland has invested heavily in educating its workforce.

JOB OPPORTUNITIES

Forty per cent of the population live within 100 kilometres of Dublin, which is the country's only sizable city, and it's here that the vast majority of opportunities are to be found. Ireland is the base in Europe for many multinational companies,

particularly those in the hi-tech sector. Companies such as Intel, Microsoft, Apple and Corel all have major operations here. It is the second-biggest exporter of software after the USA.

FINDING A JOB

Nationals from other EU countries are entitled to be treated like an Irish applicant when applying for jobs in Ireland, except positions to do with the security of the Irish state, such as the army or police. There are many job websites where you can look for vacancies in Ireland, and some give you the facility to register your CV for prospective employers. Thanks to the booming economy, there's a lot of casual work on offer, which can often be secured by simply responding to advertisements in shop windows or local papers.

LANGUAGE REQUIREMENTS

English is the main language spoken in Ireland, although Gaelic is the country's other official language. This is taught in schools but it isn't widely spoken, other than in some areas in the far west of the country. ●

Who moves there?

Plentiful job opportunities, economic growth and high quality of life are the key factors attracting immigrants to Ireland

IRELAND

LEFT: Ireland enjoys picturesque and lush countryside, a scenic backdrop to life here

"It is said that Ireland has the best quality of life in the world"

Among them are the job opportunities, along with continued economic growth and a better quality of life. On average, 14 per cent of a business's staff are immigrants, and 22 per cent of businesses say they interview immigrants for jobs. As immigration has increased, unemployment has dropped to a rate of four per cent, and job opportunities have grown. Ireland faces the necessity of securing immigrant workers in order to better its economic output and continue functioning in the global market place, so employment opportunities for immigrants are unlikely to dry up.

ALTHOUGH IMMIGRATION IS A RELATIVELY new phenomenon for Ireland, it is predicted that it will increase as investment and global integration continue. In 2002, the Irish government issued 40,322 work permits, 43 per cent of which were from the UK.

Who moves there?

Most immigrants to Ireland are aged between 25 and 44, but a large number of students also move to Ireland in order to carry out their studies. Thanks to the working holiday visa for 18 to 30 year olds, young people have been encouraged to spend time working in Ireland, generally in the tourist industry. The largest number of immigrants (49 per cent) is employed in hotels and restaurants, the second largest group (31 per cent) is employed in agriculture and 20 per cent are in construction. Of the total number of work permits issued in 2002, 37 per cent were for jobs in the service industry and 25 per cent in catering. Out of 40,322 work permits issued, 16,367 were for County Dublin.

Why move there?

A number of reasons have been cited by immigrants as to why they have moved to Ireland.

There has also been increased investment into the country. Ireland is home to Microsoft's operations and development centre, The Hartford Financial Services Group (one of the USA's largest insurance and finance companies) and AutoEurope (who have a call centre in County Dublin). Yahoo! is set to establish a European operations headquarters in Dublin, and Colgate-Palmolive is expanding its business park in the city, creating a number of new jobs. The Irish government are continuing to develop and promote foreign investment. Economically, Ireland has doubled its GDP over the last decade, with the number of people in work increasing by more than half a million since 1991. Unemployment has dropped by 12 per cent since 1991, and productivity is up, with a 20 per cent growth in the economy seen in the 1990s.

It is said that Ireland has the best quality of life in the world. *The Economist* placed the country top in a poll of 111 countries worldwide because it boasts the world's fourth highest GDP, low unemployment figures, political liberties and the preservation of family life. Since Ireland joined the EU, it has seen a boost in fortunes, with many Irish emigrants returning to the country of their birth. ●

Employment hotspot

Dublin's "fair city" has a colourful mix of culture and nightlife, plus excellent job opportunities

1 Dublin

The capital of Ireland, Dublin nestles in the shadow of the Wicklow Mountains on the coast of the Irish Sea. It was founded in 988 by the Norman Vikings, but it wasn't until 1171, when the Danes were expelled, that the Irish could claim Dublin as their own. Famous for chaotic St Patrick's day celebrations, it is as cosmopolitan as it is traditional.

Dubliners are by reputation hard-drinking and fiercely proud of their city, which is a colourful mix of culture and nightlife. It has become the mecca for stag and hen parties, as well as for cultured weekend city breaks.

Whether you want Grafton Street and O'Connel Street, with their shops and pubs, or the Georgian elegance of Merrion Square and St Stephen's Green, harking back to the heydays of Dublin's previous economic boom, Dublin comes up trumps. It boasts a plethora of theatres, museums and art galleries. Among the most famous are Dublin's National Gallery and Yeats collection, which boasts paintings by some of Ireland's finest and Yeats's entire work.

There are many literary landmarks to be found throughout the city, such as the James Joyce Tower in Sandycove, and Trinity College, home to the Book of Kells, Ireland's celebrated medieval manuscript.

Once the culture is over, you can choose from one of the 1,000 pubs that grace the streets of Dublin. Food is high on the list of Dubliners' priorities, and there are a number of eateries,

ranging from chic and contemporary to basic and homely. The nightlife culture attracts many party animals and it ranges from hedonistic partying to clubs that feature some fantastic Irish music and dancing.

Living in Dublin can be a wonderful experience. Over recent years, the economy has turned itself around and this has attracted many people, especially the younger generation, to enjoy some of the wealth. EU membership and increased prosperity have transformed Dublin into a multicultural city with a thriving economy.

In terms of employment, Dublin experiences the largest influx of immigrants in the whole of Ireland, and employs the majority of foreign workers. Of the 40,322 work permits issued in 2004, 41 per cent of them were for immigrants heading for Dublin. Dublin is driving the country's economy and advancing GDP growth. With a fixed business tax rate of 12.5 per cent, an unemployment rate of 4.7 per cent, and voted one of the best countries for entrepreneurship, Ireland – and the city of Dublin – have a lot to recommend them.

The last decade has seen employment in Dublin grow by 31 per cent. It accounts for 48 per cent of the country's value. The leading sectors are ICT, electronics, engineering, food, drink, tobacco, paper and printing. Eight hundred leading multinational companies are based in the city, and 77 per cent of national employment is based in international services.

In terms of property, the

© FÁILTE IRELAND PHOTOGRAPHIC

IRELAND

ABOVE: Dublin is the destination for 41% of Ireland's immigrants

past four years have seen a significant rise in property prices throughout Ireland. Dublin has lagged behind most major European cities until recently, but following a period of sustained demand, prices rose by 8.9 per cent in 2004. There is a large amount of urban renewal underway in Dublin, particularly around the Docklands, and this is good news for investors. With prices set to continue on an upward trend and the economy destined to continue booming, now is a good time to invest in property in Dublin.

KEY FACTS

■ **Population:** 3,917,203
■ **Airport:** Dublin Airport, Tel: 00353 181 411 11
■ **Medical:** Mater Hospital,

Tel: 00353 180 320 00 ■ St James Hospital, Tel; 00353 141 030 00
■ **Schools:** Balbriggan Community College, Tel: 00353 184 12388
■ St Finian's Community College, Tel: 00353 184 02623
■ **Rentals:** Attracts many short-term renters ■ Ample prospects for long-term rents
■ **Pros:** A cultured city that boasts a number of distractions for the party animal and cultured theatre-goer alike ■ A good city for property investors ■ A huge number of jobs available ■ More than 800 international businesses based here
■ **Cons:** There is a certain air of economic uncertainty throughout Europe, which could impact upon Dublin's economy ■ This is not a city for those seeking a peaceful weekend retreat ■ Property prices have been increasing rapidly and are set to continue to rise throughout 2005. ●

Property price guide

Ireland's property market focuses on Dublin, where property can be expensive. However, if you are willing to look elsewhere you can find some real bargains

APARTMENTS FOR RENT

The rental market is booming, with something to suit all budgets

€1,000 PER MONTH
1-BED MONKSTOWN
£690 PER MONTH
- Fully furnished ✔
- Pool ✘
- Parking ✔   **CODE** LIS

€1,200 PER MONTH
2-BED DUBLIN
£830 PER MONTH
- Fully furnished ✔
- Pool ✘
- Parking ✔   **CODE** LIS

€1,200 PER MONTH
2-BED DUBLIN
£830 PER MONTH
- Fully furnished ✘
- Pool ✘
- Parking ✔   **CODE** LIS

€1,700 PER MONTH
5-BED DUBLIN
£1,170 PER MONTH
- Fully furnished ✘
- Pool ✘
- Parking ✔   **CODE** LIS

APARTMENTS FOR SALE

Luxurious city centre apartments dominate the Dublin market

€200,000
2-BED CLONDALKIN
£138,000
- Fully furnished ✘
- Pool ✘
- Parking ✔   **CODE** PIE

€250,000
1-BED DUBLIN
£172,500
- Fully furnished ✘
- Pool ✘
- Parking ✔   **CODE** PIE

€360,000
2-BED LUCAN
£248,500
- Fully furnished ✔
- Pool ✘
- Parking ✔   **CODE** PIE

€370,000
2-BED DUBLIN
£255,000
- Fully furnished ✘
- Pool ✘
- Parking ✔   **CODE** ABC

HOUSES FOR SALE

There are some modern and stunning period homes to be procured

€710,000
4-BED DUBLIN
£490,000
- With furnishings ✘
- Pool ✘
- Parking ✔   **CODE** LIS

€810,000
3-BED DUBLIN
£559,000
- With furnishings ✔
- Pool ✘
- Parking ✔   **CODE** LIS

€1,500,000
3-BED DUBLIN
£1,035,000
- With furnishings ✘
- Pool ✘
- Parking ✔   **CODE** LIS

€2,590,000
3-BED DUBLIN
£1,787,000
- With furnishings ✘
- Pool ✘
- Parking ✔   **CODE** LIS

Italy

Known as the land of art, culture and Prada

FACT BOX

- ■ **Population** 58,057,477
- ■ **Population growth rate** 0.09%
- ■ **Economic growth rate** 0.4%
- ■ **Inflation rate** 2.7%
- ■ **Capital** Rome
- ■ **Hotspots** Milan, Florence, Rome
- ■ **Average house price** (4-bed) €378,200
- ■ **Average rental price** (2-bed) €910

FACT FILE

AREA	301,230km²
POPULATION	58,057,477
CAPITAL	Rome
LIFE EXPECTANCY	80 years
LITERACY	98.6%
GOVERNMENT	Republic
GDP PER CAPITA	US$26,700
UNEMPLOYMENT RATE	8.6%
CURRENCY	Euro (€)
EXCHANGE RATE	€1 = £0.69; £1 = €1.45
LANGUAGES	Italian, German, French, Slovene

ITALY

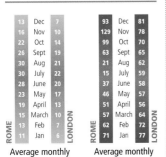

ABOVE: The Piazza del Plebiscito is situated in the heart of Naples

CLIMATE

ROME		LONDON	ROME		LONDON
13	Dec	7	93	Dec	81
16	Nov	10	129	Nov	78
22	Oct	14	99	Oct	70
26	Sept	19	63	Sept	65
30	Aug	21	21	Aug	62
30	July	22	15	July	59
28	June	20	37	June	58
23	May	17	46	May	57
19	April	13	51	April	56
15	March	10	57	March	64
13	Feb	7	62	Feb	72
11	Jan	6	71	Jan	77

Average monthly temperature °C   Average monthly rainfall mm

Living in Italy

Michelangelo, Ferrari, Pavarotti, Gucci – whether your tastes are classical or contemporary, Italy's got the lot

IT ISN'T DIFFICULT TO SEE THE APPEAL of relocating to Italy. From the relaxed Mediterranean lifestyle to the wonderful fresh food and wine, the glorious climate to the art and architecture, the ancient history to the effortlessly stylish culture – what other country has so much to offer?

Politics and economy

Italy is a stable country, but it is not without its political, economic and social problems. The country is now on its 59th government since 1945, corruption is widespread and organised crime seems to touch everything, right up to the highest levels of the government. The current prime minister, Silvio Berlusconi, drafted legislation to prevent high-ranking officials being charged with corruption, just as he was being investigated for tax evasion. However, apart from the infamous Italian bureaucracy, these issues are unlikely to have any day-to-day impact on those looking to settle in the country.

Italy is the world's fifth largest economy and major industries include everything from agriculture to automobiles, but it has a strong north-south divide. Milan and the industrialised north are the powerhouses behind the economy, but, in the south, unemployment is high and the inhabitants are noticeably less affluent.

Climate

Italy has a temperate climate, but due to its range of latitudes and mountainous terrain this varies wildly throughout the country. The north, in the shadow of the Alps, has the more extreme temperatures while, in the south, the climate is distinctly Mediterranean. The whole country is extremely hot during the summer months, and in August the cities see mass evacuations, as citizens head for the coast to escape the stifling heat.

Education

Italy has provided free state education for all since 1946 and standards are excellent. Education is compulsory between the ages of 6 and 15, and the vast majority of students continue into further education – where minimal fees are payable. The system comprises *Scuola Elementare* (primary, ages six to ten), *Scuola Media* (secondary, ages 11 to 13) and *Scuola Superiore* (high school, ages 14 to 18). Education is free for the children of foreigners

© ENIT

"Italy has made an enormous contribution to world cuisine, going way beyond the all-familiar pizza and pasta"

living in the country, regardless of whether they are actually residents. Foreign students also have the same entitlement to university education as nationals. Private schools are available, but are not regarded as being any better than state schools.

Lessons are taught in Italian, but there are a number of international schools throughout Italy, especially in the larger, northern cities. These follow the UK or US curriculum. Younger children adapt to a new language with an ease that confounds most adults, but you may feel it is best to continue English-language-based education for children of secondary school age.

Healthcare

Italy does have a national health service (*Servizio Sanitario Nazionale*, or SSN), which provides free or low-cost healthcare to all residents, including those from other EU countries. The SSN is, however, somewhat under-funded. Standards vary wildly between hospitals, with those in the south generally being worse than those in the north. Italy's spending on health is just six per cent of its GDP – one of the lowest in the EU. For this reason, many Italians and the majority of foreigners take out private health insurance.

Food and drink

Italy has made an enormous contribution to world cuisine, going way beyond the all-familiar pizza and pasta through to wonderful *formaggio* (cheese), including parmesan and gorgonzola, and delicious desserts and *gelati* (icecreams). Italians make abundant use of fresh, natural ingredients in their cooking, with liberal amounts of locally produced olive oil. You will find mouthwateringly tasty dishes throughout the entire country – every region seems to have a speciality named after it, from Bolognese sauce to Parma ham to pizza Neapolitan.

Italy is a nation of coffee drinkers, but newcomers should note that, to Italians, cappuccino is strictly a breakfast beverage, and ordering a cup after dinner will bring quizzical looks. Italy is, of course, also justly renowned for its wines. As well as the world–famous Chianti, Tuscany also produces the notable red wines Brunello di Montalcino and Vino Nobile di Montepulciano. Other regions have their own speciality – Frascati in Rome, Soave around Venice and sweet Marsala down in Sicily.

Expat communities

Official statistics for the 2001 census (Italy carries out a census every ten years) showed that there were close to 19,000 British citizens resident in the country. It is hardly surprising that many of the foreigners working in Italy are in the cities to the north and centre of the country. But there also are a fair number of people who have relocated to the countryside in search of peaceful rural living, particularly to the hills of Tuscany and Umbria.

Pets

An individual may bring up to five pets into Italy. These may include cats, dogs and birds, plus some of our more unusual furry friends too. Monkeys, rodents and turtles are welcome but, curiously, rabbits and pigs are specifically barred from entry. Since October 2004, it has been necessary to obtain a European Community veterinary certificate for each pet you wish to introduce into the country. It is essential that all animals are microchipped, and they must also be vaccinated against rabies. ●

TRAVEL FILE

AIR Flights are available to Italy from most UK airports, and the choices are extensive because Rome, Milan and Venice are each served by multiple airports. **Ryanair** (www.ryanair.com; 0871 246 0000) has comprehensive routes to Italy, flying to an exhaustive list of regional airports: from Stansted to Rome, Milan, Venice, Genoa, Pisa, Bologna, Trieste, Turin, Verona, Ancona, Pescara, Bari, Brindisi, Palermo and Alghero; from Liverpool to Rome, Milan, Pisa and Venice; from Glasgow to Rome, Pisa and Milan; from Luton to Milan, Venice and Rome; from Teeside and East Midlands to Rome; and from Newcastle to Milan. **Easyjet** (www.easyjet.com; 0871 244 2366) offers the following services: from Bristol and East Midlands to Venice and Rome; from Stansted to Milan and Naples; and from Newcastle to Rome. **British Airways** (www.ba.com; 0870 850 9850) has the following routes: from Gatwick to Venice, Pisa, Genoa, Rome, Naples and Brindisi; from Heathrow to Milan and Rome; from Manchester to Milan, Bologna, Venice, Pisa, Rome, Palermo and Alghero; and from Birmingham to Milan and Rome. National Italian airline **Alitalia** (www.alitalia.co.uk; 0870 544 8259) flies from Heathrow to Milan and Rome, and from Gatwick and Birmingham to Rome. **BMI** (www.flybmi.com; 0870 607 0555) flies from Heathrow to Milan, Venice and Rome. **Jet 2** (www.jet2.com; 0871 226 1737) flies from Leeds to Venice, and begins flights from Manchester to Pisa and Venice in May 2005.

RAIL Taking the train from London to Rome takes more than 19 hours and can be more expensive than flying, see **Rail Europe** (www.raileurope.co.uk; 0870 837 1371). The Channel Tunnel (www.eurotunnel.com; 0870 535 3535) is useful for drivers who can board at Folkestone from the M20.

SEA You can take a ferry to France then drive to Italy. **P&O** (www.poferries.com; 0870 520 2020) sails from Portsmouth and Dover, **Hoverspeed** (www. hoverspeed.co.uk; 0870 240 8070) goes from Dover and Newhaven. **Brittany Ferries** (www.brittany-ferries.co.uk; 0870 366 5333) sails from Portsmouth, Plymouth and Poole. **Condor Ferries** (www.condorferries.co.uk; 0845 345 2000) goes from Portsmouth, Weymouth and Poole. **SpeedFerries** (www.speedferries.com) operates a fast route from Dover to Boulogne.

GETTING AROUND Cars drive on the right in Italy, but other than this most rules are similar to the UK – except for a law requiring you to have your headlights on at all times of the day on motorways. A UK driving licence is acceptable. The Italian train network (www.trenitaliaplus.com) is extensive, reasonably priced and generally the most efficient way to get around the country. Local bus services take up the slack. Most large cities, including Rome, Naples and Milan, have metro systems.

© ENIT

ABOVE: **The stunning city of Florence with the Ponte Vecchio**

I did it!

Name: Morrena Francis

Occupation: Director of Pozzuoli Holidays

Where: Pozzuoli, near Naples, Italy

Contacts: info@pozzuoliholidays.co.uk and www.pozzuoliholidays.co.uk

ITALY

Relocating to Italy

Buying a house in a foreign land can be tricky. Morrena Francis describes how she relocated to Campania

WHEN MORRENA DECIDED THAT SHE HAD had enough of the rat race, she pursued her childhood dream of moving to Italy. She now runs a successful business introducing foreigners to the town of Pozzuoli, near Naples, which she very proudly calls home.

Q: What made you decide to live in Italy?
A: For many people, the place where they spend their childhood holidays always remains close to their heart. My father used to take us to Italy, and it was that place that I grew to love. I knew that one day I would have to live there. I used to work as a PA in various fields, but mostly in tourism so that I could look through the Italian brochures. My life was quite mundane – work, cook, clean, shop – which is probably why I longed for my holidays so much. I always used to think that there had got to be more to life than that. Five years ago, after my first marriage had come to an end, I met Stefano. He was from a place called Pozzuoli near Naples. "Ah, you're Italian," I said to him. He very proudly replied in excellent English, "No, I'm a Neapolitan." A few months later, Stefano took me to Pozzuoli in Campania to meet his family. He drove me around the Gulf

of Pozzuoli, to the towns of Arco Felice, Lucrino, Port of Baia, and the lovely beach at Miseno. Everywhere I turned there was a stunning view – a wonderful combination of the sea, mountains and volcanic lakes.

Q: What drew you to the Italian lifestyle?
A: The thing that hit me most about Pozzuoli was that the people walked around as if they had not got a care in the world. This was a far cry from my hectic life back in London. People had time for one another and they were happy to help you. I was hooked and fell in love with Pozzuoli almost immediately. The thought of living in Italy was mind-blowing and scary and I wondered if it was really possible. It turned out it was!

Q: How did you become a tour operator?
A: There wasn't much work in Pozzuoli. Stefano suggested living and working in England for six months during the winter and living in Italy for six months during the summer, but that was definitely not for me. We considered buying a property out of London, but eventually decided we wanted to live in Italy permanently. I could afford to buy a house there with no mortgage, with the money from the sale of my house in London. We wanted to make a living doing something that we would enjoy, and that's when we thought about introducing British tourists to this magnificent unknown part of Southern Italy. With the experience we both had, we put our heads together and Pozzuoli Holidays Ltd was born.

LEFT: The Gulf of Pozzuoli in Campania, an unspoilt area of southern Italy

ABOVE: Fruit trees and cacti flourish in the garden

RIGHT: Morrena's traditional-style home in Pozzuoli

Q: How difficult was it for you to start your business?

A: Starting up a business wasn't as difficult as I thought it would be. We just took it a step at a time. First, we went to the bank to set up a business account. When I told the business advisor that I was going to use my own money, he said, "Anyone who puts in their own money to start up a business must be serious about it," and we got our account. Then we set up a website. Stefano got us on as many search engines as he could, and this has proved to be the most effective way of reaching our clients.

Q: How did you go about finding and buying your property?

A: Life became manic and we had to look for a place to buy in Pozzuoli. It is not essential to go to an estate agent to buy a property because many Italians buy and sell privately. If you're in the market to buy or sell, you simply spread the word. Stefano's father did just that for us, and fortunately a friend of his was selling his villa in Licola. It was the first house we looked at and it was everything we wanted. Then came a lot of bartering between the two old friends. Stefano's father told me to stop smiling and act unsure about the house, which was very difficult! We got the house for €95,700 (£66,000). The process was made a lot easier for us because we had the help of an excellent solicitor who did all the groundwork, making sure the land was correctly owned by the seller and there were no outstanding taxes on the house. (Normally the buyer picks up the tab for the solicitor.) We then had the first "preliminary", whereby we paid half the money. Once this was paid, we were given the keys, by law, and were allowed to move in. Six weeks later we paid the rest of the money and the solicitor's fee of €3,600 (about £2,500).

Q: How have you found your last two years in Italy?

A: Relocating here was the best move I have ever made. The cost of living is cheap and I have a far better quality of life than I had back in London. I love going to the fish, fruit and vegetable markets. Everything is so fresh and tastes much better than in London. I can enjoy peace, tranquillity and long walks along the

"Relocating here was the best move I have ever made. The cost of living is cheap and I have a far better quality of life than I had back in London"

beach, but in 20 minutes I can be in the centre of Naples and be the city girl again. My neighbours are fantastic, always ready to give me bags of fruit, vegetables and salad. I now speak enough Italian to get by, but I'm far from perfect. I make myself understood and the locals are very patient. We all have a good laugh when I come out with something strange. As for missing England, well I certainly don't yearn for the climate. I do miss my family, but flights to and from Naples are quick and cheap, so I fly back and forth quite frequently. ●

Top tips

● If you are thinking of buying property in Italy, visit your chosen area and get to know it really well before you buy, because if you buy a property and sell it within five years, you will be liable for tax.

● Get in with the locals and find out from them if there are any properties up for sale in the area. Be cheeky. Don't be afraid to ask anything – Italians love to take you under their wing and they are very protective.

ABOVE: Italy is full of breathtaking monuments and ancient buildings

Who moves there?

The appeals are obvious, but who are the people forgetting the pipe dream and living the dream instead?

"It is the warm climate and the friendliness of the people that are the greatest draw for many British people"

OVER THE PAST FOUR YEARS, ITALY HAS SEEN an increase of 40 per cent in the amount of people wishing to relocate there. The most popular regions are Le Marche, Tuscany and The Lakes. Umbria is also becoming popular.

With the advent of low-cost flights over recent years and the short travel time, many people flit between the UK and Italy. Advances in communications technology – especially email, the Internet and mobile phones – allow people to work remotely, and this has opened many doors for people in a wide variety of businesses.

Who moves there?
According to the latest census, there are approximately 19,000 British expats permanently resident in Italy. Those coming to work will find the best opportunities close to some of the larger cities such as Milan, Florence and Rome.

The age of people relocating is getting very much younger. In 1988, there were very few people relocating, and most of those who did were in the 50 to 55 age group and looking to retire. 1998 saw the average age drop to 45 and the numbers increase by about 15 per cent.

Recent years have seen the most dramatic change. The average age for relocating to Italy is now 35, with an increase in numbers of 40 per cent.

Why move there?
The main reason for the increase in numbers relocating to Italy is that people have realised that they can afford property in Italy. The cost of living is lower than in the UK, plus there is no capital gains tax after five years and no inheritance tax.

Italy is a country full of culture and famous for its fantastic food and wine. But it is the warm climate and the friendliness of the people that are the greatest draw for many British people. It is common for people to visit on holiday, fall in love with the lifestyle then decide to make the move permanently. Relocators are made most welcome – there's none of the resentment from locals that can be characteristic of some other European countries. While English is not spoken everywhere, you are likely to get a warm response and help from the locals if you make just a little effort to speak the language.

The main sectors in which you could expect to find work are media and communications, tourism, finance and international business. But, whatever sector you are looking to work in, you will need to be well qualified. In Italy, qualifications are of the utmost importance.

While many relocators are drawn to the Italian countryside and the rural lifestyle, finding work in the country is somewhat more difficult, so you will have to use your initiative. Some people set up alternative therapy centres, or open hairdressing salons. Teaching English is another popular choice with British expats, but to do this successfully you will need to have some skills in the Italian language.

Unemployment in Italy is, on average, in line with the Eurozone, and currently stands at 8.6 per cent. This is the lowest unemployment rate in Italy since 1992, and has dropped from 9.6 per cent in 2001. But this is an average, and the rate is much higher in the south of the country and far lower in Bergamo, in Milan and other northern industrial cities. The variation is roughly 3.5 per cent in the north and 15 per cent in the south. ●

LEFT: **The church of Santa Maria del Carmine, one of Florence's many artistic treasures**

ITALY

Working in Italy

There are plenty of opportunities for English teachers, but when looking for any other job, you will need to learn Italian

■ LABOUR MARKET

Unemployment has come down dramatically in recent years, from 11.4 per cent at the end of the last millennium to 8.6 per cent today. It is still an emotive issue, however, and jobs tend to go to Italians first then EU citizens, with anyone else way down the list. Non-EU citizens are likely to have problems getting permission to work in Italy in the first place. Jobs given to non-EU nationals tend to be senior executive roles for multinational companies.

Employment conditions in Italy are among the best in the world and, in Europe, only Switzerland takes better care of its workers. There are strict employment laws, which enhance job security and increase benefits. Under Italian law, all employees must have a contract outlining salary, job description and benefits.

Despite the excellent working conditions, Italy has one of the worst records for industrial relations in the EU. Unions are less powerful than they were, but strikes are frequent.

Everyone in Italy must have a tax code number (*codice fiscale*), which is required for most paperwork – opening a bank account, signing contracts, starting a job, buying a car and so on.

■ JOB OPPORTUNITIES AND KEY INDUSTRIES

About seven per cent of the working population is employed in agriculture, 33 per cent in manufacturing and the remaining 60 per cent in the service industries. The principal industries are tourism, iron and steel, machinery, chemicals, food processing, textiles and ceramics. Italy is the world leader in fashion, and is home to famous houses such as Benetton, Gucci and Diesel.

Many British expats earn a living by teaching English. There are hundreds of English schools, with the biggest concentration in the large, northern cities. Most schools require a TEFL qualification.

Au pair (*alli pari*) work is a popular choice for women aged between 18 and 30. It is possible to work for up to 12 months, and is a great way to improve your Italian.

Self-employment is possible, but even if you're intending to start your own business, it is still often necessary to hold a relevant qualification. Failure to do so can incur stiff penalties.

■ FINDING A JOB

If you're job hunting from the UK, it is best to use job sites that allow you to post your CV. National and regional newspapers are another useful resource. If your profession has a trade body, try to find out whether there is an equivalent organisation in Italy, and whether they can help you find employment.

Actually being in the country is a great advantage. You can visit your local employment office (*Uffici di Collocamento*), ask around and then apply in person. More often than not, simply being in the right place at the right time is the most important factor.

■ LANGUAGE REQUIREMENTS

In order to get any decent form of employment, apart from teaching English, you will need to speak fluent Italian and be well qualified in whatever field you wish to work. ●

ABOVE: The Piazza del Duomo at the heart of Milan

■ USEFUL WEBSITES

www.bestjob.it Job hunters' website that allows you to post your CV (in Italian only)

www.jobs-in-europe.net/italy.html Provides useful links to many English language job sites

www.corriere.it/lavoro The website of *Corriere della Sera*, one of the top Italian newspapers

www.ergonline.it Useful Italian government website (in Italian only)

www.embitaly.org.uk Home page of the Italian Embassy in London

VISAS AND WORK PERMITS

As a British or EU citizen, you are entitled to live and work in Italy. That does not, however, help you to avoid the infamous Italian bureaucracy.

● PERMITS

You may stay for up to 90 days with just a passport, but to stay any longer, you'll need to apply for a permit at the local police headquarters (*questura*). There are a number of categories under which this can be applied for, depending on the principal reason for your extended stay, including *permesso di soggiorno per lavoro* (a work permit for employees) and *permesso di soggiorno per lavoro autonomo/indipendente* (a work permit for independent workers). You must apply for a work permit within eight days of arriving in the country, and it can take up to three months to be processed. Once you have it, you can apply for a residence permit (*certificato di residenza*), which entitles EU citizens to full residency for at least five years and is automatically renewable.

● VISAS

Non-EU citizens need a visa to work in Italy. These are hard to get, and you will need an employment offer from an Italian company. Check with your local Italian Embassy for further information.

Finding a home

Buying your dream home in Italy is straightforward, and there are always bargains to be found

THE PERCENTAGE OF HOME OWNERSHIP in Italy is one of the highest in the world, at about 85 per cent. Property is generally good value, especially in rural areas. Homes can be much more expensive in the cities, where supply is limited and demand is high. The fashionable coastal, mountain and lakeside resorts are also pricey.

Italians tend to prefer modern homes to old farmhouses and view property as a home rather than an investment, so the market has not seen the same dramatic rises as many parts of Europe.

Renting

It is wise to rent initially, unless you are specifically looking for a long-term investment in the housing market. Most property is rented unfurnished, and this usually means it will be completely empty, with no curtains, carpets or kitchen cupboards. On the other hand, when a property is rented as furnished, it will usually come with everything, right down to crockery and linen.

Properties get snapped up quickly in the cities, and you'll need to be quick off the mark. Check adverts in local papers, visit estate agents (*agenzie immobiliare*) and look out for properties displaying a "to rent" (*affittasi*) sign. The best way to find a property, though, is simply to ask around friends and colleagues.

If you rent through an agent, expect to pay about ten per cent of a year's rent as a fee. The landlord will usually ask for a deposit of one to three months' rent.

Buying

Italian law offers a high level of protection to homebuyers, and the buying process is carried out by a public official called a *notaio*. Fees are usually paid by the buyer and amount to about 2.5 per cent of the declared value of the property. Once the *notaio* has carried out the searches and a *geometra* has surveyed the property, a preliminary contract is signed and a deposit of 10 to 30 per cent is paid. If the buyers pull out of the purchase, they lose this deposit, but if the sellers pull out, they must pay back twice the deposit.

It is possible to take out a fixed or variable rate mortgage with an Italian bank. The Woolwich and Abbey National building societies have local offices in Italy and are experienced in arranging loans for those wishing to buy in the country.

ABOVE: Neptune's fountain in the Piazza Navona, Rome

Restrictions on foreign buyers

There is a purchase registration tax of four per cent if the property is your main residence, and you may buy at this rate if you become an Italian resident within a year of the purchase. Otherwise, you will pay at the higher rate of 11 per cent, as for a second home. The cost of amenities is up to 50 per cent higher for second homes, so it is very much in your financial interests to buy as a resident.

Property tax

Local property tax ranges from 0.4 to 0.7 per cent of property value. This rate is set by the government. It is based on land registry prices and may differ from the amount you buy the property for. ●

AVERAGE RENTAL/SALE PRICES

Hotspot	2-bed apartment rentals	2-bed apartment sales	4-bed house sales
Milan	€1,310 (£903)	€376K (£259K)	€595K (£410K)
Florence	€1,040 (£717)	€438K (£302K)	€800K (£552K)
Rome	€1,730 (£1,193)	€419K (£289K)	€528K (£364K)

TAX

The state-wide income tax in Italy is known as *Imposta dei Redditi delle Persone Fisiche* (IRPEF) and is chargeable on the following bands:

Up to €15,000	**23%**
From €15,001 to €29,000	**29%**
From €29,001 to €32,600	**31%**
From €32,601 to €70,000	**39%**
Over €70,000	**45%**

A foreign resident citizen who is employed in Italy pays tax only on income earned in Italy. This is because Italy has double taxation treaties with more than 60 countries, including all other members of the EU. Note that there is no wealth or inheritance tax in Italy.

ITALY

© ENIT

Employment hotspots

Italy boasts a number of sophisticated and wealthy cities, abundant in employment opportunities

1 Milan

Wealthy and sophisticated, Milan is home to the famous fashion week and is a mecca for shoppers; it is also full of stunning monuments, theatres, museums and galleries.

Italy's stock exchange and most of its major corporations are located in Milan, including Alfa Romeo and Pirelli, as well as telecommunication agencies and Silvio Berlusconi's media empire. The city also contains the country's largest concentration of industry. Foreign investment has increased rapidly over the last ten years, with a leap from 261 to 433 foreign businesses registered here. Unemployment is half the national average and there are a large number of foreign workers. The services sector employs 66.7 per cent of Milanese inhabitants.

Property is expensive, but some small towns outside the city, such as Arese, have areas populated mainly by expats. Renting is the best option, and this market is thriving.

KEY FACTS
- **Population:** 1.6 million
- **Airport:** Milan Malpensa, Tel: 00 39 274 852860
- **Medical:** Hospital San Raffaele, Tel: 00 39 226 431
- **Schools:** Sir James Henderson British School, Tel: 00 39 221 0941
- **Rentals:** Large number of professionals and students who rent ▨ Shortage of top-quality residential apartments in popular areas
- **Pros:** Extremely efficient city ▨ Italy's richest city and the marketplace for fashion
- **Cons:** Smog can become very thick ▨ Very hot in August ▨ Pickpockets and thieves create problems in the city centre.

ABOVE: The magnificent Colosseum in Rome, once the site of gladiatorial combats

2 Florence

Nestled in the Tuscan hills by the River Arno, Florence is surrounded by vineyards and olive groves and is a cradle of Renaissance culture and history. Full of churches and adorned on every corner with murals and sculptures, it is visited by millions of tourists every year.

Tourism supports Florence's economy but the city is also one of Italy's leading industrial heartlands and home to small businesses and multinationals alike. Textiles, metalwork, ceramics, jewellery and embroidery are important sectors within the Florentine economy. For centuries, the Milanese have sent their fashion designs to be created in Florence, and this remains an important part of the city's trade.

Tuscany has always been popular with international property buyers, and the Italians are just starting to buy into this region. Prices are above average in this area and demand is sky-high. Florence itself is a rentals market, which is sustained by students.

KEY FACTS
- **Population:** 461,000
- **Airport:** Amerigo Vespucci Airport, Tel: 00 39 553 0615
- **Medical:** Policlinico di Careggi, Tel: 00 39 554 277111
- **Schools:** International School, Tel: 00 39 556 61007
- **Rentals:** Tourists take much of the accommodation during the summer ▨ Year-round demand
- **Pros:** One of the most beautiful cities in Italy ▨ Easily accessible
- **Cons:** Relentless traffic, stifling heat and pollution during the summer ▨ Outskirts are an industrial sprawl ▨ Tourists take over during the summer.

3 Rome

Rome is a centre of history and legend, as well as being a modern business centre. The capital of Italy and home to the Pope, it attracts a huge number of tourists, and 17 per cent of city-centre residents are foreign.

Tourism is the main industry, but the city is also a hub of banking, publishing, insurance and fashion. There is work for IT specialists and English teachers, and many associations hire English speakers to give tours of the major attractions.

Outside the city, "Tiburtina Valley" is home to a range of electronic and satellite industries. Temporary jobs in agriculture are also available, but they don't pay well.

Property prices in Rome are among the highest in Italy, and rose by about six per cent last year. Rents of central properties are rising at nine per cent per year. Aventino, Cassia, Flaminia, Eur and Parioli are favoured by foreigners because they are close to international schools.

KEY FACTS
- **Population:** 3.8 million
- **Airport:** Rome Leonardo da Vinci, Tel: 00 39 665 951
- **Medical:** International Medical Centre, Tel: 00 39 648 82371
- **Schools:** St George's British International School, Tel: 00 39 630 860021
- **Rentals:** Very expensive ▨ Wide variety, but much is taken by tourists
- **Pros:** Concentration of history, archaeology and culture ▨ Excellent climate
- **Cons:** Very expensive ▨ Traffic is chaotic and pollution is extreme ▨ Large number of thieves around stations and tourist attractions. ●

© ENIT

ITALY

Property price guide

Italy is the country for buyers seeking quiet country retreats nestled among gentle hills and boasting stunning views

PROPERTIES FOR RENT

A selection of strikingly affordable homes to rent

€122 PER WEEK

1-BED METAPONTO
£85 PER WEEK
- Fully furnished ✔
- Pool ✔
- Parking ✔   **CODE** CAT

€425 PER WEEK

1-BED LAKE COMO
£294 PER WEEK
- Fully furnished ✔
- Pool ✘
- Parking ✔   **CODE** CAT

€456 PER WEEK

2-BED LAKE BOLSENA
£315 PER WEEK
- Fully furnished ✔
- Pool ✘
- Parking ✔   **CODE** RRR

€1,015 PER WEEK

2-BED PORTO MAURIZIO
£700 PER WEEK
- Fully furnished ✔
- Pool ✘
- Parking ✔   **CODE** CAT

APARTMENTS FOR SALE

Some stunning flats with glorious views and great locations

€44,000

1-BED LAZIO
£30,000
- Fully furnished ✘
- Pool ✘
- Parking ✔   **CODE** RRR

€67,000

2-BED LAZIO
£46,000
- Fully furnished ✘
- Pool ✘
- Parking ✔   **CODE** RRR

€120,245

1-BED ABRUZZO
£83,000
- Fully furnished ✘
- Pool ✔
- Parking ✔   **CODE** CAT

€300,000

2-BED LAKE COMO
£207,000
- Fully furnished ✘
- Pool ✔
- Parking ✔   **CODE** CAT

HOUSES FOR SALE

Traditional Tuscan villas and rural farmhouses can be yours for a snip

€131,000

3-BED NORTHERN LAZIO
£120,000
- Fully furnished ✘
- Pool ✘
- Parking ✔   **CODE** RRR

€179,000

3-BED PESCAGLIA
£123,000
- Fully furnished ✘
- Pool ✘
- Parking ✔   **CODE** RRR

€233,000

RENOVATION PROJECT VOLTERRA
£161,000
- Fully furnished ✘
- Pool ✘
- Parking ✔   **CODE** CAT

€1,050,000

4-BED NORTHERN LAZIO
£724,000
- Fully furnished ✔
- Pool ✔
- Parking ✔   **CODE** CAT

ITALY

Thinking of buying abroad?

Buy a Red Guide first!

AVAILABLE TO ORDER NOW!

A new generation of definitive illustrated guides to buying property and living abroad, the Red Guides offer a wealth of expert advice on top property hotspots to help you realise your dream.

- An unrivalled blend of expertly researched, up-to-the-minute information and authoritative practical advice
- Step-by-step guide to the legal and financial stages of buying a property
- Fact-filled regional profiles highlight top hotspots, their key facilities and taxes
- Inspirational real-life stories reveal how to turn a dream into reality
- Illustrated price guides show you what to expect for your money, with photographs of hundreds of sample properties
- Extensive listings of useful contacts and addresses, from estate agents and solicitors to tradesmen and surveyors

CALL OUR ORDER HOTLINE TODAY ON 01225 786850
Please quote order code FR27 when ordering

--->✂- -

YES! I would like to buy a copy of *Buying a Property in France 2005* at £16.99 plus p+p **NEW!**

YES! I would like to buy a copy of *Buying a Property in Eastern Europe 2005* at £16.99 plus p+p **NEW!**

YES! I would like to buy a copy of *Buying a Property in Spain 2005* at £16.99 plus p+p **NEW!**

YES! I would like to buy a copy of *Buying a Property in Florida 2005* at £16.99 plus p+p **NEW!**

YES! I would like to buy a copy of *Buying a Property in Portugal 2005* at £11.99 plus p+p **NEW LARGER FORMAT!**

Title ____ Initial ____ Surname _____

Address _____

Postcode _____ Telephone _____

ORDER CODE FR27

POSTAGE & PACKAGING
UK: £2.50 per order
Air Europe: £3.50 first book (£1 per extra book)
Air Worldwide: £5 first book (£1 per extra book)

Quantity	Price plus p+p (see above rates)	TOTAL

CREDIT CARD

VISA   MASTERCARD   SWITCH   AMERICAN EXPRESS

Card no. ☐☐☐☐ ☐☐☐☐ ☐☐☐☐ ☐☐☐☐ ☐☐☐☐

Expiry Date ___ / ___   Issue/Valid Date ___ / ___

Signature _____   Date ____ Date ____

CHEQUE

☐ I enclose a cheque/postal order payable to *Merricks Media Ltd*

Please return this form with payment to:

French Magazine Property Buying Guide Offer
Merricks Media Ltd
FREEPOST
(SWB 10668)
Bath
BA1 2ZZ
UK

Please allow up to 14 days for delivery

Japan

A country of kimonos, cultural delights and blossom trees

FACT BOX

- **Population** 127,333,000
- **Population growth rate** 0.08%
- **Economic growth rate** 2.7%
- **Inflation rate** -0.3%
- **Capital** Tokyo
- **Hotspots** Tokyo, Osaka, Kyoto
- **Average house price** (4-bed) ¥83,000
- **Average rental price** (2-bed) ¥332,000

Living in Japan

Enjoy life in the fast lane in Tokyo, or a more sedate lifestyle in Kyoto

FACT FILE

AREA	374,744km²
POPULATION	127,333,000
CAPITAL	Tokyo
LIFE EXPECTANCY	81.1 years
LITERACY	99%
GOVERNMENT	Constitutional monarchy
GDP PER CAPITA	US$28,200
UNEMPLOYMENT RATE	5.3%
CURRENCY	Japanese Yen (¥)
EXCHANGE RATE	¥1 = £0.005; £1 = ¥200
LANGUAGE	Japanese

COST OF LIVING

PETROL (1L)	¥110
WINE (0.75L)	¥1,500
MEAL (3-COURSE)	¥2,000
BEER (375ML)	¥200
LOAF OF BREAD (650G)	¥150
MILK (1L)	¥180

WITH ITS HISTORIC POLICY OF ISOLATION, Japan was a mystery to foreigners until 1854, when it opened its borders after signing a treaty with the USA. Since then, it has rapidly modernised and industrialised to become one of the world's strongest economies. An archipelago made up of four islands – Hokkaido, Honshu, Shikoku and Kyushu – Japan is about the same size as Italy, and spans 20 degrees of latitude in eastern Asia. Half of the land is covered by forested mountains, so urban areas tend to cling to the coast. The Japanese are friendly people, and foreigners are guaranteed a warm welcome.

Politics and economy

Japan has the third-largest economy in the world after the USA and China, and the second-highest GDP after the USA. The Japanese economy relies heavily on industries such as car exports, electronic goods and computers, with agriculture making up just two per cent of its GDP. Lifetime employment and cooperation between manufacturers, suppliers and distributors have been marks of the Japanese system. These values are being eroded today, but Japan still has a strong work ethic, excellent government-industry cooperation and an unemployment rate of about five per cent.

Since the Allied occupation in 1946, Japan's political system has been based on a constitution. Structurally, it includes the parliament, called the diet, and a cabinet normally made up of members of the diet. The role of emperor has become a purely ceremonial one. Japan's ruling figure is the prime minister, currently Junichiro Koizumi of the Liberal Democrat party. The age at which men and women can vote is 20.

Climate

Japan's climate varies widely from north to south. The seasons are well defined, with hot, humid summers and cold winters bringing lots of snow to the western side of the country. The rainy season occurs for about 40 days during June and July, and typhoons are likely between August and October. Average summer temperatures range from the low to high 20°sC. In winter they drop to around 7°C, except on the northernmost island of Hokkaido where winter temperatures are usually below

BELOW: **The Cosmo Clock ferris wheel in Yokohama**

RIGHT: o-sechi, a traditional dish eaten to celebrate New Year

© JAPANESE TOURIST BOARD

freezing and there is a lot of snow. There is an annual Snow Festival here each February.

Education

The Japanese have an extremely efficient education system, based on the American principle of six years in elementary school followed by three years each in junior and senior high school. Elementary and junior high are compulsory. After that, students may choose to spend four years at university or two years in junior college. The school year starts in April and consists of three terms, with short holidays in spring and winter and a month-long summer break. About 90 per cent of Japanese students graduate from high school, with around 40 per cent going on to get a qualification from university or college. The education system is very competitive, with entrance exams for most levels. Students often attend after-school classes at a *juku*, or preparation school, in order to pass these exams.

"Since it opened its borders in 1854, Japan has rapidly modernised and industrialised to become one of the world's strongest economies"

Healthcare

Japan's healthcare system is highly regulated and on a par with the West. Unlike in the UK, patients can go straight to a specialist without referral from a GP. Doctors' offices are usually referred to as clinics, and small, privately owned practices make up 80 per cent of what the Japanese call hospitals. The best time to visit a doctor is first thing in the morning or after lunch, when queues are shortest.

Service is provided mainly by private practitioners, but about 70 per cent of costs are met by insurance policies – the Social Insurance System (SIS) for those in employment and National Health Insurance (NHI) for everyone else. Some international organisations provide lists of clinics with experience in dealing with foreigners.

Food and drink

The best-known Japanese dish is *sushi*, but there is a great deal more to the country's cuisine than uncooked fish. Other delicacies include *gyouza* (dumpling filled with pork and vegetables), *ramen* (noodles in *miso* or soya soup), *yakitori* (grilled chicken skewers) and *tempura* (deep-fried battered seafood and vegetables). Western food – everything from pasta to take-away burgers – is also available. Restaurants tend to be rather expensive, but good, cheap food can be found in eateries near train stations, built to serve Japanese commuters. Vegetarians may find it difficult to find acceptable food, because vegetarianism is not a popular concept in Japan. The Japanese tend to enjoy a drink, and beer is widely available, not only in bars but also in vending machines on the side of the street. Traditional *sake*, or rice wine, is served hot and is significantly stronger than normal wine.

Expat communities

There are a large number of expat communities in Japan, not just English but people from all around the world. There are also plenty of English publications, such as *Kansai Scene*. This magazine is aimed at English-speakers in the Kansai area (midwest Japan) and features pages of personal advertisements, where expat clubs and other social groups are advertised. Another good place to find other British people is in the nearest British pub. Not only will you be likely to bump into someone from back home, but you can enjoy a pint of Guinness and a plate of fish 'n' chips. ●

TRAVEL FILE

AIR It takes about 12 hours to fly from London to Tokyo. **Korean Air** (00 8000 656 2001, www.koreanair.eu.com) and **Lufthansa** (0870 837 7747, www.lufthansa.com) are usually cheapest. **British Airways** (0870 850 9850, www.britishairways.com) also flies to Japan. Late April to early May, known as Golden Week, is one of the most expensive times to travel, as are Christmas, New Year and the summer holidays. Japan has two national airlines, **Japan AirLines** (0845 774 7700, www.jal-europe.com) and **All Nippon Airways** (0870 837 8866, www.anaskyweb.com). The main Japanese airports are Tokyo's Narita airport and Osaka's Kansai airport.

GETTING AROUND The public transport system, whilst crowded at peak times, is efficient and popular. It is fairly expensive, but economic rail passes are available to tourists. Japan has overland and underground trains, as well as the famous bullet train that travels at more than 300km/h. Tickets can be bought in person or from vending machines. There are maps to help you plan your journey, like those in the London Underground.

The Japanese operate a left-hand drive system and accept international drivers' licences for up to a year, providing the driver is over 18. Insurance and parking are expensive, and toll systems operate on many main roads.

The cheapest way to travel is by bicycle, which is very popular in Japan. Everyday bicycles tend to be fairly low-tech and cheap to buy. Be careful where you leave your bike, though – it may get towed away. Look out for bicycle parks, which charge a small fee – considerably less than paying to get your bike out of the pound.

JAPAN

CLIMATE

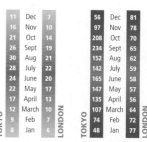

TOKYO		LONDON
11	Dec	7
16	Nov	10
21	Oct	14
26	Sept	19
30	Aug	21
28	July	22
24	June	20
22	May	17
17	April	13
12	March	10
9	Feb	7
8	Jan	6

Average monthly temperature °C

TOKYO		LONDON
56	Dec	81
97	Nov	78
208	Oct	70
234	Sept	65
152	Aug	62
142	July	59
165	June	58
147	May	57
135	April	56
107	March	64
74	Feb	72
48	Jan	77

Average monthly rainfall mm

I did it!

Name: Chris Braham

Job: Chris runs her own media agency and consultancy business in Tokyo, and has been living and working in Tokyo for six years

RIGHT: **Japanese apartments are compact and cosy**

BELOW: **Space is used differently in Japanese properties**

Moving to Japan

Chris moved to Japan and set up her business six years ago. She tells us about the differences in lifestyle

THE DESIRE FOR A NEW CHALLENGE AND A different environment led media consultant Chris Braham to move to Japan. We asked her how she'd gone about it.

Q: When you first came to Japan, did you move here by yourself?
A: Yes I did, and it was an exciting as well as difficult experience to begin with. At the time, it was great to be constantly discovering new things, but it was tough dealing with all the practical issues such as the different cultural environment, especially because I did not understand the language.

Q: Where did you move to and what is the job you are doing?
A: I moved from London to Tokyo, just over six years ago. Initially, I worked for a Japanese book-distribution company that imports foreign books from the USA, UK and Europe. I also worked for their subsidiary book publishing company. Now, I run my own media agency and consultancy company with a Japanese business partner.

Q: Why did your work take you abroad, and what are the advantages of working in Japan?
A: I moved abroad for a change of environment and to experience something challenging and new. Since the object of my current business is to trade between Japan and the UK and USA, it is an advantage to be here and to have an understanding of the Japanese market. I'm building up a good insight into Japanese business practice and gaining experience of working with Japanese companies.

Q: How does the work ethic and etiquette in Japan compare with that in the UK?
A: There is much more emphasis on teamwork and networking in Japan, and you have to pay a great deal of attention to relationship-building. One of the main differences is the emphasis on customer satisfaction in Japan. The customer is a king – if not a god!

Q: Have you noticed any major differences in terms of business practices?
A: In many industries, there are rigid standards of behaviour and procedure. The decision-making processes differ. In Western companies, decisions tend to be taken by a manager, or at least by a small management team. In Japan, it is necessary to secure an agreement by a consensus from the ground up. Even a president can't always make his or her own decision. In terms of new projects, the Japanese examine every small detail first, build many prototypes, establish all the processes and procedures in advance, and then follow them to the letter.

Q: How easy is it to find work in Japan?
A: The main types of job for foreigners are teaching languages or working in entertainment. However, there are strict requirements for these jobs, and without the appropriate qualifications and documentation, it is very difficult to get a visa. After living in Japan for a while, it's possible to find jobs outside these areas. I had specialist experience that matched the requirements of the company offering me a job. To secure a

JAPAN

ABOVE: Chris uses one room as her office, from which she runs her business

RIGHT: The Japanese are great believers in storage space, and every apartment comes with an array of cupboards

JAPAN

visa you have to find a company to sponsor you, and then you must complete all the right forms in the right way. The visa system follows a strict formula, and you have to do things the right way or you will be turned down.

Q: How does the lifestyle differ in Japan?
A: If you have a reasonable income, the lifestyle is very good and it can be great to live here, but it is expensive! Everything runs smoothly, and once you find out how things are done, it's very easy and convenient to live here. There are many things to do and see. Art galleries and museums abound, and the restaurants are fantastic. It is a vast consumer society, so there are many shopping malls and department stores.

Q: How easily did you settle in Japan?
A: I underestimated the problems of adapting to the culture and working style, but I've been here a while now and forgotten some of that. It is important to respect the community and the expectations of society. It is a very polite culture, and doing things the right way and showing that you are considering the feelings of other people is important. The Japanese have many small "rituals" in their everyday life, and social pressure to adhere to them is strong. They don't expect foreigners to comply with all the social obligations, but a lack of respect for them will cause offence. Misunderstandings can happen because foreigners do not always understand when, how or why they have caused offence.

Q: How did you cope with the language barrier?
A: Japanese is not the easiest language to learn, so communicating was quite tough in the early days. However, the use of English is increasing for things such as directions in stations, street signs and some restaurant menus. I do try to speak Japanese, but it is really difficult.

"It was great to be constantly discovering new things, but it was tough dealing with all the practical issues such as the different cultural environment"

Q: How did you find your property?
A: Initially, I rented a semi-furnished apartment, which I found through an agency that specialises in short-term rentals for foreigners. It's hard and expensive to rent in Japan because you have to pay key money, gift money and a six-month deposit, so you need a lot of cash up front. Agencies that deal with foreigners often provide property without such stringent requirements, but the standard can be low.

I then saved up enough money to go to a Japanese estate agency, but I still needed an agency that dealt with foreigners to make the introduction – many Japanese landlords won't take foreign tenants. Once accepted though, and as long as you are a responsible tenant, there is no hassle and you are quite secure.

Q: Is property more or less expensive than the UK, and is it better value for money?
A: My instinct tells me that the UK is better value, but now that prices have risen so much in the UK that may no longer be true. I live in a suburb just outside Tokyo city. My apartment could be described as a two-bedroom flat in a modern block. Space is used a bit differently here, which is why I say "could be described". I pay the equivalent of around £725 per month, which includes a maintenance fee. ●

Top tips

● Many Japanese landlords won't deal with foreign tenants, so get a foreign agency to make an introduction – it's better to deal with a local agent.

● Don't underestimate, as I did, the problems of assimilation. The language and culture are very different so be prepared and maybe do some research before you go.

● Be prepared – life is expensive!

● Ensure you have the appropriate qualifications and requirements for your field of employment – Japanese employers place heavy emphasis on these.

Who moves there?

A hotspot for gap-year students and financial executives alike, and a popular choice with Europeans

© JAPANESE TOURIST BOARD

JAPAN

LEFT: Tokyo's stunning backdrop of Mt Fuji and Lake Kawaguchi

In 2003, 155,800 foreigners entered Japan on working visas, a 20 per cent increase since 2000. One per cent of Japan's entire labour force (670,000) is of foreign origin, an increase of 70,000 since 1994. This trend is set to continue as the requirements and demands for skilled labour rise. Currently, 0.3 per cent of labourers in agriculture and fishing, 59.8 per cent of those working in mining and manufacturing 0.2 per cent in construction, 8 per cent in trade and hotels, and 29.6 per cent in other services are foreigners. Unemployment rates have been gradually falling since 1999.

"Japan offers a wealth of opportunities and gives foreigners high financial return for their work"

MORE THAN 10,000 BRITISH PEOPLE live and work in Japan. With so many people choosing to relocate to the hub of the Asian economy, Japan is regaining position as a global market leader, and the economy and employment rates are on the up.

Who moves there?

The largest age group of foreign migrants to Japan is 20- to 25-year-olds. Many are students, and a large percentage spend time teaching English to Japanese students. It is possible to earn up to ¥52,000 (£260) for two days teaching, and there are plenty of openings for English language teachers in schools. A large number of foreigners also work in the finance markets and Japan's equivalent of Wall Street in Tokyo. Most of these foreign workers have either relocated through companies back home, or have sufficient language skills to be able to fulfil the job requirements independently. Many families move to Japan when one spouse is relocated through their company. But there are also a large number of single men working in finance, mainly in Tokyo and Osaka.

Why move there?

There are a huge amount of openings for skilled foreign workers in Japan, and a high financial return for hard work. Japanese people have a firm hard-work ethic, but they still find time to socialise.

If you have no knowledge of the language, it may still be possible to find a job with one of Japan's larger companies. The majority of people will find that work opportunities are focused around Tokyo, a world-class city where excellent money can be made, which is necessary to fund increasingly expensive living costs.

One major reason to consider relocating to Japan is the culture of the country. With Buddhist gardens, temples and shrines at every turn, picturesque cherry blossom trees and wonderful architecture, Japan truly appeals to the senses. An added benefit is that it is relatively close to Thailand, Australia, Hawaii and Bali, which makes it an excellent base for travel and holidays. Many Westerners find Japan's culture alien, and the prospect of learning the language daunting, but most enjoy their time in Japan and find the contrast exhilarating. ●

Working in Japan

A knowledge of Japanese business etiquette and of the language will reap dividends in the job market

■ LABOUR MARKET

Japan has few natural resources and little land suitable for extensive agriculture, so the labour market is industry centred, with manufacturing, construction, distribution, real estate, services and communication all contributing significantly to its GDP. Advanced technological abilities make Japan a leading producer and exporter of motor vehicles, electronic equipment, machine tools, steel and chemicals.

■ JOB OPPORTUNITIES AND KEY INDUSTRIES

Job opportunities for Japanese speakers are wide ranging, but most jobs tend to be in the business sector, especially IT and investment. The main opportunities for foreigners without Japanese language skills are in teaching – the Japanese are keen to learn English from native speakers. The JET scheme is particularly well paid at about ¥3,600,000 (£18,000) per annum.

■ FINDING A JOB

A transfer within an international company to a Japanese branch is the best way to secure a job in Japan, but international recruitment agencies are also good places to start. There are many ways to find teaching jobs, from notice boards in international centres to publications, such as e-newsletters, that list current vacancies.

■ LANGUAGE REQUIREMENTS

To get work other than teaching or a holiday job, it is essential that you have some knowledge of the language. The Japanese Language Proficiency Test is the most recognised qualification, and the *nikyu* (second-highest) level will be sufficient. It will require 9 to 12 months of intensive training and you will learn to write about 1,000 characters and have a moderately advanced conversation.

■ BUSINESS ETIQUETTE

One easy rule to remember is to bow – always bow to greet a colleague. The more prestigious the colleague, the deeper and longer you hold the bow. Business cards have a high significance in Japan, and if you are there on business you should carry some of your own. If you are presented with one in a meeting, accept it with both hands, read the information on it and then leave it on the desk for the duration of the meeting. Afterwards, put it away carefully – it is disrespectful to just shove it in your back pocket. ●

BELOW: Tokyo's stylish shopping district Shibuya

© JAPANESE TOURIST BOARD

JAPAN

VISAS

There are seven types of visa available for those entering Japan, only some of which let you work. Note that visas recommend that you be allowed to stay in Japan, but it is landing permission (which can be refused for any number of reasons) that actually grants you permission. It can be secured at any port of entry into Japan. For more information on any of these visas, contact the Japan Consulate.

● TOURIST VISAS

Two types of visa are available to tourists – the transit visa, which allows you to stay for 15 days en route to another destination, and the temporary visitor's visa, or tourist visa. UK citizens are entitled to stay in Japan as a tourist for three months, and may then apply for a further three months. Japan has signed a visa waiver agreement, so you may not need to apply for a visa before you leave home. You can simply fill out a landing card at the airport.

● WORK VISAS

There are three types of work visa – one for diplomats, one for government officials and one for everyone else. Standard work visas are valid for three years and are categorised by type of job. You cannot change from a non-working visa to a working one within Japan. Instead, you will need to apply to an embassy or consulate in another country. But if you already have a visa that allows you to work, you can apply for a change of status within Japan.

● STUDENT VISAS

Student visas will allow you to study or work as a trainee, but do not allow you to get paid.

● RESIDENTS

To stay in Japan for a longer period of time, you will need a specified visa, which may or may not allow you to work, depending on the specification. Once you have lived in Japan for five consecutive years, you may apply for permanent residence.

■ USEFUL WEBSITES

www.ohayosensei.com
A bi-monthly e-newsletter listing current vacancies for English teachers in Japan.

www.daijob.com An online recruitment agency specialising in jobs for English-speaking professionals with Japanese language skills.

www.embjapan.org.uk
The Japan Consulate

Finding a home

Securing accomodation can be tricky – look out for agencies that specialise in dealing with foreigners

FINDING ACCOMMODATION IS THE MOST difficult thing for Westerners wanting to live in Japan. Estate agents are often loath to deal with foreigners. You will need a lot of money and possibly a Japanese guarantor.

Renting

Apartments are rented for two years at a time and are tiny – usually no more than one or two rooms with a cupboard-sized kitchen and bathroom. They are assessed on a LDK (living, dining, kitchen) basis. For example, a 1K apartment has one bedroom plus kitchen, a 2DK has two rooms plus dining area and kitchen and so on. Toilets are included, but bathrooms may be shared.

Extra costs include a reservation fee and deposit, which are refundable, and a service fee and key money, which are non-refundable and often amount to several months' rent. *Gaijin* (foreigner) houses or guest houses are rented by the month or week rather than for the standard two years, and cost from ¥104,000 (£520) per month for a basic private apartment.

Buying

Although mortgage interest rates are low, land is expensive and a sizable deposit is usually required. If you do decide to buy property in Japan, you may do so without permanent residence. Property tax is paid by the owners listed in the local property register the previous January and is usually paid in four instalments. Property is valued every three years, and tax rates are assessed annually by local authorities. ●

ABOVE: The striking landmark of Yokohama Bay Bridge

AVERAGE RENTAL/SALE PRICES

Hotspot	2-bed apartment rentals	2-bed apartment sales	4-bed house sales
Tokyo	¥435,000 (£2,174)	¥59.7M (£298,350)	¥97M (£484,760)
Osaka	¥335,000K (£1,674)	¥57M (£284,360)	¥83M (£414,794)
Kyoto	¥227,000K (£1,134)	¥42M (£207,395)	¥69M (£334,829)

TAXES

The taxation system in Japan combines a withholding system (where your employer deducts taxes from your wages and pays them on your behalf) with self-assessment. As well as income tax, tax payers are expected to contribute to a number of national social insurance policies, including Unemployment Insurance and Health Insurance. If you are not sure what your status is, the National Tax Organisation's web site (www.nto.go.jp) has an extremely thorough income tax guide for foreigners.

● **TAXABLE INCOME**
Anyone who has their domicile in Japan, or has lived in the country for a year, is considered a resident for tax purposes. Permanent residents are taxed as Japanese nationals would be, and non-permanent residents are taxed on all income except that paid abroad by a non-Japanese company. In that case, only the amount of money transferred into Japan would be taxable. Finally, non-residents are taxed only on domestically earned income, at a fixed rate of 20%.

● **TAXATION SYSTEM**
Where people are taxed by the withholding method, a year-end adjustment is made to correct any fluctuations in income throughout the year. As a result, your final pay packet could see an increase in tax, a decrease in tax or even a rebate. Those with salaries in excess of

¥20million (about £100,000) and employees of Japanese companies receiving money abroad are not subject to year-end adjustments, and are therefore required to complete a self-assessment. Assistance with filling out tax forms is available from regional tax offices.

Income tax rate:
¥1 – ¥3,300,000: 10 per cent
¥3,300,001 – ¥9,000,000: 20 per cent
¥9,000,001 – ¥18,000,000: 30 per cent
¥18,000,001 and over: 37 per cent

Employment hotspots

Japan's bustling cities offer a fast-paced lifestyle coupled with numerous job opportunities, from teaching English to the financial sector

1 Tokyo

A colourful city of neon and high-rise buildings, Tokyo is a fascinating blend of old and new, epitomised by ladies in kimonos jostling with suit-clad commuters. It operates at break-neck speed and has long been regarded as one of the world's leading economic centres. Everyday, five million workers descend on the city, where jobs are widely available. Most are in teaching English as a foreign language, but there are also openings in the financial sector – Japan's stock-exchange and leading financial institutions are located here.

Tokyo is Japan's most expensive real-estate market. Land is limited and apartments are the norm. Major redevelopment is concentrated around the city centre. The general belief is that prices have bottomed out and will now begin rising, but generally the market is still declining and the investor should be wary.

KEY FACTS
■ **Population:** 12.3 million
■ **Airport:** Tokyo Narita International Airport, Tel: 00 81 476 322 802
■ **Medical:** Tokyo Saiseikai Central Hospital, Tel: 00 81 334 518 211 ■ Tokyo University Hospital (Todai Byoin), Tel: 00 81 338 155 411
■ **Schools:** The American School in Japan, Tel: 0081 422 345 300
■ **Rentals:** Demand is very high for apartment properties in the centre ■ Properties are very small ■ Prices continue to decrease, but are still expensive compared with the UK
■ **Pros:** A vibrant city ■ Property prices are at an all-time low ■ Transport network is second to none ■ Good work opportunities for foreigners ■ Some properties are specifically designed for Westerners

■ **Cons:** Unstable property market
■ The lifestyle is difficult to adjust to
■ High levels of pollution and smog.

2 Osaka

Osaka has been a major trade hub since its creation, and is the heartland of western Japan. A concrete jungle by day and a neon-dominated nightspot by night, it holds a strange appeal and is reputedly 20 per cent busier than Tokyo. Its inhabitants are renowned for their love of fine food.

Osaka has been integrated into the Asian economic community and the jobs market and economy are very healthy. There are many Western businesses here. TEFL, embassy postings and work in the media are other options for foreigners.

As confidence in the property market grows, so property prices are rising. Rentals have increased in volume by ten per cent over the last year. There has been increased investment, particularly along the in-demand waterfront.

KEY FACTS
■ **Population:** 2.6 million
■ **Airport:** Kansai International Airport, Tel: 00 81 724 552 500
■ **Medical:** National Hospital Organization, Osaka National Hospital, Tel: 00 81 669 421 331
■ **Schools:** Osaka YMCA International School, Tel: 00 81 643 951 002
■ **Rentals:** Most are apartments and tend to be located in the city centre ■ Rentals are expensive
■ **Pros:** The largest jobs market for foreigners outside Tokyo ■ Enjoys a buoyant economy ■ Investment and revitalisation of the city are continuing ■ Healthy future as Osaka opens her doors to Asia ■ Some estate agents deal specifically with Westerners

ABOVE: The upmarket district of Ginza in Tokyo

■ **Cons:** Overcrowded and overpopulated ■ Property is expensive ■ Can be difficult to get used to the lifestyle of the city.

3 Kyoto

At first, Kyoto appears to be a modern city dominated by high-rise buildings, but it is a cultural delight with 13 World Heritage sites. Boasting over 2,000 temples and shrines, Kyoto is the epitome of a Westerner's image of Japan, with kimono-clad geisha and cherry blossom in spring.

The city is a thriving industrial centre, but it can be difficult for a foreigner to find work. There is a push to encourage foreign investment into Kyoto, which will make the job search easier. The major industry is the service sector, followed by electronics, publishing and print, textiles and food production. Rapidly expanding sectors are medical research, biotechnology and IT.

It isn't easy for a foreigner to find property here. Prices are

expensive due to high demand. Land prices haven't risen over the last year, but property prices have increased by one per cent, a trend that is set to continue.

KEY FACTS
■ **Population:** 1.5 million
■ **Airport:** Kansai International Airport, Tel: 00 81 724 552 500
■ **Medical:** Kyoto City Hospital (Kyoto Shiritsu Byoin), Tel: 00 81 753 115 311
■ **Schools:** Kyoto International School, Tel: 00 81 754 511 022
■ **Rentals:** Difficult to find a rental property ■ Demand is high for holiday lets ■ Rental income is guaranteed to be high and regular ■ Rentals are cheaper here than in Tokyo and Osaka
■ **Pros:** A stunning city with a huge number of cultural attractions ■ Prices are more affordable than in other areas ■ Rapid economic and industrial expansion planned, which will bring more jobs to the city
■ **Cons:** It is difficult to find property in the city ■ Industry is generally tourist-based so a knowledge of the language is essential in order to secure a job. ●

JAPAN

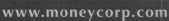

Property price guide

The Japanese property market is dominated by apartments, and there are a number available in a range of prices, and a variety of styles

PROPERTIES FOR RENT

Japanese apartments are much smaller than UK ones

¥45,000 PER MONTH

1-BED TOKYO

£225 PER MONTH
- Fully furnished ✘
- Pool ✘
- Parking ✘   **CODE** ABC

¥45,000 PER MONTH

1-BED TOKYO

£225 PER MONTH
- Fully furnished ✘
- Pool ✘
- Parking ✔   **CODE** ABC

¥65,000 PER MONTH

1-BED TOKYO

£325 PER MONTH
- Fully furnished ✘
- Pool ✔
- Parking ✔   **CODE** ABC

¥65,000 PER MONTH

2-BED TOKYO

£325 PER MONTH
- Fully furnished ✘
- Pool ✘
- Parking ✘   **CODE** ABC

¥200,000 PER MONTH

1-BED TOKYO

£1,000 PER MONTH
- Fully furnished ✘
- Pool ✘
- Parking ✔   **CODE** RET

¥200,000 PER MONTH

1-BED TOKYO

£1,000 PER MONTH
- Fully furnished ✘
- Pool ✘
- Parking ✔   **CODE** RET

¥200,000 PER MONTH

1-BED TOKYO

£1,000 PER MONTH
- Fully furnished ✘
- Pool ✘
- Parking ✔   **CODE** RET

¥200,000 PER MONTH

1-BED TOKYO

£1,000 PER MONTH
- Fully furnished ✘
- Pool ✘
- Parking ✔   **CODE** RET

HOUSES FOR SALE

Houses are harder to come by and more expensive than apartments

¥24,000,000

3-BED TOKYO

£120,000
- Fully furnished ✘
- Pool ✘
- Parking ✔   **CODE** AOI

¥150,000,000

4-BED TOKYO

£749,625
- Fully furnished ✘
- Pool ✘
- Parking ✔   **CODE** RET

¥150,000,000

4-BED TOKYO

£749,625
- Fully furnished ✘
- Pool ✘
- Parking ✔   **CODE** RET

¥178,000,000

3-BED TOKYO

£889,555
- Fully furnished ✘
- Pool ✘
- Parking ✔   **CODE** RET

JAPAN

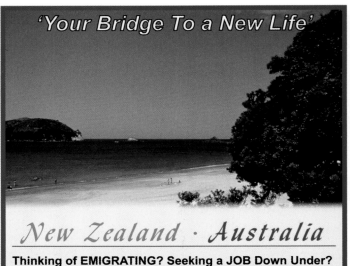

New Zealand

Spectacular scenery and a healthy, outdoor lifestyle

© NEW ZEALAND TOURIST BOARD

FACT BOX

- **Population** 3,993,817
- **Population growth rate** 1.05%
- **Economic growth rate** 3.5%
- **Inflation rate** 1.8%
- **Capital** Wellington
- **Hotspots** Auckland, Christchurch, Wellington
- **Average house price** (4-bed) $420,000
- **Average rental price** (2-bed) $1,093

Living in New Zealand

From volcanoes to fjords, this is the country for lovers of nature and the great outdoors

FACT FILE

AREA	268,680km²
POPULATION	3,993,817
CAPITAL	Wellington
LIFE EXPECTANCY	78 years
LITERACY	99%
GOVERNMENT	Parliamentary democracy
GDP PER CAPITA	US$21,600
UNEMPLOYMENT RATE	3.6%
CURRENCY	New Zealand dollar (NZ$)
EXCHANGE RATE	NZ1$ = £0.37; £1=NZ$2.68
LANGUAGES	English, Maori

COST OF LIVING

PETROL (1L)	$1.20
WINE (0.75L)	$15
MEAL (3-COURSE)	$50
BEER (375ML)	$1.90
LOAF OF BREAD (650G)	$2
MILK (1L)	$1.80

CLIMATE

AUCKLAND — Average monthly temperature °C

Dec	21
Nov	19
Oct	17
Sept	16
Aug	14
July	13
June	14
May	17
April	19
March	22
Feb	23
Jan	23

LONDON — Average monthly temperature °C

Dec	7
Nov	10
Oct	14
Sept	19
Aug	21
July	22
June	20
May	17
April	13
March	10
Feb	7
Jan	6

AUCKLAND — Average monthly rainfall mm

Dec	79
Nov	89
Oct	102
Sept	102
Aug	117
July	145
June	137
May	127
April	97
March	81
Feb	94
Jan	79

LONDON — Average monthly rainfall mm

Dec	81
Nov	78
Oct	70
Sept	65
Aug	62
July	59
June	58
May	57
April	56
March	64
Feb	72
Jan	77

NEW ZEALAND

NEW ZEALAND IS ABOUT AS FAR AWAY AS IT is possible to get from the UK and Europe. But despite the distance, it was voted the most popular long-haul destination in a 2004 UK newspaper poll. With its spectacular scenery, friendly locals and spirit of adventure, it is easy to see the attraction.

New Zealand consists of two islands, North and South, separated by the Cook Strait. Most people live on North Island, particularly around Auckland and the capital, Wellington. South Island is larger and less populated. Queenstown on South Island is the "adventure capital" and is home to a host of extreme sports, ranging from bungee jumping and white water rafting to skiing and snowboarding.

New Zealand is a rugged, mountainous country, moulded by powerful geological forces. It boasts just about all the extremes that nature can muster, from active volcanoes and steaming geysers to frozen glaciers and fjords, all of which featured prominently in the recent *Lord of the Rings* trilogy.

New Zealand is proud of its natural assets, and it is an extremely environmentally conscious country. Virtually all its electricity is produced from non-polluting hydroelectric plants. It has been a nuclear-free zone since 1986, and refuses entry to nuclear-powered or -equipped warships, which has put it at odds with the USA.

New Zealand's indigenous people are the Maoris, and there have been bloody battles with British colonisers in the past. For the most part New Zealand is now an amiable, integrated society.

© NEW ZEALAND TOURIST BOARD

RIGHT: New Zealand cities are embracing the European café culture with zeal

Politics and economy

New Zealand is a parliamentary democracy, with Helen Clark the current prime minister. The head of state remains Elizabeth II, and unlike in Australia there has been little call for Republicanism within the country. Currently the economy is performing well, with a growth of 4.9 per cent in 2004. It is increasingly reliant on tourism, and agriculture and manufacturing remain central. The crime rate is very low, with New Zealand considered to be one of the world's safest countries. Petty crime is present in the cities, but in much of the countryside it is common to leave doors unlocked.

Education

New Zealand has what is widely regarded as being one of the best education systems in the world. In a recent survey, which ranked 15-year-olds in 32 countries, New Zealand came third, beaten only by Canada and Finland. More than 95 per cent of children attend state schools, and the government spends more than 10 per cent of its total budget on education. Education starts at five or six and is compulsory until 16

ABOVE: Three-quarters of New Zealand's population live in North Island

years of age. Children attend primary school up until age 10, then move to intermediate school until they reach 12 years of age. Secondary school is attended between 13 and 16. Upon leaving secondary school, pupils take the National Certificate for Education Achievement (NCEA), which is broadly equivalent to GCSEs. Those who choose to stay at school into the sixth form go on to take NCEA levels two and three, which are roughly equivalent to A levels.

"With its spectacular scenery, friendly locals and spirit of adventure, it is easy to see the attraction"

Healthcare

New Zealand has a long, proud history of social reform. Compulsory free schooling was introduced in 1877, and the National Health Service was established in 1938. (By contrast, education was not free in Britain until 1880, and the NHS didn't appear until 1948.)

State healthcare in New Zealand is excellent and is subsidised for those with resident status. There are agreements with the UK, Ireland and certain other nations to provide the same healthcare benefits that are available to New Zealanders, but visitors from other countries have to pay the full costs.

Hospital and emergency treatment is largely free, while visits to a doctor cost about $45 (£17) plus the costs of any prescribed medicines. Private health insurance is also widely available, but is by no means regarded as a necessity.

Food and drink

Traditional New Zealand tucker is of the meat-and-two-veg variety (usually lamb), but international cuisines abound in even the smallest towns – albeit with a local flavour. New Zealand is a prolific producer of foods, and virtually everything you eat will be made from fresh, local ingredients. The country has a well-established wine industry, and its whites are particularly renowned. There is a thriving pub, and in the larger places club, scene throughout the country.

Expat communities

New Zealand is a nation of immigrants, and as it is an English speaking country and member of the British Commonwealth, there is little difficulty in integrating with the locals. In fact, New Zealanders are openly friendly to foreigners. Many will have visited Britain and the rest of the world as part of the "Great Overseas Experience" that young Kiwis inevitably embark upon in their 20s.

Pets

New Zealand has strict rules on importing pets, and you must obtain an import permit. Cats and dogs must be microchipped and all animals must be vaccinated against rabies. For further information, contact the Ministry of Agriculture and Forestry, Wellington (www.maf.govt.nz). ●

TRAVEL FILE

AIR The main gateway into New Zealand is Auckland International Airport, with ongoing connections to the capital, Wellington, and to Christchurch on South Island. Flying from Europe requires at least one stop en route, and minimum flying time is 26 hours. The most direct flights are offered by national flag carrier **Air New Zealand** (0800 028 4149; www.airnewzealand.co.uk). Other airlines with reasonably direct flights are **Qantas** (0845 774 7767; www.qantas.co.uk), **British Airways** (www.ba.com; 0870 850 9850), **Singapore Airlines** (0870 609 9996; www.singaporeair.com) and **United Airlines** (0845 844 4777; www.unitedairlines.co.uk).
Air New Zealand has the most comprehensive schedule of internal flights. Other internal airlines are **Origin Pacific** (00 64 3 547 2020; www.originpacific. co.nz) and budget airline **Freedom Air** (www.freedomair.co.nz). **Sounds Air** (00 64 3 520 3080; www.soundsair.co.nz) has a service crossing the Cook Strait.

ROAD Most roads in New Zealand are single carriageway and of good quality. Driving is pleasant, with uncrowded roads passing through spectacular countryside. Be aware, however, that New Zealand has one of the highest rates of road deaths per capita of any nation – double that of the UK.

GETTING AROUND There are just two main railway lines in New Zealand: one on North Island and one on South Island. Auckland and Wellington have local rail networks, called **Tranz Metro**. For long-distance travel, buses are more useful. Most towns have a good bus service, but it tends to stop in the early evening.

I did it!

Name: Nigel Greening

Job: Wine-maker

Where: Wanaka, South Island, New Zealand

Contacts: www.feltonroad.com and www.cornishpoint.com

Starting a business

Nigel Greening spends part of the year in the UK and the rest at his vineyard in Bannockburn in Wanaka

AS A SUCCESSFUL ENTREPRENEUR, NIGEL WAS able to buy a plot of land and build a dream home for himself and his family. He tells us how he set up and developed his own business in New Zealand.

Q: Where are your wines distributed?
A: Our wines, Cornish Point, are distributed worldwide They are distributed widely in the UK through private merchants such as Berry Brothers, but they can be quite hard to find because demand tends to be high. We also supply top restaurants run by celebrity chefs such as Gordon Ramsey and Jamie Oliver.

Q: What influenced your decision to buy property in New Zealand?
A: We decided to buy land for vineyards over there so it was a natural progression. We ended up buying eight hectares of land for vineyards at Cornish Point in Bannockburn. We realised there was huge potential to create top-quality pinot noir in that part of New Zealand and we decided on a life change. I sold my UK creative agency to take up wine-making instead. We don't intend to emigrate permanently. We live from January to May in New Zealand and May to January in the UK.

Q: How long did it take to find the right property?
A: We purchased the land for our house in Wanaka in April 2000 after a relaxed period of looking. We were living in rented accommodation, which was fairly easy to come by, so there was no urgency to buy somewhere quickly. Having found a site, we had to wait until we could afford to build. We designed it in 2001 but did not start construction until April 2003.

Q: How did you choose where to make your purchase?
A: Wanaka is a strong contender for the most beautiful town in the world in terms of location. It is populated almost entirely by people who came for the weekend and forgot to leave. Property there is very expensive compared with most of New Zealand, and possibly the most expensive property in the country. It is about 40 minutes from our vineyards in Bannockburn.

Q: Would you mind telling us how much you paid for your property?
A: The property will have cost us more than $2m (£760,000) by the time it is finished. This is extraordinarily expensive compared with

ABOVE: Nigel's purpose-built home was designed by architect Fred van Brandenburg

LEFT: The view across lakes and vineyards from Nigel's home

NEW ZEALAND

property in other areas of New Zealand, but it is not expensive for Wanaka because the location is so special.

Q: How did you fund your purchase?
A: We used the income from our wine business and the sale of my UK agency. Mortgages in New Zealand are expensive right now because interest rates are high compared to the UK.

"Wanaka is a strong contender for the most beautiful town in the world. It is populated by people who came for the weekend and forgot to leave"

Q: Can you describe your property?
A: The house is a dramatic modern house designed by Fred van Brandenburg. It has six bedrooms and three bathrooms, which are in a separate sleeping wing. There is a single large, open-plan living area as a separate building. The house overlooks vineyards (not our own), with a lake and snow-capped mountains beyond. The property is designed for comfortable family living (I have two small children and a grown-up daughter), and has plenty of guest accommodation. This is important because friends may be coming halfway round the world to see us, so they are not going to be spending just a single night! The property is nearly finished, and we are moving in at the end of October 2005.

Q: Do you feel it has been a good investment?
A: Too early to say. This is a very expensive property in an area where multimillion-dollar homes are the norm. Property prices in Wanaka have more than trebled in the past eight years. This brings the risk that in an economic downturn there could be a substantial drop in prices. However, the continued investment from the USA into this area has been very strong. (It seems to be a favourite hideaway for a number of top film stars and musicians.)

Q: Are the local people friendly and welcoming?
A: Locals are always friendly in New Zealand. It would have to be one of the easiest places on Earth for people from the UK to feel at home.

Q: What's the best thing about life in New Zealand?
A: In many ways, life in Wanaka is like village life as it used to be in the UK. Everybody knows everybody here and we can't walk up the main street without seeing a few friends. Life is built around the outdoors: you can always go walking, fishing, skiing, climbing, camping or boating. Nobody can say they are stuck for something to do.

Q: Are there any downsides?
A: It takes 37 hours to get from our UK house to our New Zealand one, not to mention the cost of the journey. Also, we have to own two of everything!

Q: What are your plans for the future?
A: More of the same. This is my working life, not an extended holiday, so for me the journey is simply my commute to work. The family do the January to May stint with me, but I do other trips on my own. ●

ABOVE: **Nigel's vineyard, only 40 minutes from his home in Wanaka**

NEW ZEALAND

Top tips

● Don't be over-ambitious. New Zealand is small, and big ideas and ambitions don't work well. People earn less than in the UK, and in general, opportunities for generating wealth from business are considerably fewer.

● Simple ideas to create practical businesses can generate good returns on which you can live very well. Don't look to make millions in New Zealand, it just won't happen.

● The cities and the rural communities are very different. Population is very thin once you leave the cities. So, come to New Zealand for open spaces and a rural life, but bear in mind that earning opportunities in rural New Zealand are thin, because the population is thin too.

Who moves there?

Unemployment among immigrants is low, but be prepared to do things the New Zealand way

"The climate is pleasant, the scenery spectacular and the lifestyle is healthy and relaxed"

CURRENTLY, 28 PER CENT OF VISA applications to New Zealand are from UK residents, and in 2004 8,700 British people relocated there. A massive 70 per cent of New Zealand's population are of European extraction.

Who moves there?
In 1996, 17.5 per cent of the resident population were migrants and 37 per cent of these were from the UK and Ireland. The majority were of working age – between 15 and 64 – but a quarter of UK immigrants were over 65, with the dominant overall age group being 30- to 49-year-olds. New Zealand also receives large numbers of immigrants from Asia and the Pacific, but these tend to be unskilled and unqualified workers rather than the skilled workers the country requires. Of migrants to New Zealand, 92.5 per cent live in urban areas and Auckland is the prevailing destination. Most UK immigrants tend to work in a professional occupation, and more immigrants make up the professional workforce than New Zealanders. Immigrants currently represent 18 per cent of the total workforce, and can expect to earn an average wage of $34,000 (£13,000). This may not seem much in terms of European wages, but the cost of living is fairly low.

Why move there?
New Zealand is a vast land mass and, with the population only just reaching 4 million, it is refreshingly uncrowded. The climate is pleasant, the scenery spectacular and the lifestyle is healthy and relaxed.

New Zealand's economy has diversified, moving away from the traditional reliance on farming and agriculture. Exports are key to the economy, so more emphasis is now placed on manufacturing. The economy has opened up in recent years, with GDP growth averaging four per cent per annum, the New Zealand dollar trading well and inflation at a maximum of three per cent. This, however, is putting pressure on the labour market. There are skills shortages in certain areas and a saturation in others. More than 40 per cent of companies have reported problems in finding skilled staff. There are a number of skills in demand, and these include ICT technicians, computer programmers, nurses, engineers, financial executives, marketing executives and tradespeople. Unemployment levels currently stand at 3.6 per cent, which is the lowest they have been for 16 years, despite the continued influx of immigrants. Unemployment rates among established immigrants are higher than those of New Zealanders, at 6.05 per cent. ●

LEFT: **Maoris make up 18 per cent of New Zealand's total population**

Working in New Zealand

Traditionally reliant on agriculture, New Zealand's workers have become more skilled, and their economy has diversified

■ ECONOMY

New Zealand is still largely reliant on agriculture (there are 13 sheep for every person in the country), but the past 20 years have seen a shift towards a service-based economy. About 75 per cent of the workforce is now employed in the service industries. The early 90s saw deep recession in the country, but the economy recovered in the late 90s and unemployment is down from 11 per cent to less than four per cent today.

■ JOB OPPORTUNITIES AND KEY INDUSTRIES

Many newly qualified young New Zealanders leave the country to work in Australia or further afield. To compensate for this, the country is keen to encourage those able to contribute to its society to apply for residency. The Immigration Service publishes a Priority Occupations List and awards points to those with relevant skills, speeding up the residency process. Healthcare, education and IT workers are particularly sought after, and people in these professions usually have little difficulty obtaining work and residency.

■ MAIN EMPLOYMENT CENTRES

The best prospects for employment are in Auckland followed by Wellington, where the government and civil service are based. It is here that you will find the majority of office-based employment.

■ FINDING A JOB

Nothing beats applying for a job in person, and it is not uncommon for those on a visitor's visa to check out the job situation first hand. New Zealand is an English-speaking country, so a good standard of English is a prerequisite to finding work and being granted a working visa or residency permit. ●

© NEW ZEALAND TOURIST BOARD

ABOVE: Auckland is New Zealand's principal and most popular city

■ USEFUL WEBSITES

www.monster.co.nz This worldwide job hunter's resource has a local website in New Zealand

www.kiwicareers.govt.nz Run by the New Zealand government, this site is a mine of useful information and has links to search sites

www.netcheck.co.nz Highly searchable NZ-specific job site

www.immigration.govt.nz Immigration information and forms

WORK PERMITS

British citizens can stay for up to six months on a visitor's visa. Irish citizens, and those from many other countries, can stay for three months.

● WORK VISAS

Work visas are issued for $160 (£60) to those on short-term contracts – you need a firm job offer in order to apply. This allows you to work only for a limited time, but stands you in good stead if applying for permanent residency. If you do wish to live or work in New Zealand for longer, you will have to apply for residency. If granted, this allows you to stay indefinitely.

● SKILLED MIGRATION

There are two main types of residency application. Skilled migration uses a points system, where you are allocated a score depending on your qualifications, age, experience and numerous other factors. The first step is to lodge an Expression of Interest. For this, you must score at least 100 points and be able to demonstrate that you are of good character, in good health, speak English and are under 55 years of age. Your application then goes into a pool, and those with the highest number of points are invited to apply for residency. Unsuccessful applications remain in the pool for three months and are re-assessed every fortnight. If you are invited to apply for residency, you will need to submit a number of supporting documents with your application. Subject to a series of checks and final approval from the New Zealand Immigration Service, residency will be awarded shortly afterwards.

● FAMILY SPONSORSHIP

You can apply for family sponsorship if you are married to, or in a stable relationship with, a New Zealander or have a close relative living in the country. Close relatives include dependent children and siblings and adult children with a permanent job offer. If awarded residency from outside the country, you will be given a Residency Visa allowing you a year to reach New Zealand and get the visa replaced with a Residency Permit. If you are already in the country, you will be granted a permit straight away.

Finding a home

New Zealanders are a nation of homeowners, with more than 75 per cent owning their own home

HOUSES TEND TO BE DETACHED AND ON LARGE 1,000-square-metre plots, even in city suburbs. This goes back to the early days of the colony, when land was granted to settlers in quarter-acre plots. Buildings tend to be constructed from simpler materials than is traditional in Europe. Weatherboard walls and corrugated tin roofs are the norm, but while this may seem flimsy and primitive, it suits the climate and such buildings are better able to withstand New Zealand's frequent earthquakes.

In the city centres, properties are more compact and apartment blocks are common. Property is cheaper than in the UK, but Auckland is significantly pricier than the rest of the country.

Renting

There are a limited number of rental properties available in New Zealand, and they tend to get snapped up quickly. The Ministry of Housing issues standard tenancy agreements, which you can rely on as being fair to both parties. A bond, equivalent to up to four weeks' rent, is paid to the Tenancy Services Department, who refund it to you, less any damage, on termination of the contract.

Buying

The first step is to make a formal offer in writing. Then, once surveys and searches prove satisfactory, a price is agreed upon, a contract is signed and a ten per cent deposit is paid. This legally binds you to go through with the purchase or forfeit the deposit. The title search is carried out by the Department of Survey and Land Information, which is very efficient – so much so that the services of a lawyer are not strictly necessary. Mortgages are generally straightforward to obtain, and there will be a variety of banks and brokers competing for your custom and offering a dazzling choice of products. Mortgages can be 90 per cent of the purchase price and can last for up to 25 years. Repayments are usually limited to about 30 per cent of your income, which is combined for a couple.

© NEW ZEALAND TOURIST BOARD

ABOVE: New Zealand boasts stunning scenery and mountain ranges

Restrictions on foreign buyers

Non-residents may buy a property on a plot of land up to 4,074 square metres in size. For larger plots, permission is required from the Land Value Tribunal or District Land Registrar. If you have been granted residency, then no such restrictions apply.

Property tax

New Zealand uses a rates system in which properties are awarded a rateable value depending on size and location. Expect to pay between $1,000 (£380) and $2,000 (£760) per year for a three-bedroom house. The money is used for local authority services. ●

TAXES

In order to work in New Zealand, you need to apply for an IRD number from the Inland Revenue Department. You should do this as soon as you start work, or preferably before, because if you don't give your employer an IRD number, you will be taxed the higher non-declaration rate of 45 per cent. You can download the form from www.ird.govt.nz and will usually be issued with your IRD number within a week. The tax year runs from 1 April to 31 March, and tax returns have to be filed by 7 July. Until recently, everyone who worked in New Zealand had to fill in a tax return; however, the system has been overhauled. Now, most employees have tax deducted at source by their employers as part of a PAYE scheme and, if no other income is received, it is not necessary to file a tax return.

New Zealand operates a fairly straightforward three-tier tax system:

Up to $38,000	**19.5% ($0.195 per dollar)**
$38,001 to $60,000	**33% ($7,410 + $0.33 per dollar over $38,000)**
Over $60,001	**39% ($14,670 + $0.39 per dollar over $60,000)**

The equivalent tax on a salary of £25,000 would be: $67,000 - (14,670 + (7,000x0.39 = 2,730)) = $17,400 or 26% of income.

In addition to the above, there are various allowances (called "rebates") that you can deduct from your gross salary to reduce your tax bill.

AVERAGE RENTAL/SALE PRICES

Hotspot	2-bed apartment rentals	2-bed apartment sales	4-bed house sales
Auckland	$1,370 (£520)	$330K (£125K)	$725K (£275K)
Christchurch	$960 (£365)	$340K (£129K)	$465K (£177K)
Wellington	$950 (£361)	$234K (£89K)	$370K (£141K)

Employment hotspots

New Zealand is rich in culture and tradition; her major cities, though, are becoming more bohemian and multi-cultured

1 Auckland

This city is a flagship for growth and dynamism. It is the major gateway into New Zealand and the country's largest city. Twice the size of London with a fraction of the population, it is the least populated city in the world. Attractions include the National Art Gallery and Museum and the Skycity complex – the Skytower is the tallest structure in the southern hemisphere. The inner city suburbs boast excellent bars, restaurants and cafés, while there are surfing beaches and wineries on the west coast.

Auckland has had economic growth of 4.5 per cent, out-performing the country as a whole. It generates 34 per cent of the national GDP. The largest growth sector is education, with ICT, film, fashion and music also experiencing huge growth.

The property market in Auckland is strong. Investment is continuing to grow due to a strong economy, low interest rates and continued migration. Since 2003, there has been a 12 per cent increase in prices.

KEY FACTS
■ **Population:** 367,737
■ **Airport:** Auckland International Airport, Tel: 00 64 927 50789
■ **Medical:** Auckland Hospital, Tel: 00 64 937 97440 ■ Starship Children's Hospital, Tel: 00 64 930 78900
■ **Schools:** Kristin School, Tel: 00 64 941 59566
■ **Rentals:** Soaring demand due to the presence of international students ■ Buying to let is a strong investment
■ **Pros:** New Zealand's largest, most vibrant city ■ Home to the best of New Zealand's entertainment venues
■ **Cons:** The city is small by international standards.

© NEW ZEALAND TOURIST BOARD

ABOVE: New Zealanders enjoy a healthy beach lifestyle most Europeans would envy

2 Christchurch

Voted one of the nicest cities to live in, Christchurch is located between the Pacific Ocean and the vineyards, fields and beaches of the Canterbury Plains. It is a relaxed, lush city with a bustling "downtown" full of pubs, cafés and bars. To the south-east is the Banks Peninsula, used as a weekend retreat.

Only five per cent of businesses in Christchurch are foreign, and these employ only 17 per cent of the workforce. There are a number of finance, insurance, communications and utilities companies. Several head offices are here, mostly national firms such as FoodStuffs, Fulton Hogan and Meridian Energy.

Property here is cheaper than in Auckland. In 2000, prices peaked. Since then they have levelled out, but still continue to rise gradually.

KEY FACTS
■ **Population:** 316,227
■ **Airport:** Christchurch International Airport, Tel: 00 64 335 85029
■ **Medical:** The Christchurch Hospital, Tel: 00 64 336 40640

■ The Accident and Acute Medical Care Centre, Tel: 00 64 336 57777
■ **Schools:** St Andrew's College, Tel: 00 64 394 02000
■ **Rentals:** Significant increase in the demand for rental property ■ Prices are much more affordable than in much of the country
■ **Pros:** Exquisite gardens, Gothic architecture and wooden villas ■ A compact city, easy to get around on foot ■ Beaches are accessible by bus ■ An array of eateries with low prices and high standards
■ **Cons:** One-way streets can make driving around the centre complicated.

3 Wellington

The cultural and economic centre of the country, this is the capital of New Zealand. The city combines historical buildings with a modern café, restaurant and entertainment scene. The pedestrianised waterfront is home to theatres, museums and the town hall, while on the hillsides stand striking multi-coloured houses.

Wellington has the highest wage earners in the country. There is continued expansion within the city, and jobs are constantly being created. The largest employers are manufacturing, retail and wholesale. Unemployment is low, and changes to visas and work permits have made it easier for UK citizens to relocate to Wellington.

The city boasts a stable property market. Vacancy rates are at a record low although demand has continued.

KEY FACTS
■ **Population:** 163,824
■ **Airport:** Wellington International Airport, Tel: 00 64 438 55100
■ **Medical:** The Wellington Hospital, Tel: 00 64 438 55999 ■ The Accident and Urgent Medical Centre, Tel: 00 64 438 44944
■ **Schools:** Aotea College, Tel: 00 64 423 73166 ■ Bishop Viard College, Tel: 00 64 423 75248
■ **Rentals:** Market experiencing a high level of confidence, which is likely to continue
■ **Pros:** Excellent museums, theatres, shops, restaurants, cafés and bars ■ Many beautiful natural features
■ **Cons:** Very windy ■ Land-right struggles between European settlers and local Maoris. ●

NEW ZEALAND

Property price guide

Offering some stunning waterfront homes at remarkably reasonable prices, as well as cheap rental properties, New Zealand is an affordable prospect

PROPERTIES FOR RENT

Rentals are a highly affordable type of accommodation

$200 PER WEEK

3-BED TAITA

£82 PER WEEK
- Fully furnished ✗
- Pool ✗
- Parking ✔　　**CODE** RED

$230 PER WEEK

2-BED CENTRAL HUTT

£87 PER WEEK
- Fully furnished ✗
- Pool ✗
- Parking ✔　　**CODE** RED

$230 PER WEEK

2-BED CENTRAL HUTT

£87 PER WEEK
- Fully furnished ✗
- Pool ✗
- Parking ✔　　**CODE** RED

$280 PER WEEK

1-BED EASTBOURNE

£114 PER WEEK
- Fully furnished ✗
- Pool ✗
- Parking ✔　　**CODE** RED

APARTMENTS FOR SALE

Luxurious homes, many fully furnished and with lovely waterfront views

$389,000

2-BED BOTANY TOWN

£147,300
- Fully furnished ✗
- Pool ✔
- Parking ✔　　**CODE** RAY

$425,000

2-BED QUEENSTOWN

£161,000
- Fully furnished ✗
- Pool ✗
- Parking ✔　　**CODE** OPT

$750,000

3-BED WELLINGTON

£305,000
- Fully furnished ✔
- Pool ✗
- Parking ✔　　**CODE** BAY

$1,195,000

3-BED CHRISTCHURCH

£486,000
- Fully furnished ✔
- Pool ✗
- Parking ✔　　**CODE** BAY

HOUSES FOR SALE

Stunning homes, in a range of prices and styles, suitable for all potential buyers

$249,000

2-BED PAKURANGA

£94,300
- Fully furnished ✗
- Pool ✗
- Parking ✔　　**CODE** RAY

$595,000

4-BED AUCKLAND

£225,400
- Fully furnished ✗
- Pool ✗
- Parking ✔　　**CODE** OPT

$700,000

3-BED QUEENSTOWN

£265,000
- Fully furnished ✗
- Pool ✔
- Parking ✔　　**CODE** OPT

$2,100,000

3-BED GREENHITHE

£795,455
- Fully furnished ✗
- Pool ✗
- Parking ✔　　**CODE** RAY

Wherever you want to go...
Merricks Media can take you there

PICTURE: SIMPLY CORSICA: 020 8541 2205

The No.1 publisher in the Travel and Property sector

It's official. Nothing on earth comes close to African hospitality.

When you fly Business Class between the United Kingdom and South Africa, you won't only experience flat bed seats and award winning South African wines on every flight, you'll also experience something no one else can offer: the magic of African hospitality. And that's why South African Airways has been voted Best Airline to Africa* fourteen years in a row.

JNB - London 14 flights per week, CPT - London 7 flights per week.   *Voted by United Kingdom's Travel Weekly Global awards.

South Africa
Guaranteed sunshine and a laid-back lifestyle

© SOUTH AFRICAN TOURIST BOARD

FACT BOX

- **Population** Nearly 43 million
- **Population growth rate** -0.25%
- **Economic growth rate** 1.9%
- **Inflation rate** 5.9%
- **Capital** Pretoria
- **Hotspots** Cape Town, Durban, Johannesburg, Port Elizabeth
- **Average house price** (4-bed) R2,285,000
- **Average rental price** (2-bed) R6,150

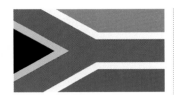

Living in South Africa

A spectacular country with mountains, beaches, desert and game reserves, South Africa also has a low cost of living

FACT FILE

AREA	1.2 million km²
POPULATION	nearly 43 million
CAPITALS	Pretoria
LIFE EXPECTANCY	44 years
LITERACY	86%
GOVERNMENT	Republic
GDP PER CAPITA	US$10,700
UNEMPLOYMENT RATE	30%
CURRENCY	South African Rand (ZAR)
EXCHANGE RATE	ZAR1 = £0.09; £1 = ZAR11.3
LANGUAGES	11 official languages, including Afrikaans, English, Zulu and Xhosa

COST OF LIVING

PETROL (1L)	R4.21
WINE (0.75L)	R25
MEAL (3-COURSE)	R80
BOTTLE OF BEER (33CL)	R8
LOAF OF BREAD	R3

BELOW: South Africa has some stunning beaches such as this one in the Northern Cape

SOUTH AFRICA'S 1.2 MILLION SQUARE kilometres (more than nine times England's land area) stretch across the southern tip of Africa, bordering Namibia, Botswana, Zimbabwe and Mozambique. The country boasts 2,500 kilometres of gorgeous coastline, which gives way to mountains as you move inland, eventually levelling out to a plateau, which forms the interior. One of the most developed countries on the continent, South Africa has a thriving economy and is attracting more and more people each day to its sunny climate and laid-back way of life.

Politics and economy

After gaining independence from the British in 1910, South Africa became a republic in 1961. But the biggest shake up in its political history has been the abolition of apartheid in the first democratic elections in 1994. This was the start of a democratic era in which the new "rainbow nation" has been fully embraced by the international community. Thabo Mbeki succeeded Nelson Mandela as President in 1999 and is currently serving his second term. He represents the ruling African National Congress (ANC) party, which governs in a coalition with the Inkatha Freedom Party (IFP).

South Africa is a middle-income, emerging market, although it still feels the hangover effects of poverty and inequality from the apartheid era.

Half of the population lives below the poverty line, and high rates of crime and HIV/AIDS infection are seen to be a deterrent to investment. However, things are improving every day. South Africa has the tenth largest stock exchange in the world with well developed financial, legal, communications, energy and transportation sectors.

Real wages and productivity have increased by more than 20 per cent since 1994, and although unemployment is fairly high at 30 per cent, this is primarily due to the fact that much of the labour market is unskilled. The government is actively seeking skilled workers, especially in healthcare, and financial investment from abroad.

Climate

Although South Africa's climate is classified as semi-arid, it varies widely across the country from Mediterranean in the south west, through the dry inland Karoo to the lush east coast. Temperatures average in the mid-20°Cs during the summer but can peak at as much as 40°C. In winter, they rarely drop below the low teens, but the high peaks of the Drakensberg Mountains in the east provide excellent skiing.

Education

At least 20 per cent of the government's budget is devoted to education each year, ensuring that it is

RIGHT: Cape Town is a colourful city, set against the backdrop of Table Mountain

© SOUTH AFRICAN TOURIST BOARD

well up to international standards in the more affluent areas. There is a wide variety of public and private, large and small, good and not so good schools, colleges and universities. School lasts over a period of 13 years or grades, although matric (the equivalent of the A-level period) is not compulsory unless students wish to go on to study at university. There are 21 universities in South Africa, many of them internationally renowned, as well as countless colleges and vocational institutes.

Healthcare

South Africa has some of the best healthcare on the continent, especially in the urban coastal areas, although there is a big gap between the best and the worst. The large public sector, although fairly well funded by the government, is over-stretched, and most middle- to high-income earners prefer to use private healthcare. There is no equivalent of the NHS and only the most basic primary healthcare is offered free. Many practitioners require payment up front, and although they accept credit card payments, it is a good idea to take out a medical aid scheme, which will help to cover these costs.

"South Africa is attracting more and more people each day to its sunny climate and laid-back way of life"

You can obtain a list of schemes registered with the representative organisation, the Board of Healthcare Funders (BHF) (Tel: 011 880 8900).

Lifestyle

Because of the vast amount of land in South Africa, houses are relatively big, which makes social gatherings at home easy. Barbecues (known as *braais*) are very popular, and with an average of 8.5 hours of sunshine per day there's no worrying about what the weather will do. South Africa

makes some of the best fine wines in the world in well known wine-producing areas such as Stellenbosch and Paarl. Food-wise, South Africa is fairly international, but *biltong* (dried, salted meat), *bobotie* (a sort of shepherds pie/stew) and *boerwors* (literally "farmer's sausage") are all local favourites.

Expat communities

South Africa is a very international country, and especially in the urban areas you will find yourself among a wide variety of nationalities. Even people who consider themselves to be South African are often of European descent a couple of generations back. There is no specific British community like the thriving South African community in the UK, but South Africans are extremely friendly and always happy to welcome newcomers into their social circle. You are bound to bump into a few fellow expats, because 55 per cent of foreign buyers, not to mention the growing number of tourists, business people and students in South Africa, are British. ●

TRAVEL FILE

AIR KLM (www.klm.com) provides some of the cheapest flights, usually via Amsterdam, as does **AirFrance** (0845 0845 111; www.airfrance.com/uk), although these normally require two stops.
British Airways (0870 850 9850; www.britishairways.com) also operates flights to South Africa. Booking early will ensure the lowest prices. It takes 12 hours to fly from London to Cape Town, and a little less if your destination is further north, such as Johannesburg.

For internal travel, domestic airlines, such as **South African Airways** (00 27 11 978 5313, www.flysaa.com), **South African Airlink** (www.saairlink.co.za) and **South African Express** (www.saexpress.co.za) fly between all major and some smaller cities. **kulula.com** provides low-price flights on popular routes and **Comair** (www.comair.co.za) operates **British Airways** flights between key cities.

ROAD South Africa's world-class infrastructure of roads means it is geared towards driving, and most middle- to high-income earners have a car. There is the usual host of car hire companies. A UK driving licence is sufficient to allow you to drive in South Africa, and although you will need to get used to measuring your speed in kilometres, at least you will still be driving on the left-hand side.

GETTING AROUND Public transport is limited and relatively expensive. There is a variety of train services from the quasi-state railway, **Spoornet**, to the luxury **Blue Train**. Many South Africans will say that train travel is not safe, but although the metro service in Johannesburg is notoriously dangerous, overall, trains need not be feared. Bus travel is also available within cities and for longer journeys with companies such as **Intercape** (www.intercape.co.za) and **Greyhound** (www.greyhound.co.za).

SOUTH AFRICA

CLIMATE

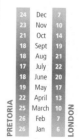

PRETORIA		LONDON
24	Dec	7
23	Nov	10
21	Oct	14
18	Sept	19
18	Aug	21
17	July	22
18	June	20
19	May	17
22	April	13
25	March	11
26	Feb	7
26	Jan	6

Average monthly temperature °C

PRETORIA		LONDON
10	Dec	81
18	Nov	78
31	Oct	70
43	Sept	65
66	Aug	62
89	July	59
84	June	58
79	May	57
48	April	56
8	March	64
8	Feb	72
15	Jan	77

Average monthly rainfall mm

Who moves there?

An increase in global trade and an influx of international companies are creating job opportunities for relocators

"A ten-fold increase in global trade makes South Africa one of the most promising markets in the world"

ABOUT 10,500 IMMIGRANTS SETTLED IN South Africa in 2003 (roughly a 39 per cent increase from 2002), and more than 8,500 by August in 2004. The UK contributed 1,032 of these permanent settlers, and UK tourists also make up 37 per cent of all overseas visitors. There is increasing interest among relocators and businesses as South Africa rebuilds, both economically and politically.

Who moves there?

South Africa is currently undergoing a significant "brain drain", with 25,000 professionals emigrating every year. Consequently, the 668 permanent immigrants from the UK in 2002 have ample job prospects. But immigrants to South Africa tend to be older than those to other long-haul destinations and less inclined to work. Most are aged between 34 to 39 and nearly 80 per cent are economically inactive. Most of those who are economically active work in the professional and technical sector in managerial and executive roles.

Many large corporations, in particular finance houses, software firms, insurance companies and consultancy firms, have set up offices in South Africa. Both Cape Town and Johannesburg have developed a demand for experienced IT professionals, while Johannesburg remains the country's main banking and commercial sector. Most people who immigrate for work purposes are on short-term contracts and most return to their country of origin once the project is completed. There is a growing number of foreign-based companies within South Africa, despite the fact that the economy is vulnerable.

Why move there?

There are many reasons to consider South Africa as a potential investment and relocation opportunity. With the country moving away from a labour-intensive economy, there are increased openings for skilled foreign workers. And a ten-fold increase in global trade makes South Africa one of the most promising markets in the world.

One of the country's major industries is mining. It is the world's largest producer of platinum, gold and chromium. Financial services make up 26 per cent of the economy, manufacturing 24 per cent, wholesale and retail trade 17 per cent and transport, storage and communication 13 per cent. Tourism is the third largest foreign exchange earner after manufacturing and mining, and is poised to overtake mining in the near future. Tourism employs one in every 16 workers, and international tourism makes up 11.7 per cent of the country's GDP.

With the abolishment of apartheid and the lifting of world trade sanctions, there has been an influx of international companies into the country. South Africa has the strongest economy in Africa, with a GDP four times the size of Egypt, its closest rival. Wages are much lower than in the UK but the cost of living is also cheaper and your money goes a lot further. The government is currently working hard to encourage international investment into South Africa. Housing is extremely affordable, with the average four-bedroom property fetching R2,258,000 (£200,000) and there are no restrictions on foreign buyers. ●

BELOW: Wildlife lovers will be pleased to know there are five game reserves in South Africa, the largest being Kruger National Park

Working in South Africa

From tourism to diamond mining, finance to IT, South Africa offers excellent prospects for skilled workers

■ ECONOMY

South Africa now has a growing economy with a modern infrastructure of international standard. There has been a move from labour-intensive to capital-intensive industry, and South Africa is steaming ahead in the financial and communications markets. It contributes a quarter of Africa's GDP and has the tenth largest stock exchange in the world.

■ JOB OPPORTUNITIES

Unemployment is around 30 per cent for the country overall, but only four per cent among the white community. The government is trying to eradicate this inequality, and "affirmative action", i.e. positive discrimination, is common practice. The major problem for the South African economy is a shortage of skilled workers. As a result, the government is keen to attract people, especially IT and medical professionals, engineers, nurses and teachers. Mining is a key industry, including the R7.8 billion diamond industry, which employs 28,000 in mining and the jewellery trade. South Africa has a thriving financial sector, a large telecommunications industry and a healthy tourist industry. Where an industry has sufficient local workers, foreigners are unlikely to be able to find work.

■ FINDING A JOB

An international recruitment agency is a good place to start job hunting. It will be able to put you in touch with employers, and can advise on any legal requirements. Internet applications have increased in popularity over the last few years and an estimated 20 per cent of jobs in South Africa are appointed in this way. A work-seeker's permit is available to those wishing to come to South Africa for a job interview.

© SOUTH AFRICAN TOURIST BOARD

ABOVE: Cape Town is a thriving ship-building centre, accounting for 14% of the country's GDP

SOUTH AFRICA

■ LANGUAGE REQUIREMENTS

There are 11 official languages in South Africa. Although Xhosa and Zulu are the most widespread, English and Afrikaans are the most commonly used in business. You will find that most Afrikaans-speakers also speak English.

■ BUSINESS ETIQUETTE

Business etiquette is similar to the UK. There are still hangovers from the apartheid era, so it is best to avoid race debates. ●

VISAS

Anyone wishing to visit to further their career (eg a photographer on a shoot or a musician performing in a concert) must obtain a visa, as do those who are looking to work or live in South Africa. All visas and permits can be applied for at the South African High Commission, South Africa House, Trafalgar Square, London WC2N 5DP.

● WORK VISAS

Work visas are dependent on your having a firm job offer, and will not usually be issued if there are already enough local people in that field.

● STUDY PERMITS

Study permits are required for any level of study in South Africa. You must have a firm offer of a place to study and be able to prove you have enough funds to get home again. These visas are granted on a yearly basis after which they have to be renewed.

● RESIDENTS' PERMITS

The South African government's requirements for permanent residence are based on its wish to protect the country, the economy and the people. You should be of good character, a desirable inhabitant, unlikely to harm the welfare of the country and offer job skills that are needed.

To retire in South Africa, you need either sufficient financial assets or an income. People with no claim to living in South Africa must bring with them R1.5 million (£130,000) and invest half of it in the economy (e.g. by depositing it at a bank or buying property) for at least three years. If you then wish to work, you will need to consult the Department of Home Affairs, Pretoria.

■ USEFUL WEBSITES

www.southafrica.info Official "gateway" with lots of useful in-depth information
www.gov.za South African government website
www.dha.gov.za Department of Home Affairs, South Africa
www.aipsa.org.za Association of Immigrant Practitioners of South Africa
www.sars.gov.za South African Revenue Services
www.absa.co.za Associated Banks of South Africa
www.jobs.co.za South African job site
www.mortgagesa.com Information about buying property

Finding a home

Whether you're looking to rent or buy, South Africa has a wide range of attractive properties at truly affordable prices

T HE PROPERTY MARKET HAS BEEN GROWING SUBSTANTIALLY in recent years, but Amalgamated Banks of South Africa (ABSA) have said that there is no "bubble" at the moment. It is important to shop around because some people have become wise to the fact that foreigners have money, so they charge above market value. The Western Cape is slightly more expensive than most areas, but it is where most of the buying is going on. There are beautiful homes available, and the abundance of land means even the most modest property is impressive by British standards.

Renting
Renting is fairly straightforward and generally done through an agency. Expect to pay a deposit of two to three months' rent, plus one month's rent in advance.

Buying
Mortgages can be obtained in South Africa through a mortgage advisor. Interest rates are high (about 7 or 7.5 per cent), so it is best to borrow in England. It is also wise to use a currency specialist because the rand is volatile. As prices in South Africa remain fairly stable, this is likely to have a great effect on buying power.

There has been talk of restricting foreign property buyers to maintain affordability for local residents, but this is unlikely to happen. The government is keen to increase foreign investment, and there is no proof that foreign property purchases are having an adverse effect.

Security
Property crime is prevalent. Most windows have burglar bars, and houses in wealthy areas have additional security such as alarms or electric fences, or are situated in gated communities.

Property tax
Property tax applies to anyone who owns a fixed property, and is based on the value of that property. South Africa has strict policies on the amount of capital that can be taken out of the country. ●

© OCEAN ESTATES

ABOVE: Spectacular ocean views can be enjoyed from this home in Cape Town

AVERAGE RENTAL/SALE PRICES

Hotspot	2-bed apartment rentals	2-bed apartment sales	4-bed house sales
Cape Town	R8,500 (£750)	R1.9m (£168K)	R3m (£266K)
Durban	R6,750 (£600)	R1.3m (£112K)	R2.3m (£200K)
Johannesburg	R3,200 (£285)	R395K (£35K)	R1.6m (£140K)

TAXES

There are three main taxes that need to be taken into account for those planning to live and work in South Africa.

● **INCOME TAX**
The income tax system is based on residency for a period of 185 days over three years, and you will be taxed on all income, whether it is internally earned or from abroad. The scale runs from 17% to 45%:

R0 to R15,000: 17% of each R1
R100,000 +: R34,500 plus 45% of the amount over R100,000

● **CAPITAL GAINS TAX**
Capital gains tax affects all investments, including shares, property and luxury items. The rate of tax depends on status, i.e. whether it is an individual, company or trust fund being taxed. Non-residents are exempt from paying capital gains tax, except in the case of property, which in all cases is taxed.

● **DONATIONS TAX**
Donations tax applies to donations or gifts in excess of R30,000 (about £2,600) per year at a rate of 20 per cent, unless the recipient is a registered public benefit organisation or a non-government organisation run on a not-for-profit basis.

Employment hotspots

From the spectacularly situated capital to Durban with its Golden Mile Beach, all three cities attract immigrant workers with their range of industries

1 Cape Town

The parliamentary capital of South Africa, Cape Town is situated in one of the world's most spectacular locations, dominated by the 1,073-metre-tall Table Mountain. It is a cultural melting pot, which stems from the mix of French, British, Dutch, German, Indonesian and African settlers.

Cape Town is an important seaport, with a strong shipbuilding and repair industry. Other important business sectors include agriculture, ICT, oil and gas, manufacturing and media. There are also many opportunities in the service sector. Cape Town has a skilled workforce, and accounts for 14 per cent of the country's GDP.

Cape Town has a buoyant property market, where prices are rising annually by 20 per cent, and houses sell quickly. Due to the variety of property, finding an ideal home is easy.

KEY FACTS
■ **Population:** 3.1million
■ **Airport:** Cape Town International Airport, Tel: 00 27 21 937 1200
■ **Medical:** Groote Schuur Hospital, Tel: 00 27 21 406 6101
■ **Schools:** International School of Cape Town, Tel: 00 27 21 761 6202
■ **Rentals:** Strong rentals market ■ Increasing number of foreign employees needing to rent ■ Recent increase in available rental properties
■ **Pros:** High quality of life and good job prospects ■ Diverse industries ■ Thriving international community
■ **Cons:** Big difference in quality of housing between white and black areas ■ Some areas have extreme poverty ■ High crime levels in the townships ■ Strong winds in winter.

RIGHT: **Cape Town enjoys a colourful and diverse social life**

2 Durban

A sophisticated city with a subtropical climate, Durban attracts many foreigners. A thriving industrial centre with efficient transport links, it is one of the world's fastest growing urban areas.

The largest sector of the local economy is manufacturing followed by tourism. Sugar and petroleum-refining industries both employ many. Durban is the second most important seaport in South Africa and the main export centre for minerals. It is also a centre for shipbuilding and repair. Finance, government, transport and communications also have a role. Unemployment here is high, but efforts are being made to combat the problem.

Durban is a good choice for property investment. Between 2002 and 2004, prices rose by around 40 per cent.

KEY FACTS
■ **Population:** 3.2 million
■ **Airport:** Durban International Airport, Tel: 00 27 31 451 6666
■ **Medical:** Addington Hospital, Tel: 00 27 31 327 2000
■ **Schools:** Durban Girls College, Tel: 00 27 31 268 7200

■ George Campbell Technical High School, Tel: 00 27 31 260 2212
■ **Rentals:** Properties fetch good rents ■ Many houses have a pool ■ Rental prices have risen recently
■ **Pros:** Favourable climate and good quality of living ■ House prices are lower than in Cape Town ■ Property sells quickly ■ Good transport
■ **Cons:** Economic development has damaged the environment ■ High unemployment ■ Can be hot and humid ■ Huge number of tourists.

3 Johannesburg

Home to an excitingly diverse population, this city is the economic, financial and cultural powerhouse of the country. It sprang up during the gold rush of the 1880s, and is now the wealthiest city in South Africa.

Johannesburg is the base for most international companies who do business in South Africa, and 74 per cent of African companies are based here. Despite this, 37 per cent of residents are unemployed. Most jobs are in mining, telecommunications, banking, manufacturing and the media.

Although Johannesburg has typically been viewed as dangerous with the only desirable properties in the walled suburbs, analysts have detected a shift in buying to central areas. Johannesburg has a healthy property market, where house prices are rising but remain affordable.

KEY FACTS
■ **Population:** 4.9 million
■ **Airport:** Johannesburg International Airport, Tel: 00 27 11 921 6911
■ **Medical:** Johannesburg General Hospital, Tel: 00 27 11 488 4911
■ **Schools:** American International School of Johannesburg, Tel: 00 27 11 464 1505
■ **Rentals:** Prices have recently risen by 33% ■ New properties near the centre are expected to fetch high rents
■ **Pros:** English is used in the workplace ■ An important industrial and commercial centre ■ Property is affordable and a good investment
■ **Cons:** High crime rates ■ Large gap between rich and poor ■ Some no-go areas ■ High unemployment.

OTHER HOTSPOTS
■ **Port Elizabeth** Set along the shores of the beautiful Algoa Bay, Port Elizabeth is a major tourist destination and there are many jobs to be had in the service industries. There is a wide range of excellent properties available, at surprisingly low prices. ●

Property price guide

South Africa is a country which represents an excellent investment opportunity, with affordable homes ideal for a single relocator or family alike

APARTMENTS FOR RENT

Attractive apartments all ready for habitation

R5,500 PER MONTH

2-BED PORT ELIZABETH

£495 PER MONTH
- Fully furnished ✔
- Pool ✘
- Parking ✔   CODE PAM

R6,000 PER MONTH

2-BED GREEN POINT

£540 PER MONTH
- Fully furnished ✔
- Pool ✘
- Parking ✔   CODE PAM

R10,000 PER MONTH

4-BED PORT ELIZABETH

£900 PER MONTH
- Fully furnished ✔
- Pool ✔
- Parking ✔   CODE PAM

R13,200 PER MONTH

2-BED BANTRY BAY

£1,190 PER MONTH
- Fully furnished ✔
- Pool ✘
- Parking ✔   CODE PAM

APARTMENTS FOR SALE

Many come fully furnished and with all mod cons, all in an excellent setting

R525,500

STUDIO CAPE TOWN

£47,000
- Fully furnished ✔
- Pool ✘
- Parking ✔   CODE OCE

R1,460,000

3-BED CAPE TOWN

£131,500
- Fully furnished ✔
- Pool ✘
- Parking ✔   CODE OCE

R1,917,000

2-BED CAPE TOWN

£172,500
- Fully furnished ✘
- Pool ✘
- Parking ✔   CODE OCE

R4,000,000

2-BED NOORDHOEK

£360,000
- Fully furnished ✘
- Pool ✘
- Parking ✘   CODE PAM

HOUSES FOR SALE

Luxurious coastal homes, many with a pool and stunning views of the countryside

R995,000

4-BED GRAAFF-REINET

£90,000
- Fully furnished ✘
- Pool ✘
- Parking ✔   CODE PAM

R2,384,000

4-BED CAPE TOWN

£214,500
- Fully furnished ✘
- Pool ✔
- Parking ✔   CODE OCE

R4,204,500

6-BED KNYSNA

£378,500
- Fully furnished ✘
- Pool ✔
- Parking ✔   CODE OCE

R8,514,000

5-BED NATAL

£766,000
- Fully furnished ✘
- Pool ✔
- Parking ✔   CODE OCE

Spain

A mix of the picturesque, the peaceful and the exuberant

© TOBY POCOCK

FACT BOX

- **Population** 40,280,780
- **Population growth rate** 0.16%
- **Economic growth rate** 2.4%
- **Inflation rate** 3%
- **Capital** Madrid
- **Hotspots** Barcelona, Benidorm, Malaga
- **Average house price** (4-bed) €325,750
- **Average rental price** (2-bed) €755

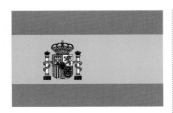

Living in Spain

Widely known as the home of flamenco, bullfights, fabulous beaches and sunshine, Spain has much more to offer

FACT FILE

AREA	504,782km²
POPULATION	40,280,780
CAPITAL	Madrid
LIFE EXPECTANCY	79.37 years
LITERACY	97.9%
GOVERNMENT	Parliamentary Monarchy
GDP PER CAPITA	$22,000
UNEMPLOYMENT RATE	11.3%
CURRENCY	Euro (€)
EXCHANGE RATE	€1 = £0.69; £1 = €1.45
LANGUAGES	Castilian Spanish, Catalan, Galician, Basque

COST OF LIVING

PETROL (1L)	€0.86
WINE (0.75L)	€1.79
MEAL FOR TWO	€34
LOAF OF BREAD (650G)	€1.82
MILK (1L)	€0.69

© SPANISH MAGAZINE

ABOVE: Costa Blanca enjoys many fiestas

CLIMATE

MADRID		LONDON		MADRID		LONDON
9	Dec	7		48	Dec	81
13	Nov	10		47	Nov	78
19	Oct	14		53	Oct	70
25	Sept	19		32	Sept	65
30	Aug	21		15	Aug	62
31	July	22		11	July	59
27	June	20		27	June	58
21	May	17		47	May	57
18	April	13		48	April	56
15	March	10		43	March	64
11	Feb	7		34	Feb	72
9	Jan	6		39	Jan	77

Average monthly temperature °C
Average monthly rainfall mm

A CULTURAL HAVEN WITH BEAUTIFUL traditional and futuristic architecture, a plethora of colourful fiestas and breathtaking landscapes, Spain has a real independent spirit, and its people are individual and proud. Each Spanish region, in particular Catalonia, the Basque Country and Andalucia, has a strong identity.

Spain is located on the Iberian peninsula in the southwest of Europe. The Pyrenees in the north form a natural border with France and Andorra, while the Mediterranean Sea and Atlantic Ocean circle most of the country. Spain has five mountain ranges, with the highest point being Pico de Teide (3,715 metres) on Tenerife. Geographically, Spain's diversity is immense – in the same day it is possible to ski in the Sierra Nevada, lounge on a sunny beach and explore the deserts of Almería.

Politics and economy

Parliamentary democracy was restored to Spain in 1975, following the death of General Franco, who had ruled since 1939. The government is involved in a long-running campaign against Basque separatists ETA, who have targeted Spanish security forces, military personnel and government officials by carrying out bombings. Spain's economy is healthy and has recently been growing significantly. 2003 saw GDP growth of 2.4 per cent, and growth in 2005 is expected to equal this. Unemployment has been falling and crime rates are among the lowest in Europe, with only 2,337 crimes per 100,000 of the population. Spain's major industries are textiles, food and drink production, agriculture, production of metals and chemicals, shipbuilding, cars, tourism and construction.

Climate

The climate of Spain varies tremendously, due to the large size and varied landscapes of the country. Peninsular Spain experiences three main climatic types: continental, maritime and Mediterranean. The bulk of inland Spain, including the central plateau or *meseta*, has a continental climate, characterised by hot, dry summers and cold winters with snow on higher ground but low rainfall. The area to the north, including the Basque Country, Asturias, Cantabria and Galicia, has a maritime climate, which is temperate with warm summers, mild winters and abundant rain, somewhat similar to the UK. The coastal areas of Andalucia and the east have a Mediterranean climate with high temperatures and low rainfall. Murcia is the hottest area of the country, with a climate not unlike that of North Africa.

Education

School attendance in Spain is compulsory for all children aged between 5 and 15. For families with young children settling in Spain, state education is free and is conducted in Spanish. Children attend primary school (*escuela primaria*) until the age of 14, when they will obtain a leaving certificate and go on to either a secondary school (*instituto de enseñanza secundaria*) or vocational training. Young children will pick up a new language quickly, and attending a Spanish school can help them integrate into the local community. To enrol your child, you must apply to the provincial governor's office, which can be done before leaving the UK. If a child is at GCSE or A-level stage, it may be more suitable to choose an international school, of which there are many in popular expat areas. Most offer a joint Spanish and English curriculum and the chance to take examinations that are recognised by overseas and Spanish universities. There are fees for these schools, which can be quite substantial.

Healthcare

If you get an E111 form from a UK post office or the Inland Revenue, you are entitled to receive free medical treatment in Spain for three months. This applies only to emergency treatment and to those in temporary residence; it is not valid if Spain is your permanent country of residence or you have a job there. If you are below retirement age and are living in Spain, you are required to make a monthly contribution to the health service. This is deducted from your salary and entitles you to free treatment. It is also recommended that you get top-up health insurance because payments do not cover all treatments. This will give you a wider choice of hospitals and you can avoid waiting lists. Healthcare in Spain is good, but if you live in a rural area, facilities can be limited. Also, around 40 per cent of hospitals will treat only private patients.

ABOVE: Almería's stunning coastline

RIGHT: The traditional town of Ajuntamiento, Majorca

Food and drink

Gastronomy and wine are central to Spanish culture, and meals are an extremely important social activity, whether at home or in a restaurant. Eating out is relatively cheap, and wherever you are, the meals will be substantial and the food will be varied. Lunch is the most important meal of the day. It is usually taken between 1pm and 4pm and may well include three courses.

Early evening *tapas* in a bar are popular. These are small dishes that include anything from fish to vegetables. Typical examples include *albondigas* – meatballs in a tomato sauce – and *boquerónes* – white fish fillets in oil. Dinner is generally eaten between 9pm and 11pm.

Spanish specialities include *churros*, a fried doughnut usually eaten for breakfast; *gazpacho*, a cold soup made with cucumber and tomato; *paella*, a rice dish made with shellfish, chicken, sausage, peppers and spices, and the very thin, salty *serrano* ham. Spanish wines include the famous Rioja, Valdepeñas, sangria, cava and sherry.

Expat communities

Spain has a large number of expat communities concentrated mainly in the coastal resorts and the larger cities. Areas such as Marbella on the Costa del Sol, Torrevieja and Benidorm on the Costa Blanca and certain areas of Barcelona and Madrid are particular expat hotspots where there are communities in which you will hear very little Spanish, and you will not need to learn the language to survive. Expat publications include *Metropolitan* for Barcelona, *Sur* for Malaga and *The Broadsheet* for Madrid.

Pets

A rabies vaccination must be given to your pet at least 30 days ahead of your date of travel to Spain.

"Spain has a real independent spirit and its people are individual and proud. Each region has a strong identity"

Microchipping is not essential for living in Spain, but it is imperative when travelling overland. An export health certificate can be obtained from the Animal Health Division of your local Department for the Environment, Food and Rural Affairs (DEFRA) office. Your vet will have to examine your pet and issue the necessary documents.

Retirement and pensions

When you become a resident in Spain, your pension remains unchanged. Pensions can be paid into a Spanish bank or into a sterling account outside the UK. Spanish state pensions are paid to residents who have contributed to the Spanish social security system for at least 15 years and are paid independently of any UK state pension. ●

TRAVEL FILE

AIR The main gateways into Spain are Madrid Barajas, Barcelona El Prat de Llobregat and Malaga airports. There are also international airports in Bilbao, Valladolid, Zaragoza, Girona, Reus, Valencia, Alicante, Murcia, Seville, Jerez, Santander, Almería, The Balearic and Canary Islands. Airlines flying to Spain include **British Airways** (www.ba.com; 0870 850 9850), **Easyjet** (www.easyjet.co.uk; 0871 244 2366), **Ryanair** (www.ryanair.com; 0871 246 0000), **Iberia** (www.iberia.com; 0845 601 2854), **Bmibaby** (www.bmibaby.com; 0870 264 2229), **Monarch** (www.flymonarch.com; 0870 040 5040), **ThomsonFly** (www.thomsonfly.com; 0870 190 0737), **Jet2** (www.jet2.com; 08712 261 737), **MyTravelLite** (www.mytravellite.com; 08701 564 564) and **Flybe** (www.flybe.com; 0871 700 0535).

GETTING AROUND The state-owned rail service, **RENFE** (www.renfe.es), is cheap and punctual and spans the whole country. It has been undergoing a complete overhaul since 2000, due for completion in 2007. New high-speed links have been completed to complement the local trains, which stop at every station, giving Spain a fast, world-class rail service.

The long-distance coach company **Eurolines** (www.eurolines.co.uk; 0870 514 3219) goes to more than 60 towns and cities in Spain, and connects them with destinations all over Europe.

They drive on the right in Spain and speed limits and distances are in kilometres. Speed limits are 120km/hr on motorways, 100km/hr on dual carriageways, 90km/hr on country roads, 50km/hr on urban roads and 20km/hr in residential areas.

All EU driving licences are valid. If you don't already hold a licence, you have to be a resident in Spain to get one by taking a Spanish driving test. Licences do not simply last until the age of 70. A car licence is usually valid for ten years if you are under 45, and for five years if you are between 45 and 70. Drivers over 70 must renew their licence every year.

Who moves there?

Spain is still the number one location for British looking to move abroad, and there are currently 900,000 in Spain

SPAIN

"Each region is different from the next, with many areas of outstanding natural beauty"

THERE ARE ABOUT 900,000 BRITISH PEOPLE living in Spain, and between them they have bought about 500,000 properties. Many more British people are renting property. It is estimated that British buyers make up 40 per cent of the international total on the mid-costas alone, and they accounted for 100,000 sales last year. There are also a large number of Scandinavian, French, German and Russian buyers relocating to Spain. It is expected that 800,000 Europeans will move to Spain in the next four years.

Who moves there?

Traditionally, it has been the 50 plus age group who have bought property in Spain, as holiday homes and for retirement, and this group still forms a large sector of the market. Most of these people do not want to pursue full-time careers, but often take part-time jobs, perhaps painting and decorating villas or cleaning and servicing pools, both of which can be quite lucrative with the large number of new foreign buyers. Due to this type of work, the cash economy is very strong, and official unemployment rates are higher than the actual ones.

The age group of those choosing to live in Spain has steadily fallen over recent years. Agents are now witnessing 25-year-olds, disillusioned with their pension prospects in the UK, investing their pension contributions in bricks and mortar, while their friends and relatives rent out the property from them to help meet the overheads. Young professionals are also moving to Spain to take up new careers or continue existing ones. This group is more likely to integrate into the local Spanish society because they need to learn Spanish for their jobs. For those preferring to remain in their own catchment, there are plenty of opportunities to service the tourist industry. The season typically stretches from Easter to the end of October, although regions such as Torrevieja have available work all year round, not only in bars and restaurants, but also in offices, as the infrastructure that supports the burgeoning property developments continues to expand.

Young families are another group who are choosing to make the move over to Spain, to provide a good quality of life for their children and take advantage of the excellent schools, pleasant climate and lower cost of living.

Why move there?

There are a number of reasons why Spain has become the number one destination for those buying property overseas. The weather is a major factor, and the World Health Organisation concludes that the country boasts a healthy climate and a high standard of living. The varied terrain and climate make Spain attractive to different types of people. Each region is different from the next, with many areas of outstanding natural beauty.

Spain has a stable political framework, a good health system, top-class schools and a low crime rate. The more relaxed way of life and "*mañana*" attitude appeal to those wanting to retire and those who are just tired of the rat-race in the UK. The cost of living can be half that of the UK, and rates and utility bills are far lower. Another appeal is that it is not far from the UK and there are many cheap flights, making it easy to return home.

Property prices are lower than in the UK on average, and profits can be made if you choose the right area and type of property. Spanish banks are ready to finance property purchases.

Work is easy to find – jobs in the construction industry in particular are readily available – and tradespeople are always in demand. Expats are increasingly finding lucrative work in the leisure services sector. Renovation of country *fincas* and properties that come with arable land are popular with many buyers who want the challenge of a new project. However, Spain is hot and water is scarce in summer, so crop-growing can be very difficult without a good irrigation system. And unless you are very competent at DIY, the project may become a burden. ●

BELOW: The café culture is flourishing in Spain

© MIKE LEWIS

Working in Spain

With short-term work and plentiful self-employment opportunities in the tourist industry, foreign relocators will never be short of work

■ ECONOMY

Spain's economy has been growing faster than the EU average for ten years and accounts for nine per cent of the EU output. Inflation is under three per cent, and public sector debt under 50 per cent of the GDP. The economy is expected to grow by three per cent in 2005. The driving forces behind the economy are buoyant domestic demand, a booming construction sector and the tourist industry.

■ LABOUR MARKET

The labour market in Spain has undergone a transformation in the last few years because of the progressive incorporation of women, and of immigrants. Unemployment rates have been declining since 1994, and currently stand at 10.3 per cent. Spain is experiencing a decrease in foreign direct investment, as multinationals relocate to countries with cheaper labour costs, although the Spanish property market is still experiencing huge international investment.

ABOVE: Inland Spain boasts a rugged yet green terrain, and some stunning scenery

■ JOB OPPORTUNITIES AND KEY INDUSTRIES

Although Spain is traditionally an agricultural economy, tourism and the service sector now employ more than 60 per cent of the workforce, and this is where most of the work can be found. For those who do not speak Spanish, the areas around Benidorm, Magaluf and Lloret de Mar are great places to find work within English speaking communities. Work in bars, restaurants, clubs and hotels is prevalent along all the costas for those with a grasp of the local language. Seasonal workers are in particular demand, as the number of visitors to Spain rises year on year.

Coastal areas also provide a range of roles related to property development and construction, and there is currently a shortage of all skilled workers, from bricklayers to planners.

Teaching English is a popular option, and there are many language schools looking for staff, although most will require you to have a TEFL qualification. With a growing hi-tech sector, Spain also has a shortage of IT professionals, and there has been a resurgence in the recruitment of engineers. Sales is a growth sector, and there are plenty of opportunities here for those who speak Spanish.

■ FINDING A JOB

Great places to start your search for a job are local and national newspapers. Numerous recruitment adverts can be found in the *International Herald Tribune*, *Wall Street Journal Europe*, *Overseas Job Express* and *El Pais*. Various expat publications also advertise a range of positions. In the larger cities, employment agencies are a useful resource, and the National Employment Institute (www.inem.es) specialises in helping people find work or set up their own business. Those looking for temporary work will find agencies such as Flexiplan (www.flexiplan.com), Adecco (www. adecco.com) and Select (www.select.as) useful. EU citizens have the same rights as Spaniards when applying for jobs, but make sure that any contract you have is for at least six months; this will give you the same rights as a Spanish employee.

■ LANGUAGE REQUIREMENTS

For work outside the tourist sector and English teaching, you will need to be able to speak Spanish. ●

VISAS AND PERMITS

EU citizens do not need a visa to visit Spain, although anyone planning to spend more than 90 days in the country or planning to work there must apply for a residence card – the *visado de residencia*. You can get this from the Spanish Embassy in London (tel: 0207 235 5555) before entering the country. You will need a copy of your qualifications, passport, visa application, a certificate confirming you do not have a criminal record, and a medical certificate. Alternatively, you can apply for a residence permit within 15 days of entering Spain, at a police station in the area in which you intend to live. All residence cards should be renewed every five years.

Those planning to set up a business in Spain will need an EU document called the *tarjeta comunitaria*. In order to get this, you will need to get a business licence – *licencia fiscal* – from the tax authorities.

■ USEFUL WEBSITES
www.spanishpropertyinsight.com
www.strongabogados.com
www.idealspain.com
www.nabss.org
www.spain-info.com

Finding a home

Despite recent urban myths, the Spanish market is experiencing continued demand and ever increasing prices

THE SPANISH PROPERTY MARKET IS BOOMING AND PRICES ARE sprinting up; the average rise was 17.4 per cent in 2004 and prices have increased by 89 per cent since 2001. It is expected that the upward trend will continue, albeit at a slower rate, leaving a healthy and stable market.

Renting

There are two types of rental contract in Spain: long-term lasts a minimum of one year, and short-term lasts for up to a year. It is normal practice to pay one month's rent as a deposit and the first month's rent in advance. If you rent through an agent, you may also have to pay up to one month's rent in fees.

The Spanish rental market in coastal and popular tourist resorts centres around short-term lets, but it is possible to find long-term lets. There are several useful websites, such as www.globaliza.com, www.infoinmueble.com and www.vivendum.fotocasa.es. Local newspapers are also a helpful resource.

Buying

The Internet is the best place to start your property search; many companies selling property in Spain have a website. Before you purchase a property, it is essential to check the title deed to see that the property actually belongs to the vendor and is free of debt. You must also obtain a *número de identificación extranjeros* (NIE) or identification number, which is used to control the fiscal obligations of all foreign owners.

It is common to pay a deposit to the vendor and you must sign a public deed of sale in the presence of a notary. All banks in Spain offer mortgages. Residents can borrow up to 90 per cent of the purchase price, while non-residents can usually borrow 50 to 60 per cent. The average mortgage length is 10 to 15 years.

Property tax

Most Spanish property sales involve payment of various fees and taxes, which normally amount to around ten per cent of the purchase price. For resale properties, the largest tax is the transfer tax, or ITP, at seven per cent. For new properties, seven per cent VAT, or IVA, is payable, along with 0.5 per cent stamp duty. If you buy property from a non-resident, you must keep five per cent of the price as a withholding tax, to be paid to the tax authority on account of any liability by the vendor to capital gains tax. Capital gains tax is payable at 35 per cent for non-residents and 15 per cent for residents.

A local tax based on the increase in the value of a property since it was last sold is a one-off charge paid within a month of purchase. Local rates, or IBI, are charged at 0.5 to one per cent of the official value. Finally, you can expect to pay one per cent of the sale price as a fee to your lawyer, and one per cent to the notary. ●

© MIKE LEWIS

ABOVE: Spanish properties are colourful and full of character

AVERAGE RENTAL/SALE PRICES

Hotspot	2-bed apartment rentals	2-bed apartment sales	4-bed house sales
Barcelona	€1,060 (£731)	€207K (£143K)	€474K (£327K)
Benidorm	€740 (£510)	€165K (£114K)	€255K (£176K)
Malaga	€670 (£462)	€227K (£157K)	€295K (£203K)

INCOME TAX

Anyone who lives in Spain for more than 183 days a year will have to pay income tax there. This is called *la renta*, and compares favourably with other European countries.

● The UK and Spain have a double taxation agreement, so you won't be taxed by both UK and Spanish tax authorities on either income or pension. This may, however, occur during your first period of residency, because the UK tax year runs from April to April, and the Spanish one from January to January. If this happens, you can get a refund of UK tax via the Inland Revenue.

● Those who are self employed can fill in their own tax return, and the forms are available from the local *hacienda* (Spanish tax office). UK citizens working in Spain for fewer than 183 days in a year will be liable for UK income tax only, and must declare all earnings to the Inland Revenue. You will not get a bill for income tax in Spain, but must present the declaration yourself or use a tax representative.

● The standard income tax rates for 2004 were as follows. You pay different rates on different portions of your income. For example, if you earn €20,000, you pay tax at 18 per cent on the first €3,700, at 24 per cent on the next €9,200 and at 28 per cent on the final €7,100.

Less than €3,700 = 18%
€3,700 to €12,900 = 24%
€12,900 to €25,100 = 28%
€25,100 to €40,500 = 37%
€40,500 to €67,400 = 45%
More than €67,400 = 48%

SPAIN

Employment hotspots

From Barcelona in the north to the Costa del Sol, Spain remains a hugely popular destination for second-home buyers

1 Barcelona

Famous for being cosmopolitan and avant-garde, Barcelona is the capital of Catalonia and one of Spain's largest and liveliest cities. Home to the work of Gaudi and a fascinating medieval centre, it is bursting with fine vistas and parks and often tops quality-of-life surveys.

With top-class services and an excellent infrastructure, the city is a successful commercial centre and contains a growing number of international companies. Key industries are manufacturing, textiles, electronics, publishing, advertising and tourism. In the jobs market, speakers of Spanish or Catalan have a big advantage. Others may be limited to work in the tourist sector and TEFL.

Barcelona is the most expensive city in Spain. In 2004, property prices increased by an average 18.3 per cent, and they will probably continue to rise. The areas north and west of the city are the most expensive; cheaper properties exist in the old quarter. Sixty-eight per cent of properties are owner-occupied, but with the recent price rises, renting is expected to increase because many will not be able to afford to buy.

KEY FACTS
■ **Population:** 1.5 million
■ **Airport:** Barcelona Airport, Tel: 00 34 93 298 3838
■ **Medical:** Hospital de la Creu Roja, Tel: 00 34 93 507 2700
■ **Schools:** The British School of Barcelona, Tel: 00 34 93 665 1584
■ **Rentals:** High demand ■ Long-term lets have increased; short-term lets have decreased
■ **Pros:** Eleven universities and a number of international schools in the area ■ Good access to beaches ■ A large and successful port

ABOVE: The town of Mascerat in Altea offers a fabulous marina

■ **Cons:** Chronic traffic congestion ■ Prices in popular areas are high ■ Cost of living is one of the highest in Spain ■ Petty crime levels are high.

2 Benidorm

The biggest and busiest tourist resort in the country, Benidorm has gorgeous sandy beaches, a variety of activities and a lively atmosphere, making it an all-year-round destination. It has successfully improved its image in recent years.

Unemployment is low and there are job opportunities for expats in tourism and services, particularly in catering and property sales, but many jobs are limited to the summer. A knowledge of Spanish and/or German will improve your job prospects. The town is also a commercial centre, with a large number of foreign companies and a modern infrastructure.

Benidorm has some of the cheapest housing on the Costa Blanca. It is mostly apartments in high-rise tower blocks, but some villas and more spacious apartments are available. Many properties are snapped up by those who spend a few weeks a year here, and rent out their homes for the rest of the year.

KEY FACTS
■ **Population:** 56,300
■ **Airport:** Alicante Airport, Tel: 00 34 96 691 9032
■ **Medical:** Hospital General de Alicante, Tel: 00 34 96 593 8300
■ **Schools:** Sierra Bernia School, Tel: 00 34 96 687 5149
■ **Rentals:** High demand in the summer, and properties are also occupied in the winter ■ Long-term lets can be difficult to obtain
■ **Pros:** Pleasant climate ■ Clean beaches and sea ■ Lively town
■ **Cons:** Many ugly high-rise blocks ■ Very overcrowded in summer.

3 Malaga

One of the most cosmopolitan cities in Spain, Malaga is currently home to around 6,000 British expats but it is largely untouched by mass tourism. A beautiful city with a Moorish style, Malaga is a mix of everything Andalucian. The inhabitants are proud of their city and of the most famous *Malagueños*, Pablo Picasso and Antonio Banderas.

The city is a busy port and important commercial centre. Work is available in the tourist and service sector, technology and construction. An excellent infrastructure and the recent construction of a technology park have attracted electronics, mobile phone and other hi-tech businesses. A high-speed train link to Barcelona will be completed in 2007.

Malaga is an ideal place to live. Property prices are lower than in other resorts along the coast and a variety of properties are available. Most of these are apartments; houses are limited to the more exclusive residential and suburban areas.

KEY FACTS
■ **Population:** 540,000
■ **Airport:** Malaga Pablo Picasso, Tel: 00 34 95 204 8484
■ **Medical:** Hospital Carlos Haya, Tel: 00 34 95 390 400
■ **Schools:** Sunny View School, Tel: 00 34 95 238 3164
■ **Rentals:** Year-round demand ■ It can be difficult to find rental property in high season
■ **Pros:** Reliable public transport ■ Some of the best facilities on the Costa del Sol ■ Many cheap flights from the UK
■ **Cons:** High crime rates, particularly theft ■ Traffic congestion.

OTHER HOTSPOTS
■ **Madrid:** Spain's capital city has always attracted foreign students, and offers excellent job prospects for those who speak the language. ●

SPAIN

Property price guide

Most properties come with a pool and many are within a stone's throw from the coast – the ultimate for those seeking a relaxed beach lifestyle

APARTMENTS FOR RENT

The Spanish market is full of homes for long and short rentals

€300 PER WEEK

2-BED MURCIA

£207 PER WEEK
- Fully furnished ✔
- Pool ✘
- Parking ✘   **CODE** GPG

€450 PER WEEK

2-BED DENÍA

£310 PER WEEK
- Fully furnished ✔
- Pool ✔
- Parking ✘   **CODE** GPG

€1,200 PER MONTH

2-BED NUEVA ANDALUCÍA

£828 PER MONTH
- Fully furnished ✔
- Pool ✔
- Parking ✔   **CODE** GPG

€1,400 PER MONTH

2-BED PUERTO BANUS

£966 PER MONTH
- Fully furnished ✔
- Pool ✘
- Parking ✘   **CODE** GPG

APARTMENTS FOR SALE

Everything from a bolthole on the coast to an apartment in the city centre

€137,500

2-BED VILAMARTIN

£94,800
- Fully furnished ✔
- Pool ✔
- Parking ✘   **CODE** BOL

€279,000

2-BED MIJAS COSTA

£192,400
- Fully furnished ✘
- Pool ✔
- Parking ✔   **CODE** PPA

€355,000

3-BED COTO REAL

£244,800
- Fully furnished ✘
- Pool ✔
- Parking ✔   **CODE** BOL

€594,000

2-BED BARCELONA

£409,600
- Fully furnished ✘
- Pool ✘
- Parking ✔   **CODE** YHS

HOUSES FOR SALE

There is a wide variety of homes to be found in Spain to suit all budgets

€140,000

RENOVATION ALMERÍA

£96,500
- Fully furnished ✘
- Pool ✘
- Parking ✔   **CODE** CAS

€250,000

3-BED HUERCAL OVERA

£172,400
- Fully furnished ✘
- Pool ✔
- Parking ✔   **CODE** CAS

€1,200,000

3-BED BENALMÁDENA COSTA

£827,600
- Fully furnished ✘
- Pool ✔
- Parking ✔   **CODE** PPA

€1,450,000

5-BED SANT CUGAT

£1,000,000
- Fully furnished ✔
- Pool ✔
- Parking ✔   **CODE** YHS

United States of America

The original land of opportunity

© NEW YORK TOURIST BOARD

FACT BOX

- ■ **Population** 293,027,571
- ■ **Population growth rate** 0.92%
- ■ **Economic growth rate** 3.1%
- ■ **Inflation rate** 2.3%
- ■ **Capital** Washington DC
- ■ **Hotspots** Florida, California, Arizona, Boston, New York, Washington
- ■ **Average house price** (4-bed) $801,600
- ■ **Average rental price** (2-bed) $1,175

Living in the USA

This vast country offers a kaleidoscopic range of lifestyles, from laid-back California to dynamic New York

FACT FILE

AREA	9,800,000km²
POPULATION	293,027,571
CAPITAL	Washington DC
LIFE EXPECTANCY	77.6 years
LITERACY	97%
GOVERNMENT	Democracy
GDP PER CAPITA	US$37,800
UNEMPLOYMENT RATE	5.4%
CURRENCY	US dollar (US$)
EXCHANGE RATE	US$ = £0.53
	£1=$1.90
LANGUAGES	English, Spanish

USA

THE USA WAS BUILT ON IMMIGRATION and still attracts staggering numbers of immigrants. It is a huge country, and it encompasses an incredible range of landscapes and cultures, from the mountains of Colorado to the deserts of California and the plains of Oklahoma. The culture of the east coast has been strongly influenced by immigration from Europe, while the west coast looks to Asia and Latin America. In between is the Midwest, an area of huge open spaces with just a handful of major cities.

© CALIFORNIAN TOURIST BOARD

ABOVE: In California, the USA's third largest state, you are only ever half a day's drive from the coast

COST OF LIVING

PETROL (1L)	$0.05
WINE (75CL)	$7.00
MEAL (3-COURSE)	$30.00
BOTTLE OF BEER (33 CL)	$1.30
LOAF OF BREAD	$2.00
PINT OF MILK	$1.00

Politics and economy

Politically, the USA is a capitalist democracy based on liberal principles. The President is directly elected by US citizens aged 18 and over. Members of the Congressional House of Representatives and the US Senate are elected by individual states. The Federal Government is supported by 50 state governments, which handle much of the day-to-day running of the nation. Workers pay federal and state taxes.

Climate

For many people, the USA has the perfect climate, with hot summers and cold winters. California and Florida are generally considered to have the best year-round weather, but you can escape from the winter snow in most of the southern states. It is worth remembering, however, that the USA is a land of extremes. The west coast has earthquakes, the southeast has hurricanes, the Midwest has tornadoes and the east coast has snowstorms, all of which may affect where you choose to live.

Education

All children of US citizens and other legal residents are entitled to free education provided by the state. There are also numerous private schools throughout the country, including international schools that can offer pupils the standard UK curriculum. The free state education system in the USA covers elementary school (for children between six and ten years), middle school or junior high school (for 11 to 13-year-olds) and high school (for 14 to 17- or 18-year-olds).

University in the USA begins with a Freshman year, followed by three or more years of undergraduate study. Course fees and living expenses are normally paid for by the student's parents, but private and government student loans are also available. Universities are located in all large US cities, and a degree from Harvard, Yale or the Massachusetts Institute of Technology (MIT) can dramatically improve future career prospects. This is reflected in the fees, and the competition for places at these most exclusive universities.

Healthcare

The healthcare system in the USA is based on private medical insurance. US citizens on a low income are eligible for free healthcare under the Medicare and Medicaid systems, but legal residents from overseas must take out private health cover (this is a condition of most work permits). There are hundreds of US insurance companies, and many British insurers have specialist policies for people who are working abroad.

"It is a huge country, and it encompasses an incredible range of landscapes and cultures"

Crime rates

Internationally, the USA has a reputation for high levels of violent crime, but the threat is often blown out of proportion. Crime rates are in fact dropping in many cities, and most people in the country manage to live their whole lives without ever encountering serious crime. Nevertheless,

CLIMATE

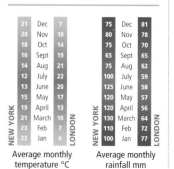

NEW YORK				NEW YORK			
21	Dec	7	LONDON	75	Dec	81	LONDON
20	Nov	10		80	Nov	78	
18	Oct	14		75	Oct	70	
16	Sept	19		65	Sept	65	
14	Aug	21		75	Aug	62	
12	July	22		100	July	59	
13	June	20		125	June	58	
15	May	17		120	May	57	
19	April	13		120	April	56	
21	March	10		130	March	64	
23	Feb	7		110	Feb	72	
23	Jan	6		100	Jan	77	

Average monthly temperature °C

Average monthly rainfall mm

there are areas in most cities that are considered "out of bounds" because of street crime, so it pays to maintain a level of awareness.

Food and drink

When it comes to Americans and food, a supersize mentality prevails. Unless you want to join the obesity statistics, try to maintain a moderate and balanced diet and avoid getting accustomed to over-sized portions. The USA is known for its fast food, but the nation also has a strong history of gourmet cooking. There is a range of distinct regional cuisines to choose from, and there is really no reason to eat unhealthily. East coast cuisine relies heavily on meat and fish, while vegetarians and health-food fans are better catered for on the west coast.

Americans tend to drink coffee rather than tea, so many expats have tea sent out from home. Coffee is available in an amazing array of flavours and configurations, from espresso and cappuccino to toffee-flavoured macchiato. The USA has a slightly puritan attitude to alcohol. The legal drinking age of 21 is strictly enforced, and photo ID is required to buy alcohol in shops and bars.

Expat communities

There are expat communities across the USA. Most major cities have areas where expats from different communities can get together and enjoy foods and culture from home. The largest British expat scenes are on the east coast, in Florida and parts of California. The west coast has large Asian and Latin American communities.

Retirement

For a comfortable retirement in the USA, you will need to make adequate provisions during your working life. The official retirement age is 65, and US citizens and legal residents are eligible for social security payments. British expats may be eligible for a government pension from the UK, but a private pension scheme is a useful back-up.

Pets

If your pets are healthy, you should be able to take them to the USA. Dogs, cats, rabbits, fish and birds are not subject to quarantine, but a rabies vaccination certificate is required to import a dog from an affected area. A vet will carry out a health check on arrival in the USA. ●

TRAVEL FILE

AIR Most visitors to the USA fly into one of the main international air hubs, from where domestic flights fan out to hundreds of smaller cities and towns across the USA. The main airlines flying between Britain and America are:

American Airlines (UK 0845 778 9789; USA 00 1 800 433 7300; www.aa.com)
Continental Airlines (UK 0845 607 6760; USA 00 1 800 231 0856; www. continental.com)
United Airlines (UK 0845 844 4777; USA 00 1 800 538 2929; www.united.com)
Delta (UK 0800 414 767; USA 00 1 800 241 4141; www.delta.com)
Northwest/KLM (UK 0870 507 4074; USA 00 1 800 447 4747; www.nwa.com)
British Airways (UK 0870 850 9850; USA 00 1 800 247 9297; www. britishairways.com)
Virgin Atlantic (UK 0870 574 7747; USA 00 1 800 862 8621; www.virgin-atlantic.com).

RAIL Trains are slow and expensive compared with air travel. **Amtrak** (USA 00 1 800 872 7245; www. amtrak.com) runs trains all over America.

ROAD Intercity bus fares are reasonable, but it can take a long time to get anywhere. **Greyhound** (USA 00 1 800 231 2222; www.greyhound.com) is the most famous US bus company.

The leading car hire firms are **Avis** (USA 00 1 800 230 4898; www.avis.com), **National** (USA 00 1 800 561 893 7470; www.nationalcar.com) and **Hertz** (USA 00 1 800 654 3001; www.hertz.com). A British driving licence is fine for short stays in the USA, but if you are staying for more than a few months you should apply for a driving licence from the state department of motor vehicles.

The US road network is excellent, but don't forget Americans drive on the right.

© VISIT FLORIDA

ABOVE: Florida offers a relaxed and healthy lifestyle

LEFT: Florida is perfect for watersports lovers

USA

I did it!

Name: Deborah Pira

Job: Deborah is a qualified realtor. Last year she set up her own business, the British Real Estate Network, which consists of British agents operating throughout Florida

Where: Deerfield Beach, Broward County

Moving to the USA

Six years after moving to the USA, Deborah Pira has put her experiences of buying real estate to good use

DEBORAH PIRA'S MOVE TO FLORIDA HAS proved more fruitful than she could have ever imagined. Successful in her chosen career as a realtor, Deborah is firm in the belief that the secret of success lies in loving what you do.

Q: What is it about living in Florida that you love?
A: One of the reasons I love living and working in Florida is the international make–up of the community. The USA is home to many foreigners who have come to start a new life, and a spirit of enthusiasm and the will to succeed are prevalent throughout the country. I believe that it is possible to do very well here if you are willing to work hard and if you believe in yourself all the way.

Q: How did you gain the qualifications for your chosen job?
A: I trained as a realtor before I became a permanent resident, but there are strict visa regulations regarding employment. It is important to remember that you are not entitled to work unless you have the correct visa. You really must ensure that you have a good immigration company working for you. Once I had secured my visa and finished

(and passed!) my exams, I began working as a sales agent in Broward County. At the moment, my company organises my visa and insurance requirements. It is very important to get this handled by a knowledgeable and competent third party, particularly because the regulations regarding visas are constantly changing.

Q: What is your property like?
A: When I first moved to Florida, and before I became a permanent resident, I purchased a two-bedroom beachside townhouse for $160,000 (£85,000). A year later I sold it for $200,000 (£106,000) and, three years on, it has doubled in value to $400,000 (£212,000). Property here is an excellent investment, and mortgages are easy to get, especially if you are a foreign investor. My second home is located on the waterfront. It cost me $365,000 (£193,000), but has more than doubled in value to $850,000 (£451,000).

Q: How did you go about purchasing your home?
A: I was not a full US resident when I purchased my home, so issues such as credit checks did not hamper the purchasing process. Anyone can purchase a property here – it makes no difference whether you are an American citizen

LEFT: Deborah loves every minute of her life in Florida, especially the daily sunshine!

ABOVE: Deerfield Beach has an island park which includes a 3.5-hectare mangrove swamp

RIGHT: Deborah runs her business from her office in Deerfield Beach

or not. The difference, however, becomes apparent when you attempt to sell your property, and this is why it is essential that you deal with a British realtor who knows the local real estate laws and will enable you to go through the conveyancing process fully clued up.

Q: How did you get to grips with the Floridian lifestyle?
A: It is important you assimilate into American society as quickly as possible. Being fully integrated into the American system will make your future dealings and conveyancing process much easier. One major reason why I set up my business was so that I could educate other British people on the important differences between the British and American way of life.

Q: What are the most important things to do when you first move to the USA?
A: One of the first things you need to establish when you arrive in the USA is a line of credit. A bank account is essential, and you need to procure a driving licence in order to establish a credit line. Your credit history can be established in a number of ways, although I recommend that it is done through a "secured credit card", which your bank can advise you on. You should also establish two other lines of credit, maybe through leasing a car or getting a foreign investor's mortgage or a department store card. This may not be straightforward, however, because some organisations will grant you these and others won't. The best advice I can give is to approach people who have moved to the USA and ask them how they did it.

Q: Can you tell us about your company?
A: I now work as an independent contractor for a real estate company called Balistreri, which I feel is the best way to conduct my business. Someone else takes care of all the headaches, while I just get on with doing what I do best, which is helping British buyers. My husband Frank joined the company two years ago; consequently we now have a somewhat family-orientated company.

"The USA is home to many foreigners who have come to start a new life, and a spirit of enthusiasm and the will to succeed are prevalent throughout the country"

Q: How did you go about claiming residency?
A: When I arrived in the country six years ago, I started out on a six-month visa. It was relatively easy to obtain at the time, but is harder now. Since getting married, my visa has become permanent, and my intention is to apply for citizenship next year.

Q: What do you love about life in Florida?
A: I enjoy every minute of my life in Florida. The sun shines almost every day, the birds are exotic and colourful and most people love the British. I am constantly asked to "just talk" so that they can listen to my accent. I have no regrets about moving to Florida, although I do wish I'd had more advice from people who had done it before me. On the positive side, my experience has inspired me to start my business with a network of British realtors throughout the state, hopefully giving British buyers the benefit and security of my own and others' experiences. People come to me and I refer them to someone who works in the area in which they want to buy. I guess I've come full circle, and now I'm helping others to find their own American dream. ●

Top tips

- It is essential to find an honest agent with an intimate knowledge of the area in which you wish to buy.

- The old adage "location, location, location" is very relevant when investing.

- You must ensure you develop a good line of credit.

- Make sure that any property you purchase will be a good investment and appreciate well.

- Try to get as much as possible of the preliminary work done before you relocate permanently. Preliminary work includes tasks such as sorting out a driving licence and opening a bank account.

USA

Who moves there?

Traditionally a land of immigrants, the USA attracts large numbers of foreign workers from all over the world

"The appeal of working in the USA is obvious. Wages and quality of life are high, and most people speak English"

THE USA IS KNOWN THE WORLD OVER AS a land of opportunity, but going there to work is harder than you might expect. There are plenty of opportunities for both skilled and unskilled workers, but finding a job upon arrival in the USA is almost impossible. Unless you have a relative living there or qualify for the diversity visa lottery, you will need a confirmed job before you can apply for an immigrant visa and work permit.

Out of 700,000 legal immigrants entering the USA every year, about 240,000 are on working visas sponsored by US companies. The vast majority of immigrants to the USA come from Mexico and Southeast Asia, but British migrants account for about three per cent. In 2003, the USA received 3,000 British immigrant workers and 8,800 temporary workers and trainees.

Who moves there?

Approximately two-thirds of British migrants to the USA are aged between 25 and 44, reflecting the fact that most immigrant visas are set aside for skilled workers. Immigrant numbers have fallen slightly as a result of the tightening of rules after 11 September 2001, but the profile of migrants has remained roughly the same.

The typical age of relocators varies with the type of work. Temporary workers tend to be single and in their 20s and 30s, while most permanent migrants are aged over 35 and are more likely to have families. Many British people relocate to the USA to retire, and the expat population there has almost as many 65-year-olds as 25-year-olds.

The age of people migrating to individual cities is strongly affected by the labour market. For example, the number of 25- to 35-year-olds moving to San Francisco dropped significantly after the "dot.com" bubble burst in 2001.

A large proportion of UK immigrants currently work in management, business and finance, but advertising, computer-aided design and media are attracting increasing numbers of recent graduates.

Why move there?

Not everyone can manage the meteoric rise from immigrant to governor like Arnold Schwarzenegger, but with hard work, dedication and a little luck, you can achieve almost anything, regardless of where you originally come from.

The appeal of working in the USA is obvious. Wages and quality of life are high, and most people speak English. The climate is warm and the government offers well-established programmes for migrant workers. And, of course, US culture is exported everywhere, so people have a good idea of what they are letting themselves in for.

Despite the recent economic slowdown, unemployment levels remain stable at about eight million people, or 5.4 per cent of the population. Most temporary workers are employed in agriculture and tourism, while permanent workers are in skilled jobs such as nursing, finance, engineering or IT. There are also opportunities for unskilled workers in construction, transport and sales in areas that have worker shortages. ●

LEFT: New York boasts a plethora of entertainment options, especially around Times Square

Visas and taxes

Securing a visa and paying your taxes in the USA are complicated procedures, and it is essential to go about it the right way

■ VISAS AND PERMITS

Foreign workers need a visa, which also serves as a work permit, and this must be obtained from outside the country. You cannot visit the USA on a tourist visa and then change your status to a working visa. The main visas used by British workers in the USA are:

E class visas – for investors in US businesses
These visas are for people who invest $100,000 (£53,000) or more in a US business. The visa is initially valid for two years, but can be extended for as long as the business is operational.

J1 visas – for students or trainees
University students can work for up to four months in casual jobs, and university graduates and professionals can work in trainee positions at US companies for up to 18 months.

H1 visas – for skilled professionals
These visas are for people taking up jobs that require degree-level education or special skills. They apply to a specific job, and a US employer must sponsor you.

H2A & H2B visas – for seasonal and agricultural workers
The H2B allows people to work in industries such as tourism and construction for up to ten months. H2A visas are for seasonal agricultural workers.

K class visas – for fiancés of US citizens
These visas allow fiancés of US citizens to visit the USA to get married. Marriage partners of US citizens are granted temporary resident status, followed by full resident status after two years.

L class visas – for intra-company transfers
These visas are used to transfer employees of multinational companies to branches within the USA.

O & P class visas – for artists, academics and athletes
These visas are reserved for people with exceptional ability in sport, science, business or the arts.

■ LAWFUL PERMANENT RESIDENCE

You can apply to become a legal permanent resident of the USA (the first step towards becoming a citizen) if you have relatives who are already legal residents, or if a US company sponsors you for a permanent job. The sponsor must file the application on your behalf. US companies sponsoring foreign permanent workers must be able to prove that no US citizen was available for the job.

■ DIVERSITY LOTTERY

Every year, the US government issues 50,000 "green cards". These grant full legal residency to citizens of countries with low levels of immigration to the US, including Ireland and Northern Ireland. The diversity lottery takes place in October. ●

© BOSTON TOURIST BOARD

ABOVE: Boston, in New England, is a sophisticated and modern city

INCOME TAX

Tax rules vary depending on whether you are legally resident or non-resident in the USA. Residents pay US tax on all their income, while non-residents pay different rates of tax on US and foreign income.

Foreign workers in the USA are liable for federal and state income tax if they spend more than three months in the country in any tax year. Tax is normally withheld from your wages at source, and personal tax returns are due on 15 April every year. If you plan to spend more than nine months outside the UK, you should inform the Inland Revenue. A single taxpayer in 2005 is taxed according to the following tax bands:

Tax rate	Portion of income	Tax rate	Portion of income
10%	Up to $7,300	28%	$71,951–$150,150
15%	$7,301–$29,700	33%	$150,151–$326,450
25%	$29,701–$71,950	35%	$326,451 or more

All states, apart from Alaska, Florida, Nevada, South Dakota, Texas, Washington and Wyoming, charge an additional state income tax. The rate and threshold for state income tax varies depending on your marital status and how many children you have.

■ USEFUL WEBSITES

http://uscis.gov The website of the US Citizen and Immigration Services, with information about all visa classes and the diversity lottery scheme
www.bunac.org Sponsoring organisation for students and trainees wishing to find casual or temporary work in the USA
www.inlandrevenue.gov.uk Features a useful guide on non-residency

Employment hotspots

Find out about employment prospects and the housing market in the USA's top six states for relocators

FLORIDA

■ PROPERTY

Florida is the destination of choice for one in ten immigrants to the USA for the same reasons that it is popular with tourists – year-round sunshine, sandy beaches and glamorous cities.

Where you live will depend on what you intend to do when you arrive. People working in tourism tend to congregate around Miami, Tampa and Orlando, while older migrants head for the northeast and northwest coast of the state. Miami offers the best opportunities for corporate employment, but homes come at big-city prices.

Many people start off by renting, and a wide range of holiday accommodation is available around the destinations of Orlando, Miami and Tampa. Alternatively, there are hundreds of local estate agents. Expect to pay $600 (£320) to $1,500 (£795) per month for a two-bedroom apartment, depending on the location and facilities.

About 18,000 British immigrants buy holiday or permanent homes in Florida every year. Interest rates are generally low, with 30-year fixed-rate mortgages hovering at about 6.26 per cent.

The maximum loan for non-nationals in Florida is 80 per cent of the value of the property, and buyers must also pay property tax to the county authorities. Prices for a two-bedroom apartment start at $100,000 (£53,000) and four-bedroom houses go for about $400,000 (£212,000). Prices go through the roof for beach properties, and you also have to insure against hurricane damage.

Florida's cities have some of the worst crime rates in the USA. Miami is consistently listed in the top five most dangerous cities in the country, and West Palm Beach, Orlando and Tampa also score badly for violent crime. Many residents choose to live in gated communities to cut down the risk of burglaries.

■ EMPLOYMENT

The main employment in Florida is in tourism, construction, retail, services, business, healthcare and agriculture. Large numbers of people are also employed in transport, particularly aviation and shipping, and technology. Unemployment is typically one per cent below the national average.

One reason for the popularity of Florida with relocators is the lack of state income tax, although workers must still pay federal income tax.

The tourist industry is vast in Florida, and it employs huge numbers of temporary workers. A significant number of foreign workers are employed by theme parks and other major tourist attractions on H2B visas. Extensions to H2B visas are easy to arrange, providing that your employer can prove that you are fulfilling a shortfall in the local labour market. Florida orange growers and other agricultural sectors employ large numbers of migrant workers on similar H2A visas.

One of the most popular ways for people to relocate to Florida is the E2 visa. This could be as simple as buying a share of a fast-food franchise or as complicated as taking over a local corporation. You must prove that the business will provide employment for US citizens.

English is the main language requirement for jobs in Florida, but Japanese speakers can do well in tourism, and Spanish is the second national language. There are temporary and permanent recruitment agencies in all the major cities, and many have websites that allow you to start your job hunt from the UK. Some people visit on holiday to find a job and then return to the UK to apply for a visa. ●

© VISIT FLORIDA

LEFT: **The old and new capital buildings in Tallahassee, Florida**

CALIFORNIA

■ PROPERTY

The sloping streets of San Francisco and the palm-lined boulevards of Los Angeles have been etched into the popular consciousness by movies, TV shows and hit records. But not everyone can afford to move to Beverly Hills, so it is vital to do some thorough research before relocating to California to ensure that the reality will live up to the expectations.

Construction of new family homes in California shot up by 15 per cent in 2004. Housing is expensive compared with average wages in the state. A typical family home cost $600,000 (£318,000) in 2004.

San Francisco and Los Angeles are among the most expensive cities in the USA. The average house price is $1,000,000 (£530,000) in Beverly Hills and $970,000 (£514,000) in San Francisco. Prices are significantly lower, however, in smaller towns and many people choose to live outside metropolitan areas and commute into the cities. California is facing a severe shortage of low-cost housing, and only about 30 per cent of residents earn enough to afford a medium-price home, compared to 60 per cent in the nation as a whole.

Many people prefer to rent, but rental prices are also steep at about $1,000 (£530) per month for a two-bedroom apartment. Los Angeles and San Francisco are by far the most expensive places to rent property.

If you are looking to buy, the average interest rate for a 30-year fixed-rate mortgage is currently 5.35 per cent, and local mortgage lenders will consider foreigners who are legal residents. Property tax is based on one per cent of the sale value of the property and is collected annually by county authorities. Crime rates are falling in both Los Angeles and San Francisco.

There are no restrictions on foreign legal residents and people on non-resident work permits buying property in California, but mortgage lenders may ask for a larger deposit than for nationals. Foreigners selling property in California are liable for a ten per cent withholding tax, but mortgage interest payments can be deducted from income tax. Earthquake reports are mandatory for property sales in high-risk areas.

Prices for two-bedroom apartments start at $175,000 (£93,000), and the cheapest four-bedroom houses start at $200,000 (£106,000), but you will pay upwards of $500,000 (£263,158) for a home in a good area.

■ EMPLOYMENT

A handful of people move to Hollywood every year to become movie stars, but the chances are that you will have less lofty ambitions. The main employment sectors in California are construction, agriculture, IT, military and industrial projects, including aviation, and entertainment. There are also good opportunities for nurses and teachers – the University of California is one of the largest employers in the state.

California has bounced back after the bursting of the "dot.com" bubble in 2001, and the state is now 24th in the world ranking of economies, out-doing many national governments. Entrepreneurs

ABOVE: The Golden Gate bridge in San Francisco connects the city with Marin county

are encouraged, and the state government is generous with licences and tax benefits for new companies that employ US workers. Unemployment in California, however, is slightly higher than the national average, at 5.8 per cent.

The IT and biomedical industries are concentrated in the Bay Area around San Francisco and in Sacramento. There are lucrative opportunities for recent graduates at infotech companies, and this is reflected by the slightly younger profile of international migrants to California compared with the national average.

Tourism is a major industry in Los Angeles and the Bay Area, and Disneyland is a major employer. There are also opportunities for temporary workers at ski resorts, hotels and national parks in the Central Sierra region. Farms in the Central Valley produce wine, fruit and vegetables, but there is massive competition for casual work from Mexican immigrants.

Everyone wants to work in Hollywood, and jobs in entertainment are heavily over-subscribed. If you are coming to Hollywood to get your big break, make sure you have a "Plan B" in case things don't work out. Mainstream business and finance jobs are concentrated in large metropolitan areas such as Los Angeles, San Francisco and San Diego. As a rule, the Bay Area has the most cosmopolitan business climate.

Spanish is spoken by more than a third of Californians, and Spanish-speakers are at an advantage in many jobs. An English accent can also be a useful foot in the door in the Bay Area. It is worth noting that California has some of the highest state income taxes in the USA – up to 9.3 per cent for high earners.

Many people move to California on transfers within multinational corporations, and company-sponsored immigrant visas are generally restricted to people with exceptional skills. California has specialist recruitment agencies for most business sectors. Agriculture and tourism employ large numbers of temporary workers. It is a good idea to try contacting larger theme parks, hotels and ski resorts to see if they offer a sponsored H2B visa programme for temporary workers. ●

ARIZONA

■ PROPERTY

Arizona is seen as cowboy country, famous for its cactus-filled deserts, pony trails and the vast chasms of the Grand Canyon. It has a strong US character, with significant influences from nearby Mexico.

The climate is hot and dry, and water scarcity has restricted urban development to a handful of major population centres. Phoenix and Tucson are expanding fast. Both cities have high crime rates, but they are still the most popular destinations for foreign workers. Housing there consists of older downtown homes, modern suburban developments and ranches in the countryside. The average interest rate for a 30-year fixed-rate mortgage is 5.8 per cent. Local lenders are not used to dealing with foreign buyers, and an international mortgage from the UK may be the best solution.

A four-bedroom house in a nice part of Phoenix will cost at least $175,000 (£93,000), and a large property in the suburbs will set you back more than $2,000,000 (£1,060,000). If you'd rather rent, two-bedroom apartments can be had for $700 (£370) per month, but $1,500 (£795) will get you somewhere in a good location.

■ EMPLOYMENT

Large numbers of illegal immigrants cross the border from Mexico to the USA in Arizona, which increases competition for casual and temporary work. Employers are unlikely to be able to claim that there are shortages in the unskilled workforce.

The overall jobs market is growing by 3.3 per cent a year, and unemployment is well below the national average at 3.7 per cent. There are plenty of opportunities for skilled migrants. Growth industries in the greater Phoenix area include the IT and biotech industries, software design and healthcare. Arizona has a large retired population, so there are opportunities for foreign nurses.

Jobs are also available in business, telecommunications and construction, reflecting the massive growth of cities such as Phoenix and Tucson. Corporate jobs are likely to be the result of transfers within companies, but company-sponsored visas are an option for skilled professionals, particularly in IT.

Being able to speak Spanish is a major advantage in Arizona. The state used to be part of Spanish-speaking Mexico, and job-hunters with a grasp of Spanish will have the most success with local recruitment agencies. Be aware, however, that wages in Arizona are some of the lowest in the country, and state income taxes range from 3.8 per cent up to 7 per cent. ●

BOSTON

■ PROPERTY

Boston is a safe and vibrant city with a huge student population and a large British expat scene. The capital, Massachusetts, is one of the USA's most historic cities, with numerous old buildings tucked in among the skyscrapers.

History and green open spaces do not come cheap. House prices are high compared to incomes, and analysts are predicting a slump in the future. A four-bedroom home in a decent area will cost upwards of $400,000 (£212,000), and a two-bedroom apartment will cost $160,000 (£85,000) or more. The average interest rate for a 30-year fixed-rate mortgage in Boston is about 5.7 per cent, and property taxes are rising. Boston mortgage lenders have traditionally been reluctant to lend to foreign buyers, but working legal residents who have a 25 to 40 per cent deposit should have few problems.

Popular areas for relocators include Fenway, Kenmore Square, Allston, Brookline and Jamaica Plain. The most exclusive areas are the Back Bay neighbourhood – full of historic brownstone townhouses – and Cambridge – home to Harvard University. Renting is more affordable than buying, and two-bedroom apartments start from $1,000 (£530) per month.

■ EMPLOYMENT

Boston has a highly educated workforce, and the city is a major centre for the biotech industry. Physical sciences and engineering are on the rise due to the presence of the prestigious Massachusetts Institute of Technology. There are also openings for skilled professionals in healthcare, education and finance.

Many British teachers and researchers move to Boston on international educational scholarships, which often come with generous research funding. Foreign nurses can take advantage of priority visa programmes, including the H1C visa, which allows nurses to work in the USA for up to three years.

Corporations in Boston rely mainly on internal transfers, but exceptionally skilled foreign workers can get sponsorship for a working visa. IT in particular is a major growth area. Many people get a foot in the door by attending university in Boston, which entitles them to work for a year in the USA after graduation.

There are jobs in hospitality, retail and services suitable for temporary workers, but competition from local students makes it hard for employers to prove that there are local worker shortages.

The cost of living in Boston is about 50 per cent higher than the national average and state income tax is 5.3 per cent. Unemployment is fairly low, but the jobs market is rather sluggish. ●

© BOSTON TOURIST BOARD

LEFT: Part of Boston's "freedom trail". Boston has more sites related to the American Revolution than any other American city

NEW YORK

■ PROPERTY

New York marks the spot where millions of early European immigrants came ashore, and the city remains culturally closer to Europe than anywhere else in the USA. New York is the second most popular US destination for international migrants, and has a huge British expat population.

Many relocators end up living in New Jersey, where rents are lower and crime is less of a problem than in Brooklyn or the Bronx. The most expensive areas are Manhattan and Long Island. New York is in the grip of a chronic housing shortage, which has pushed all property prices sky high.

In Manhattan, a two-bedroom apartment can cost up to $350,000 (£186,000), while a four-bedroom house is likely to be at least $1,000,000 (£530,000). The average interest rate for a 30-year fixed-rate mortgage is about 5.4 per cent. New York lenders are used to dealing with foreign buyers, and mortgages are available for a deposit of about 20 per cent. Rental rates for two-bedroom apartments start from $1,200 (£635) per month.

In the 1990s, New York had a reputation for violent crime, but it is now the safest large city in the USA. Public services are paid for out of New York's notoriously high property taxes.

■ EMPLOYMENT

New York City is the financial heart of the USA, and corporations in Manhattan employ huge numbers of expat workers. Many companies transfer employees from other international offices on L1 visas, and offer relocation packages that include rented accommodation. This is the easiest way to move to New York.

It is also possible to obtain a visa if you have a relative already living in New York, and people from eligible countries can obtain legal residency through the national diversity lottery scheme.

The best opportunities for skilled workers are in business, management and finance on Manhattan, but there are also jobs available in the media, local government, education and nursing. Most international recruitment agencies have New York offices, and many companies conduct job interviews in the UK.

Unskilled jobs are mainly in construction, urban transport, hospitality, and retail and services. As a popular tourist destination, New York attracts lots of temporary workers on sponsored H2B visas, but there is huge competition for casual jobs from students and other international migrants.

English is the main language requirement for working in New York, and British accents seem to go down well with US employers. Unemployment, however, is well above the national average at 6.2 per cent. High business taxes and office rental costs make New York a difficult place to set up a business. ●

WASHINGTON

■ PROPERTY

The most popular area for relocators is the Northwest quadrant. Attractive residential areas close to the centre include Adams-Morgan, Mount Pleasant and Georgetown. Many people also choose to live further from the centre in Northern Virginia or suburban Maryland, where property prices are cheaper. Arlington and Bethesda are popular suburbs.

Overall crime rates are low, but violent crime is a problem in the southern part of Washington DC and many districts are best avoided. The Northeast quadrant is an up-and-coming area, but it has a way to go to catch up with the northwest part of the city.

The average interest rate for a 30-year fixed-rate mortgage is six per cent, and property tax is about $1 (53p) per $100 (£53) of property value. Local lenders will consider international buyers who are locally employed and can provide a strong credit history, but it may be easier to get an international mortgage from home.

The housing market is soaring. The average home costs $290,000 (£154,000), and a typical four-bedroom house in a decent area will go for about $350,000 (£185,000). A two-bedroom apartment will cost about $180,000 (£95,000). Rents in Washington are famously high. It is not unusual to pay $2,000 (£1,100) per month for a two-bedroom apartment, but you can find apartments for $800 (£425) if you don't mind living further from the centre.

■ EMPLOYMENT

Average wages in Washington are well above the national average, but the cost of living is high. Income tax rates vary from five per cent to 9.3 per cent. The overall number of jobs is declining in central Washington, but growing elsewhere in the state.

Washington has plenty of museums and other cultural attractions that may provide employment for temporary workers. There are also hotels and restaurants that cater for tourists, business visitors and politicians. Demand for nurses is high, and many people take advantage of the streamlined H1C visa programme. The major skilled industries are business, finance, media, education and politics – the Federal Government is one of the largest employers in the area. There are good opportunities for intra-company transfers and company-sponsored visas for skilled financiers and journalists.

English is the standard language requirement in Washington, but speakers of other European languages are the preferred choice for some media and political jobs. The national economy seems to be slowly recovering, and prospects in Washington look set to improve at a steady rate. ●

BELOW: Capitol Hill, location of the White House

■ OTHER HOT STATES

The states we have covered offer some of the best job prospects for relocators, but many other states attract large numbers of immigrant workers from the UK and around the world. Other states to consider include Texas (particularly Dallas-Fort Worth), Illinois (particularly Chicago) and New Jersey (particularly Jersey City, for commuting to New York).

USA

Property price guide

The USA offers a home for everyone, ranging from an affordable bolt hole in New York to a stunning mansion on the beachfront in California

APARTMENTS FOR RENT

From small and stylish to spacious and luxurious

$575 PER MONTH

1-BED PHOENIX, AZ

£300 PER MONTH
- Fully furnished ✗
- Pool ✔
- Parking ✔   **CODE** APT

$595 PER MONTH

2-BED PHOENIX, AZ

£315 PER MONTH
- Fully furnished ✗
- Pool ✔
- Parking ✔   **CODE** APT

$820 PER MONTH

3-BED TALLAHASSEE, FL

£430 PER MONTH
- Fully furnished ✗
- Pool ✔
- Parking ✔   **CODE** APT

$820 PER MONTH

2-BED PENSACOLA, FL

£430 PER MONTH
- Fully furnished ✗
- Pool ✔
- Parking ✔   **CODE** APT

APARTMENTS FOR SALE

For the young professional or those seeking a quiet retirement property

$61,900

1-BED PHOENIX, AZ

£32,580
- Fully furnished ✗
- Pool ✗
- Parking ✗   **CODE** CAZ

$121,900

1-BED FREEPORT, NY

£64,160
- Fully furnished ✗
- Pool ✗
- Parking ✗   **CODE** CNY

$299,900

2-BED BOSTON, MA

£157,840
- Fully furnished ✗
- Pool ✗
- Parking ✔   **CODE** CMA

$360,000

1-BED WASHINGTON DC

£184,470
- Fully furnished ✗
- Pool ✗
- Parking ✗   **CODE** CDC

HOUSES FOR SALE

From traditional family holiday homes to elegant mansions on the waterfront

$183,344

3-BED HAINES CITY, FL

£96,500
- Fully furnished ✗
- Pool ✗
- Parking ✔   **CODE** COL

$275,900

4-BED BRIDGEWATER, FL

£145,210
- Fully furnished ✔
- Pool ✔
- Parking ✔   **CODE** COL

$420,000

3-BED CLERMONT, FL

£221,050
- Fully furnished ✔
- Pool ✔
- Parking ✔   **CODE** COL

$535,000

3-BED MASSAPEQUA, NY

£281,580
- Fully furnished ✗
- Pool ✗
- Parking ✔   **CODE** CNY

The Americans specialise in modern, spacious apartments and villas boasting all mod cons

APARTMENTS FOR RENT

$1,335 PER MONTH

1-BED LOS ANGELES, CA

£700 PER MONTH
- Fully furnished ✗
- Pool ✗
- Parking ✔   **CODE** APT

$1,750 PER MONTH

1-BED WASHINGTON DC

£920 PER MONTH
- Fully furnished ✗
- Pool ✗
- Parking ✔   **CODE** REL

$1,849 PER MONTH

2-BED ARLINGTON, VA

£975 PER MONTH
- Fully furnished ✗
- Pool ✔
- Parking ✔   **CODE** REL

$2,539 PER MONTH

2-BED PASADENA, CA

£1,335 PER MONTH
- Fully furnished ✗
- Pool ✔
- Parking ✔   **CODE** APT

APARTMENTS FOR SALE

$365,000

2-BED ATLANTIC BEACH, NY

£192,110
- Fully furnished ✗
- Pool ✗
- Parking ✔   **CODE** CNY

$470,000

2-BED BOSTON, MA

£247,370
- Fully furnished ✗
- Pool ✗
- Parking ✔   **CODE** CMA

$699,000

2-BED LOS ANGELES, CA

£367,900
- Fully furnished ✗
- Pool ✔
- Parking ✗   **CODE** CCA

$1,695,000

2-BED LOS ANGELES, CA

£892,110
- Fully furnished ✗
- Pool ✔
- Parking ✔   **CODE** CCA

HOUSES FOR SALE

$560,000

4-BED EMERALD ISLAND, FL

£294,340
- Fully furnished ✗
- Pool ✔
- Parking ✔   **CODE** COL

$790,000

3-BED PHOENIX, AZ

£415,790
- Fully furnished ✗
- Pool ✗
- Parking ✔   **CODE** CAZ

$1,149,000

5-BED NEWTON, MA

£604,740
- Fully furnished ✗
- Pool ✗
- Parking ✔   **CODE** CMA

$2,395,000

4-BED LOS ANGELES, CA

£1,260,530
- Fully furnished ✗
- Pool ✔
- Parking ✔   **CODE** CCA

USA

Up-and-coming countries

With a number of countries set to become excellent employment prospects in the near future, we showcase the top five relocation opportunities

1 Hungary

- **Population:** 10,032,375
- **Capital:** Budapest
- **Mercer cost of living:** 84.5
- **Life expectancy:** 72 years
- **Literacy:** 99.4%
- **Government:** Parliamentary democracy
- **GDP per capita:** US$4,431
- **Unemployment:** 5.9%
- **Currency:** Forint (Ft)
- **Exchange rate:** Ft1 = £0.003; £1 = Ft355
- **Languages:** Hungarian
- **Climate:** Temperate and cloudy with humid winters and warm summers
- **Expats:** There are about 40,000 expats in Budapest, many of whom are British and German.

ABOVE: Budapest is a prosperous and lively city which boasts a number of employment opportunities

HUNGARY IS A BEAUTIFUL country with a very varied topography. Land-locked and located in the centre of Europe, it is bordered by no fewer than seven other countries. Straddling Western and Eastern Europe, Hungary is ideally located for residents to enjoy the benefits of both.

Jobs and economy: Hungary joined the EU in 2004 and has been enjoying dynamic economic growth since 1997. With a current growth rate of 2.9 per cent, it is one of the most prosperous countries in Eastern Europe. Unemployment has fallen to 5.9 per cent, inflation has fallen to six per cent, wages are rising and industry has diversified. The service industry employs 65 per cent of the population. The main employment centre is Budapest, with one-third of businesses situated either in the city or the surrounding area. These businesses include a number of international companies, such as Audi, Electrolux and Samsung. The major industries are mining, metallurgy, construction, textiles, chemicals and car production. There are plenty of job opportunities in hi-tech industries, publishing, consulting, tourism, agriculture and manufacturing. Publications that feature "situations vacant" in English include the *Budapest Sun*, the *Budapest Business Journal* and *Budapest Week*.

Education: Most public and private schools in Hungary are excellent, and there are a number of international schools in and around Budapest that teach the English curriculum. It is also possible for foreigners to attend university here.

Healthcare: The health service in Hungary is state-owned and run, but the government is planning to privatise some hospitals in the near future. Residents pay social security contributions. Non-residents must take out separate health insurance.

Renting: Throughout Hungary, rental apartments are in plentiful supply, particularly in the centre of Budapest, where 33 per cent of properties are for rent. Tenants are expected to pay one month's rent in advance, and one or two months' rent as a deposit. They also pay for the utilities and contribute to the house fund, which is for maintaining common areas. Rental adverts can be found in local newspapers, and there are many English-speaking rental agencies. A two–bedroom apartment in Budapest costs about Ft183,600 (£510) per month. Rental prices are rising by about eight per cent every year.

Buying: Foreigners must apply for a permit before purchasing property. The price of property in Hungary is increasing dramatically. Since 2000, prices in parts of Budapest have increased by between 80 and 100 per cent. Even properties in the least desirable districts are set to increase by 14 to 18 per cent in 2005. There is a well-established registry system and legal apparatus, and it is usual to pay a ten per cent deposit to secure the property. Several banks in Hungary now offer mortgages to foreigners, of about 40 per cent of the purchase price. A two-bedroom apartment in Budapest will cost approximately Ft30,899,880 (£85,800), while a four-bedroom house will cost Ft44,094,000 (£124,150).

Tax: Income tax is charged on a sliding scale starting at 18 per cent, going up to 38 per cent for those who earn over HUF1,500,000. You are also taxed on any income generated outside Hungary. Property tax includes stamp duty of between two to six per cent of the purchase price, and capital gains tax of 20 per cent.

2 Malaysia

- **Population:** 23,522,482
- **Capital:** Kuala Lumpur
- **Mercer cost of living:** 67.7
- **Life expectancy:** 72 years
- **Literacy:** 88.7%
- **Government:** Constitutional monarchy

- **GDP per capita:** US$9,000
- **Unemployment:** 3.6%
- **Currency:** Ringgit (RM)
- **Exchange rate:** RM1 = £0.14; £1 = RM7
- **Languages:** Bahasa Melayu
- **Climate:** Tropical, hot and humid with two monsoon seasons
- **Expats:** More than 60,000 expats, including many British.

MALAYSIA IS A MULTICULTURAL, modern society spanning two land masses. Mainland Malaysia occupies the southern part of the Malay Peninsula, while East Malaysia occupies the top third of the island of Borneo. Malaysia is a mountainous country, and boasts some of the world's most ancient rainforest.

Jobs and economy: Malaysia has one of the best standards of living in Southeast Asia, and a booming, and continually expanding, economy. It is the world's largest producer of rubber and a major provider of tin. But the main economic driver is manufacturing, particularly electronics. Labour costs are relatively low and productivity is high. The main employment centres are Kuala Lumpur, George Town, Ipoh and Johor Bahru. English language dailies *The Star* and *New Straits Times* have good online job sections. Malaysia also has a reputation for being a largely safe country with a low crime rate.

Education: English is taught in state schools, but the main curriculum is usually in Bahasa Melayu. There are, however, plenty of private international schools for foreigners.

Healthcare: Standards are high, but foreign workers have to use private clinics. If health insurance isn't part of your employment package, you will need private insurance.

Renting: Expect to pay an initial deposit of one month's rent plus two months' rent and utilities deposit. The average cost of a two-bedroom apartment is RM9,500 (£1,335) per month.

Buying: A decent apartment starts from RM256,125 (£36,000), which is the minimum price for foreigners investing in property and obtaining a mortgage (of up to 60 per cent). Approval is needed from the Foreign Investment Committee, and properties may not be sold within three years of approval being granted. Stamp duty is 1.5 to 1.75 per cent. There is no annual property tax. Capital gains operates on a sliding scale, from zero to 30 per cent.

Visas: EU nationals can stay for up to three months without a visa. To work, you will need an Employment or Professional Pass, which your employer should apply for. Any accompanying family members need Dependents' Passes.

Tax: Income tax for residents is charged on a sliding scale of up to 28 per cent. You are classed as a resident if you are in the country for 182 days or more a year, any fewer and you are liable to pay 28 per cent as a non-resident. Malaysia has a taxation treaty with the UK, so you won't be taxed twice.

3 Singapore

- **Population:** 4,353,893
- **Capital:** Singapore
- **Mercer cost of living:** 83.6
- **Life expectancy:** 81.5 years
- **Literacy:** 92.5%
- **Government:** Parliamentary republic
- **GDP per capita:** US$23,700
- **Unemployment:** 4.8%
- **Currency:** Singapore dollar (SG$)
- **Exchange rate:** SG$1 = £0.33; £1 = SG$3
- **Languages:** English, Chinese Mandarin, Malay, Tamil
- **Climate:** Tropical, hot and humid, with frequent rainfall and two monsoon seasons
- **Expats:** There are approximately 13,000 British expats in Singapore.

SINGAPORE IS ONE OF THE world's most prosperous nations, occupying a tiny island at the tip of the Malay Peninsula. It is a major transport hub and has the world's busiest seaport. Singapore has heavily subsidised health, housing and education, and is extremely safe. Crime is virtually unheard of and the streets are litter-free.

Jobs and economy: Singapore has a highly developed and successful free-market economy, with one of the highest per capita GDP in the world. The economy relies heavily on exports. Singapore is the international centre for banking in Asia, has a large manufacturing industry and is a major centre for shipping. Many multinationals and several hundred UK companies have a base here.

Education: Education is compulsory from the age of seven. Foreign workers must pay $5,000 (£1,650) to enrol a child at a state school. English is usually taught as the first language in Singapore schools, but there are also plenty of international schools to choose from.

Healthcare: Singapore has a world-class healthcare system. The Ministry of Health offers subsidised healthcare, but private insurance is common and plans for foreign workers are readily available.

Renting: Accommodation is normally let on a one- or two-year lease, and there will be a deposit of about three months' rent.

UP-AND-COMING

BELOW: One of the world's most prosperous nations, Singapore has the world's busiest sea port

© SINGAPORE TOURIST BOARD

Buying: Property, unsurprisingly, is expensive in Singapore. A compact apartment in a decent and popular area will cost $600,000 (£200,000) or more. Solicitors' fees, stamp duty, mortgage and survey costs add another five per cent. Permanent residents can borrow up to 80 per cent of the purchase price. Foreign buyers can purchase only premises in buildings of six storeys or higher, or in other approved condominiums. Property tax is based on the annual estimated rental value.

Visas: Singapore is one of the world's most immigration-friendly nations. In most cases, all you need is an Employment Pass, which your employer or a local sponsor will secure. Passes are usually processed within a week and, if lodged online,

can be turned around in a day. Spouses and children under the age of 21 need to apply for Dependents' Passes.

Tax: Rates in Singapore are low compared with Western countries. If you are there for 60 days or fewer, you pay no tax. Those staying for up to 183 days pay at the non-resident rate of 15 per cent or the residential rate, whichever is higher. Anyone staying for more than 183 days is classed as resident for tax purposes, and pays from zero to 22 per cent. Singapore has a tax treaty with the UK, so you won't pay twice.

4 Sweden

- **Population:** 8,986,400
- **Capital:** Stockholm
- **Mercer cost of living:** 89.5
- **Life expectancy:** 80 years

- **Literacy:** 99%
- **Government:** Constitutional monarchy
- **GDP per capita:** US$26,800
- **Unemployment:** 4.9%
- **Currency:** Swedish krona (SEK)
- **Exchange rate:** SEK1 = £0.076; £1 = SEK13.01
- **Languages:** Swedish
- **Climate:** The climate in Sweden is relatively mild in spite of its northern position. Summers can be very hot, while winters are extremely cold.
- **Expats:** There is a large community of more than 11,000 British expats living in Sweden.

SWEDEN IS LOCATED IN Northern Europe between Finland and Norway, and is by far the largest of the Scandinavian countries. Due to its long, narrow shape, Sweden's landscape varies enormously. There are lakes and waterways, mountainous regions and glaciers, open areas of countryside and sandy beaches. Most of Sweden is fairly flat. The mountainous regions are in the west of the country.

Jobs and economy: Sweden's main centres of employment are Stockholm, Gothenburg and Malmö. Newspapers in Sweden are an important source of vacancies for jobseekers. The country's main exports are machinery and transport equipment, along with chemicals, paper, ceramics, iron and steel. More than 3.2 million people work in services, including 1.3 million in the public sector and 1.8 million in private companies. The economy is currently very strong, and unemployment is low.

Education: The English language is mandatory in all Swedish schools, and schooling is obligatory in Sweden from seven to 16 years of age. All children whose mother tongue is not Swedish are entitled to

be taught in their national language. There are numerous international schools throughout Sweden and all lessons are conducted in English. Swedish state education is free to all children whose parents are resident in Sweden, regardless of nationality.

Healthcare: All Swedes are covered by the National Health Insurance System, which provides medical care and hospitalisation free of charge or at a modest cost. UK nationals who are working in Sweden are entitled to healthcare on the same terms as Swedish nationals.

Rentals: About 40 per cent of Swedes live in rented accommodation, which is primarily found in blocks of flats. The majority of rental accommodation is owned by municipal housing companies, most of which are non-profit corporations. The average annual rent for a three-bedroom flat is SEK72,900 (£5,451).

Buying: There are no restrictions on UK buyers purchasing a property in Sweden. Property tax is payable at the annual rate of about 1.5 per cent of the property price, and will be charged on tax-registered foreign ownership. Surprisingly property is affordable compared with the cost of living in Sweden. A family home starts at around £85,000 (SEK1,130,483) and an apartment at around £25,000 (SEK332,464).

Visas and Permits: You need a valid passport to enter Sweden, but UK nationals do not require a visa if they are intending to stay in the country for fewer than three months. To secure residency, the Swedish Embassy can process a residency application for you before you leave, but

ABOVE: **Singapore has an excellent and lively expat community**

you can also apply for residency whilst in Sweden. UK nationals have the right to live and work in Sweden without a work permit, and share the same rights as Swedish nationals with regard to pay, working conditions, access to housing, vocational training, social security and trade union membership. If you are offered permanent employment in Sweden, a residence permit is granted for five years, but if a temporary, worker the permit is granted solely for the period of your employment.

Tax: Swedes pay notoriously high taxes, but public services are correspondingly good, and the government provides citizens with extensive welfare benefits. Income is taxed at 26 to 35 per cent, depending on municipality. There is also a national income tax of 20 per cent on annual taxable earnings starting at SEK252,000 (£19,000), to 25 per cent for income above SEK390,400.

5 Switzerland

- **Population:** 7,450,867
- **Capital:** Bern
- **Mercer cost of living:** 106.2
- **Life expectancy:** 80 years
- **Literacy:** 99%
- **Government:** Federal republic
- **GDP per capita:** 41,409
- **Unemployment:** 4.1%
- **Currency:** Swiss franc (CHF)
- **Exchange rate:** CHF1 = £0.451; £1 = CHF2.21
- **Languages:** German, French, Italian and Romansch
- **Climate:** Temperate with cold, wet, snowy winters and cool to warm humid summers
- **Expats:** There are about 65,000 British expats in Switzerland, mostly in the Geneva area.

SWITZERLAND IS A LAND OF contrasts, from mountain villages, where little seems to have changed for decades, to bustling cosmopolitan cities with modern architecture. It also has some of the most beautiful scenery in the world. The country is divided into administrative areas called cantons, and the language spoken varies from one canton to another. The standard of living is high and there is a low crime rate.

Jobs and economy: The economy is stable, although growth has dropped in recent years. Almost 70 per cent of the workforce are employed in service industries such as banking, insurance and tourism. About 26 per cent are involved in industry such as the development and manufacture of machinery, pharmaceuticals, watches, textiles and precision instruments. Many Swiss businesses are family run, but Switzerland is also home to leading producers of pharmaceuticals and chemicals such as Novartis and Hoffmann-La Roche. About 20 per cent of Switzerland's workforce is made up of foreign workers, from builders to computer scientists. The main Swiss employment centres are Zurich, Basel, Geneva and Lausanne.

Education: The state system is excellent and free, and there are classes for children who do not speak the language. There are also many private international schools.

Healthcare: There is no public health service, so you will need to ensure you have private health insurance.

Renting: Two-thirds of Swiss people rent their homes. Tenants usually have to pay a deposit of one to three months' rent and take out personal liability insurance as a condition of the lease. It can be difficult to find affordable accommodation. Rents vary from F600 (£270) for a one-

© SWISS TOURIST BOARD

ABOVE: The Alps form part of Switzerland's south-west border

room apartment to F1,220 (£550) for a four-room one.

Buying: Foreigners can buy property only in certain tourist areas, unless they have a special permit. A studio apartment costs from F100,000 (£45,000), and a three-bedroom apartment F400,000 (£180,000).

Visas: To live and work in Switzerland, you will need a Residence Permit. EU citizens also need proof that a Swiss employer is willing to take them on. Your employer should apply on your behalf before you enter the country. An L permit is short-term. It is usually issued for less than a

year, for both those with job offers and the unemployed. The standard, or B, permit is usually issued for a year for a specific job and is renewable. The C permit allows the holder to work freely in any occupation except law or medicine, but this can only be applied for by a person who has already held a B permit for five to ten years.

Tax: There is no central tax system. All taxes are levied at federal, cantonal and communal level. Rates vary between cantons but rarely exceed 30 per cent. Most foreign workers have income tax deducted directly from their pay by their employer. ●

BUYER'S REFERENCE

Buyer's reference

You'll find all the resources you need in our reference section, from a country matrix to our useful contacts listings

Country matrix

	POPULATION	EXPAT POPULATION	CAPITAL CITY	CURRENCY	INTERNATIONAL DIALLING CODE	EMERGENCY SERVICES	IMMUNISATIONS	GMT
AUSTRALIA	19,547,000	1.1 million British 8,580 British moved there in 2004	Canberra	Dollar AUS$	00 61	000	No	+8 to +11 (Canberra +11)
BELGIUM	10,275,000	903,000 foreign residents	Brussels	Euro €	00 32	112	No	+1
CANADA	31,950,000	606,000 British	Ottawa	Dollar CAN$	00 1	911	No	-3.5 to -8 (Ottawa -5)
CHINA	1,298,847,624	260,000 foreign residents	Beijing	Yuan CNY	00 86	110	Hepatitis A & B, typhoid, tetanus, yellow fever, diphtheria, rabies, tuberculosis, cholera	+8
DUBAI	1,400,000	50,000 British	Dubai City	Dirham Dh	00 971	999	Hepatitis A, typhoid, malaria	+4
FRANCE	59,766,000	150,00 British 3.26 million foreign residents	Paris	Euro €	00 33	112	No	+1
GERMANY	82,252,000	114,000 British	Berlin	Euro €	00 49	112	No	+1
HONG KONG	6,710,000	34,000 British	Victoria	Dollar HK$	00 852	999	Polio, hepatitis A & B, typhoid, tuberculosis, tetanus	+8
IRELAND	3,883,000	103,476 British	Dublin	Euro €	00 353	112	No	GMT
ITALY	57,716,000	Over 20,000 British 1.46 million foreign residents	Rome	Euro €	00 39	112	Hepatitis A in summer in South	+1
JAPAN	127,333,002	10,411 British 1.5 million foreign residents	Tokyo	Yen ¥	00 81	110/119	Hepatitis B, Japanese encephalitis, tetanus	+9
LUXEMBOURG	462,690	148,000 foreign residents	Luxembourg City	Euro €	00 352	112	No	+1
NETHERLANDS	16,068,000	678,000 foreign residents	Amsterdam	Euro €	00 31	112	No	+1
NEW ZEALAND	3,908,000	Over 178,000 British 21,238 British moved there in 2004	Wellington	Dollar NZ$	00 64	111	No	+12
SOUTH AFRICA	43,648,000	750,000 British 4.05 million foreign residents	Pretoria	Rand ZAR	00 27	107	Malaria, hepatitis A and B, polio, tetanus, typhoid and yellow fever	+2
SPAIN	38,383,000	105,479 British 50,000 British move per year 3 million foreign residents	Madrid	Euro €	00 34	112	No	+1
USA	Arizona 1,000,000 Boston 589,141 California 35,484,453 Florida 17,019,068 New York City 8,008,278 Washington DC 572,059	Arizona 714,343 (12.8%) of population foreign born Boston 151,998 (25.8%) of population foreign born California 3,360 British people moved there in 2002, 9.3 million (26.2%) of population foreign born Florida 2.8 million (16.7%) of population foreign born New York City 2,874,971 (20.4%) of population foreign born Washington D.C. 73,795 (12.9%) of population foreign born	Arizona Phoenix California Sacramento Florida Tallahassee	Dollar US$	00 1	911	No	Arizona -7 Boston -5 California -8 Florida -5 New York -5 Washington DC -5

✈ AIR TRAVEL TIME	✈ MAJOR AIRPORTS	★ EU MEMBERSHIP	∨ VISA REQUIRED	WP WORK PERMIT REQUIRED	% INTEREST RATES	% MORTGAGE RATES	🛏 AVERAGE RENTAL PRICE for a 2-bedroom property per month	🏠 AVERAGE PRICE for a 2-bedroom apartment	🏠 AVERAGE PRICE for a 4-bedroom house
22 hrs 30 mins	Canberra, Adelaide, Brisbane, Melbourne, Perth, Sydney	No	Yes	Yes	5.99%	6.46%	$1,200 / £492	$267,000 / £109,470	$385,000 / £157,850
1 hr	Brussels, Antwerp	Yes	No	Resident's permit	2%	5.5%	€827 / £566	€149,600 / £102,466	€325,273 / £222,790
7 hrs 30 mins	Montreal, Ottawa, Toronto, Vancouver	No	Not for short periods	Limited to 5 years	3.5%	4.25-7.65%	$820 / £352	$241,000 / £103,433	$330,000 / £141,631
10 hrs	Beijing capital, Shanghai Pudong, Guangzhou Baiyun	No	Yes	Yes	5.58%	5.51%	CNY 13,392 / £853	CNY 225,000 / £14,355	CNY 640,000 / £40,800
7 hrs	Dubai International	No	Not for 60 days	Yes and resident's permit	5.05%	6.5%	Dh 8,400 / £1,207	Dh 831,000 / £119,397	Dh 2,462,000 / £353,736
1 hr 5 mins	Paris CDG, Paris Orly, Nice, Lyons	Yes	No	Resident's card	2%	6.2%	€1,330 / £917	€196,000 / £135,172	€374,000 / £257,931
1 hr 25 mins	Frankfurt, Munich, Berlin, Hanover, Hamburg, Düsseldorf	Yes	No	Resident's permit	2%	5.87%	€920 / £634	€163,000 / £112,414	€273,000 / £188,276
12 hrs 50 mins	Hong Kong International	No	No	Yes	6.5%	6.5%	$20,200 / £1,414	$12,000,000 / £811,860	$58,000,000 / £3,923,989
1 hr	Dublin, Cork, Shannon	Yes	No	No	2%	4.0%	€880 / £607	€191,600 / £132,138	€302,800 / £208,828
2 hrs 30 mins	Venice Marco Polo, Rome Leonardo da Vinci, Bologna, Naples, Pisa, Milan	Yes	No	Resident's card	2%	5.0%	€910 / £628	€291,300 / £200,897	€378,200 / £260,828
11 hrs 45 mins	Tokyo Narita, Kansai International, Chubu (Nagoya)	No	Not for 6 months	Yes	0.1%	0.1%	¥396,000 / £1,980	¥55,000,000 / £274,863	¥80,000,000 / £399,800
1 hr 30 mins	Luxembourg Findel	Yes	No	Resident's permit	2%	5.0%	€980 / £676	€280,000 / £193,103	€490,000 / £337,931
1 hr 30 mins	Amsterdam, Eindhoven, Maastricht, Rotterdam	Yes	No	Not for 3 months	2%	4.5%	€1,030 / £710	€210,950 / £145,483	€355,800 / £245,379
30 hrs	Auckland, Christchurch, Wellington	No	Not for 6 months	Yes, given to those offered employment, valid for 3 years	6.89%	7.25-10.8%	$1,000 / £380	$258,000 / £98,040	$401,000 / £152,380
11 hrs 10 mins	Johannesburg, Cape Town, Durban	No	Yes	Yes	11.5%	12.5%	ZAR 3,500 / £315	ZAR 903,000 / £81,270	ZAR 1,765,000 / £156,333
2 hrs 15 mins	Madrid Barajas, Malaga, Barcelona, Bilbao	Yes	No	No	2%	3.79-6.79%	€1,320 / £910	€182,000 / £125,517	€452,000 / £311,724
Arizona 10 hrs 55 mins, Boston 7 hrs 10 mins, California 11 hrs, Florida 8 hrs, New York 7 hrs 45 mins, Washington DC 8 hrs 10 mins	Arizona Phoenix Shy Harbour, Boston Logan International, California Bob Hope Los Angeles, Oakland, San Diego, San Francisco, Florida Orlando, Fort Lauderdale, Miami, Jacksonville, New York City La Guardia, JFK, Newark, Washington DC Washington Dulles, Baltimore	No	Yes	Yes	Arizona 5-7%, Boston 5-7%, California 5-7%, Florida 6.79%, New York City 5-7%, Washington DC 5-7%	Arizona 3.78-5.21%, Boston 3.54-5.16%, California 3.64-5.18%, Florida 3.61-5.13%, New York City 3.75-5.25%, Washington DC 3.92-5.25%	Arizona $700 / £371, Boston $1,800 / £954, California $1,295 / £686, Florida $1,200 / £636, New York City $2,100 / £1,113, Washington DC $1,750 / £928	Arizona $151,000 / £80,030, Boston $516,842 / £273,926, California $285,000 / £151,050, Florida $274,876 / £145,000, New York City $850,000 / £450,500, Washington DC $410,000 / £217,300	Arizona $278,000 / £147,340, Boston $1,053,594 / £558,405, California $630,000 / £333,900, Florida $533,900 / £281,000, New York City $1,564,000 / £828,920, Washington DC $750,000 / £397,500

Useful contacts

The directory includes a wealth of companies that can help with every aspect of relocation, from accountants to architects and removal firms

Accountants

AUSTRALIA
ADELAIDE
Geoff Merritt Accountant & Tax Agent
Gilles Plains Office
1/601 North East Road
Gilles Plains, 5086
Tel: +61 882 665 388
Fax: +61 882 665 399
Email: geoff@accountantplus.com.au

BRISBANE
Fell Eales McGarry
39 Boundary Street
PO Box 3833
South Brisbane
QLD 4101
Tel: +61 732 172 477
Fax: +61 732 172 533
Email:frontdesk@fembris.com.au

Winn Stone Accountants
Suite 12
888 Boundary Road
Coopers Plains, Q 4108
Brisbane
Tel: +61 733 233 100
Fax: +61 733 233 200

MELBOURNE
Douglas Heck
161 Collins Street
Melbourne
VIC 3000
Tel: +61 392 899 999
www.dhb.com.au

EL Group
South Melbourne
VIC 3205
Tel: +61 396 863 322
www.elgroup.com.au

PERTH
ATC Chartered Accounting & Tax Consulting Pty Ltd
619 Beach Road
Warwick, WA 6024
Tel: +61 894 488 190
Fax: +61 894 488 199

Pitcher Partners
10 Ord Street
West Perth, WA 6005
Tel: +61 893 222 022
Fax: +61 893 221 262
Email: partners@pitcher-wa.com.au

SYDNEY
Thomas R Guth and Associates
13 O'Donnell Street
North Bondi
NSW 2026
Tel: +61 293 000 463
Fax: +61 291 301 641
Email: tomg@swiftdsl.com.au

Red Dalmatian Accountants
Suite 4
251–253 Canterbury Road
Canterbury
NSW 2193
Tel: +61 02 9787 9220
Fax: +61 02 9787 9223
Email: info@reddalmatian.com.au

BELGIUM
ANTWERP
SFC GROUP
Oosterveldlaan 102
Bus 1
2610 Wilrijk
Tel: +32 344 99757
Fax +32 344 07909
Email:sefico.Antwerpen@sfcgroup.be

BRUSSELS
SFC GROUP
Adolphe Lacomblélaan 59–61
1030 Brussels
Tel: +32 273 54145
Fax +32 273 64817
Email: sefico@sfcgroup.be

CANADA
MONTREAL
Paul Kamateros, CA
700 Cremazie West
Bureau 200
Montreal, QC H3N 1A1
Tel: +1 514 274 7519
Fax: +1 514 274 4309
Email: paul@kamateros.com

TORONTO
John R Mott
Chartered Accountant
2300 Yonge Street
Suite 1100, PO Box 2342
Toronto, Ontario
M4P 1E4
Tel: +1 416 487 7347
Fax: +1 416 486 6378
Email: john@johnmott.com

VANCOUVER
Colin Dowson Public Accountant Inc.
1748 2nd Avenue West
Vancouver
BC V6J 1H6
Tel: +1 604 731 0611
Fax: +1 604 731 4442
Email: dawson@telus.net

CHINA
BEIJING
Lehman Brown
6/F, Dongwai
Diplomatic Building
23 Dongzhimenwai Dajie
Beijing 100600
Tel: +86 108 532 1720
Fax: +86 106 532 3270
Email:beijing@lehmanbrown.com

SHANGHAI
ShuLun Pan Certified Public Accountants Co. Ltd
ADD Nan Jing Dong RD
Shanghai
200002
Tel: +86 216 339 1166
Fax: +86 216 339 2558
Email: sh.lixin@pcpa.com.cn

DUBAI
DUBAI
Jitendra Chartered Accountants
PO Box 43630
Dubai
Tel: +97 143 522 974
Fax: +97 143 522 975
Email:jitendra@jitendrafca.com

FRANCE
NICE
Cabinet Tressols et Associés Ltd
Groupe Eurex France
5 Rue de la Liberté
06000 Nice
Tel: +33 049 214 6060
Fax: +33 049 214 6070
Email: mail@eurex-nice.fr

PARIS
Arthur D Little France
50 Avenue Gauteur
75017 Paris
Tel: +33 155 742 900

CMS. Experts Associés
149 Boulevard Malesherbes
75017 Paris
Tel: +33 147 662 015
Fax: +33 143 800 398

GERMANY
BERLIN
Mazars Revision & Treuhand GmbH
Wirtschaftsprüfungsgesellschaft
Taubenstrasse 23
10117 Berlin
Tel: +49 302 007 740
Fax: +49 302 007 7444
Email: mrt-ber@mazars.de

COLOGNE
RSM Haarmann Hemmelrath
Köln Turm
Im Mediapark 8
D–50670 Cologne
Tel: +49 221 270 580
Fax: +49 221 270 58133

FRANKFURT
Mazars Revision & Treuhand GmbH
Wirtschaftsprüfungsgesellschaft
Rennbahnstrasse 72–74
60528 Frankfurt
Tel: +49 699 67650
Fax: +49 699 67651
Email: mrt-fra@mazars.de

MUNICH
Mazars Revision & Treuhand GmbH
Wirtschaftsprüfungsgesellschaft
Prinzregentenstrasse 91
81677 München
Tel: +49 894 199 960
Fax: +49 894 199 9630
Email: mrt-muc@mazars.de

RSM Haarmann Hemmelrath
Maximilianstraße 35
D–80539 Munich
Tel: +49 892 16360
Fax:+49 892 163 6133

STUTTGART
Mazars Revision & Treuhand GmbH
Wirtschaftsprüfungsgesellschaft
Kronenstr. 30
Postanschrift: Friedrichstr. 8
70174 Stuttgart
Tel: +49 711 601 7870
Fax: +49 711 601 787 17
Email: mrt-stu@mazars.de

HONG KONG
Chandler Partners
Room 1206-7
12/F New Victory House
93–103 Wing Lok
Street, Central
Tel: +85 228 506 560
Fax: +85 281 096 560
HongKong@chandler.com.hk

IRELAND
DUBLIN
Squires and Co.
4 Merrion Square
Dublin 2
Tel: +35 316 114 056
Fax: +35 316 114 943

ITALY
FLORENCE
Studio Commerciale e Tributario Caramella
Ariela Lucia
Caramella, Dottore
Commercialista,
Revisore Contabile
Via dei Servi, 12
50122 Firenze
Tel: +39 552 654 177
Fax: +39 552 679 361

MILAN
Studio Associato Luppi
Via Sant'Eufemia, 4
20122 Milano
Tel: +39 025 830 331726
Fax: +39 025 830 3233
Email:webmaster.luppi@luppi.it

THE LAKES
Inter Professionale SRL
Via Milano 138
22100 Como
Tel. +39 312 753 429
Fax: +39 312 43847
Email:info@interprofessionale.net

JAPAN
OSAKA
Nakamoto & Company
Edobori 2–1–1, Edobori
Center Building, 9F
Osaka-shi 550–0002
Tel: +81 662 2512 20
Fax: +81 662 251 212

TOKYO
KPMG
AZSA Center Building
1–2 Tsukudo-cho
Shinjuku-ku
Tokyo 162–8551
Tel: +81 332 667 551
Fax: +81 332 667 650
Email: webmaster@jp.kpmg.com

LUXEMBOURG
LUXEMBOURG CITY
Wood Appleton Oliver
Experts-Comptables Sárl
9B, Boulevard du Prince Henri
PO Box 740
L–2017 Luxembourg
Tel: +35 226 26911
Fax +35 226 269 1238
www.wao.lu

NETHERLANDS
ROTTERDAM
Accinterra Accountants
Heiman Dullaertplein 3
Rotterdam
3024 CA
Tel:+31 102 444 811
www.accinterra.nl

NEW ZEALAND
AUCKLAND
Howarth Asia Pacific Ltd
Level 14, Forsyth Barr Tower
55–65 Shortland Street
Auckland
Tel: +64 930 98898
Fax: +64 930 98980
Email: horwath.asia.pacific@horwath.co.nz

CHRISTCHURCH
Duns Limited
Level 16, PriceWaterhouse
Coopers Centre
119 Armagh Street
PO Box 2056, Christchurch
Tel: +64 336 50768

WELLINGTON
Paul Enoka Ltd.
Level 2, 119 Queens Drive
Lower Hutt
Wellington
Tel: +64 493 97977

SOUTH AFRICA
CAPE TOWN
MGI Bass Gordon
16th Floor
LG Building
1 Thibault Square
Cape Town
8001
Tel:+27 214 058 500
Fax: +27 214 196 720

DURBAN
Lowe & Company
Lloyd House
66 Bay Terrace
Durban
KwaZulu Natal
4000
Tel: +27 313 328 622
Fax: +27 313 321 828
Email: durban@gmn.co.za

JOHANNESBURG
De Villiers Myburgh Inc.
Registered Accountants
& Auditors
Tel: +27 118 671 400
Fax: +27 118 671 377
Email:jacques@dvmaudit.co.za

JCB Inc.
Registered Accountants
& Auditors
Tel: +27 115 371 560
Fax: +27 113 271 560
Email: jcb@jcbtwo.co.za

PRETORIA
Griesel Nel
7 Centuria Park
265 Von Willich Avenue
Centurion
0046
Tel: +27 126 631 735
Email: pretoria@gmn.co.za

SPAIN
BARCELONA
Spain Accountants
Diagonal 468,6
Barcelona 08016
Tel: +34 932 920 313
Fax: +34 933 969 075

BENIDORM
Noguerdes
C/Herrerías, 2 (1°A y 2°A)
03500 Benidorm
Alicante
Tel: +34 965 851 566
Fax: +34 965 851 158
Email:asesoria@nogueroles.com
www.nogueroles.com

MALAGA
David Crane
Certified Practising Accountant
5/14 Midas Road
Malaga
Tel: +34 920 91917
Fax: +34 920 91918
Email: dcrane@iinet.net.au

USA
ARIZONA
Brian R Lee, CPA, PC
2101 E. Broadway Road
Suite 7
Tempe, Arizona 85282–1735
Tel: +1 48 077 40852
Fax: +1 48 077 40857

BOSTON
Michael M Truman CPA
60 State Street, 7th Floor
Boston, MA 02109
Tel: +1 87 733 01040
Fax: +1 61 766 36464
Email: info@mmtcpa.com

CALIFORNIA
John W Weldon CPA
11600 Washington Place
Suite 105
Los Angeles, CA 90066
Tel: +1 310 390 7487
Fax: +1 310 390 7489
Email: jweldoncpa@
johnweldoncpa.com

FLORIDA
Newman & Associates, PA
707 East Colonial Drive
Orlando, FL 32803
Tel: +1 407 228 0700
Email: info@
orlando-accounting.com

NEW YORK
BDM Rosner, LLC
73–23 179th Street
Fresh Meadows, NY 11366
Tel: +1 718 578 9500
Fax: +1 718 732 2242
Email: info@bdmllc.com

WASHINGTON DC
J Dantini & Company
13015 NE 85th Street
Kirkland, WA 98033
Tel: +1 425 828 3611
Fax: +1 425 822 2327
Email: edantini@yahoo.com

Architects

AUSTRALIA
ADELAIDE
Woodhead International
26–28 Chesser Street
Adelaide
South Australia, 5000
Tel: +61 822 35013
Fax: +61 882 320 028

BRISBANE
Peddle Thorp Architects
Level 29 AMP Place
10 Eagle Street
Brisbane, QLD 4000
Tel: +61 073 228 6200
Fax +61 073 228 6201

MELBOURNE
Selwyn Blackstone
Architect
P.O. Box 8670, Armadale
Victoria, 3143
Tel: +61 3 956 36148
Fax: +61 3 950 56578
Email: selblack@
netspace.net.au

PERTH
Hart Architects
Level 2, 132 Murray Street
Perth, WA 6000
Tel: +61 893 266 830
Fax: +61 893 264 886
Email: team@
hartarchitects.com.au

SYDNEY
Davenport Campbell
Level 4, 122 Pitt Street
Sydney, NSW 2000
Tel: +61 28233 5600
Fax: +61 28233 5601

BELGIUM
BRUGES
Archimago
Damse Vaart Zuid 79
B–8310 Sint Kruis Brugge
Tel: +32 503 51077
Email: info@archimago.be

BRUSSELS
Modulo Architects
Chemin des Deux Maisons
Tweehuizen Weg
Brussels
Tel: +32 277 68100
Fax: +32 277 68109

CANADA
MONTREAL
Saucier and Perrotte
Architects
110 Jean-Talon West
Montreal
Qeubec
H2R 2X1
Tel: +1 514 273 1700
Email: spa@
saucierperrotte.com

TORONTO
William R Dewson
135 Alcorn Avenue
Toronto
Ontario
M5V IE5
Tel: +1 416 966 6635
Email: dewon@dewson.com

VANCOUVER
Patkau Architects
1564 West 6th Ave
Vancouver BC
V6J 1R2
Tel: +1 604 683 7633
Fax: +1 604 683 7634
Email: info@patkau.ca

CHINA
SHANGHAI
Adrianse Group Ltd
3003 United Plaza
1468 Nanjing Road West
Shanghai 200040
Tel: +86 216 247 3883
Email:shanghai@
adrianse.com

DUBAI
DUBAI
Al Khatib Cracknell
Landscape Architects
PO BOX 23563
Dubai
Tel: +97 143 445 417
Email: cracknel@
emirates.net.ae

FRANCE
PERIGNAC
French Architectural
Services
Le Maine Arnaud
Perignac
Tel + 33 545 240 825
www.french-architectural-
services@netfirms.com

LYON
Iain Stewart
8 Rue Pailleron
69004 Lyon
Tel: +33 478 300 192

LIMOUX
Robert Lyell Architects
4 Allée des Marronniers
11300 Limoux
Tel: +33 468 312 566

GERMANY
FRANKFURT
Architekturbüro PEAF
Sophienstr. 73
60487 Frankfurt am Main
Tel: +49 697 075 435
Email: peaf@peaf.de
www.peaf.de

MUNICH
Münchener Hausbau
Westermühlstr. 3
80469 München
Tel: +49 892 322 5850
Email: info@mhausbau.de
www.mhausbau.de

HONG KONG
Dennis Lau and NG Chun
Architects and Engineers
Hennessy Centre
500 Hennessy Road
Hong Kong
Tel: +85 228 956 888
Email: general@dln.com.hk
www.dln.com.hk

IRELAND
DUBLIN
Bucholz McEvoy Architects
Mountpleasant
Industrial Estate
Mountpleasant Avenue
Dublin 6
Tel: +35 301 496 6340
Email: info@bmcea.com

ITALY
FLORENCE
De vita e fici Architects
Via fra'g. angelico 71
50121 Florence
Tel/Fax: +39 055 247 7464
Email: info@devitaefici.it

MILAN
Matteo Thun
Via Appiani
20121 Milan
Tel: +39 02 655691
Email: info@matteothun.com

ROME
Architetti Associati
Pennella Pisco Esercizio
Professione Architetto
Via Botticelli Sandro, 1
00196 Roma
Tel: +39 632 00419

SKI RESORTS
Bich Enrico – Architetto
Via Innocenzo V Papa, 12/A
11100 Aosta
Tel: +39 165 43967

JAPAN
OSAKA
Kaito gumi
1544 Nagataki
Izumisano
Osaka 598–0034
Tel:+81 072 465 1878
www.kaito-gumi.com

TOKYO
Dasic Architects Inc.
2–3–3 Nishihara
Shibuya-Ku
Tokyo 151 0066
Tel: +81 354 655 155
Email: mail@dasic.com

LUXEMBOURG
LUXEMBOURG
Alain Leer Architectes
2016 Luxembourg
Tel: +35 226 473 723
Email: a-leer@architecte.lu
www.alainleer.lu

NETHERLANDS
AMSTERDAM
A+D+P Architecten
Kerkstraat 130
1017 HC Amsterdam
Tel: +31 206 233 391
Email: info@
adp-architecten.nl

ROTTERDAM
MacCreanor Lavington
Architects
Vijverhofstraat 47
3032 SB Rotterdam
Tel: +31 010 443 9060
Email: nl@
maccreanorlavington.com

NEW ZEALAND
AUCKLAND
Grant Neill Architects
3 Elizabeth Street Warkworth
PO Box 55 Warkworth
Tel: +64 942 59200
Fax: +64 942 59204
Email: gneill@xtra.co.nz

CHRISTCHURCH
Loxodonta Architecture
Level 2, 106 Gloucester Street
PO Box 10–176
Christchurch
Tel: +64 337 7 5015
Fax: +64 337 7 5016
Email: marcus@
loxoarchitecture.com

WELLINGTON
TSE GROUP
Wellington Manthel Building
23 Taranaki Street
Box 6643
Wellington
Tel: +64 438 42029
Fax: +64 438 45065
Email: admin@wgtn.tse.co.nz

SOUTH AFRICA
CAPE TOWN
Joshua and Joshua Ltd
6th Floor, Ledger House
Aden Avenue
Athlone 7764
Cape Town
Tel: +27 216 967 460
Fax:+27 216 968 522
Email: response@josharch.co.za

DURBAN
Robert Johnson Architects
and Associates
127 Essenwood Road
Musgrave
Durban, KwaZulu Natal 4001
Tel: +27 312 013 538
Fax: +27 312 022 162
Email: archirob@mweb.co.za

JOHANNESBURG
Archen Architecture
PO Box 2164
Bedfordview 2008
Johannesburg
Tel: +27 114 551 941
Fax: +27 114 553 016
Email:neal@archen.co.za
edith@archen.co.za

SPAIN
ALMERIA
Paula Puente, Architektin
Tel/Fax: +34 950 529 429
Email: info@paulapuente.com

BARCELONA
Integral, SA – Consulting,
Engineering, Architecture
Avda. Pearson, 31
08034 Barcelona
Tel: +34 932 061 550
Fax: +34 932 060 410

MALAGA
Punta de Lanza
Calle Campanian 30
Malaga
Tel: +34 952 414 765

USA
ARIZONA
Gordon Rogers
Architecture Inc.
4318 E. Rancho Drive
Phoenix
AZ 85018
Tel: +1 602 952 9662
Email:grogers@
gordonrogers.com

CALIFORNIA
Scott Neeley &
Associates Architecture
515 G Street
Davis, CA 95616
Tel: +1 530 297 7680
Fax: +1 530 297 7656
Email:info@
neeleyarchitect.com

NEW YORK
Steven Holl Architects
450 West 31st Street
11th Floor
New York, NY 10001
Tel: +1 212 629 7262
Fax: +1 212 629 7312
Email: mail@stevenholl.com

WASHINGTON DC
SKB Architecture
and Design
1818 N Street, NW
Suite 510
Washington DC 20036
Tel: +1 202 332 2434
Fax: +1 202 328 4547

Banks and building societies

AUSTRALIA
BRISBANE
ANZ
192 Albert Street
Brisbane
Queensland, 4000
Tel: +61 396 839 999

MELBOURNE
Citibank Australia
Ground Floor
350 Collins Street
Melbourne VIC 3000

PERTH
Citibank Australia
Ground Floor
37 St Georges Terrace
Perth
WA, 6000

SYDNEY
Reserve Bank of Australia
GPO Box 3947
Sydney NSW 2001
Tel: +61 295 518 111
Email: rbainfo@rba.gov.au

BELGIUM
BRUGES
KBC Bank Belgium
VZW Kantcentrum
Peperstraat 3A
8000 Bruges
Tel: +32 503 30072
Fax: +32 503 30417

BRUSSELS
ING Belgium
Avenue Marnix 24
B–1000 Brussels
Tel: +32 254 72111
Fax: +32 254 73844
Email: info@ing.be
www.ing.be/bank

CANADA
TORONTO
TD Canada Trust Bank
Branch 1104
77 Bloor Street West
Toronto
Ontario, M5S1M2
Tel: +1 416 944 4115

VANCOUVER
TD Canada Trust Bank
Branch 94W756
3401 Cambie Street
Vancouver
BC V5Z2
Tel: +1 604 654 3135

CHINA
SHANGHAI
Bank of China
Zhong Yin Mansion
200 Yincheng Road
Pudong New Area
200120 Shanghai
Tel: +86 388 24588

DUBAI
DUBAI
Standard Bank London Ltd
Dubai Representative Office
16th Floor, Emirates Towers
PO Box 504904
Dubai
Tel: +97 143 30011
Fax: +97 143 300 169

FRANCE
BORDEAUX
John Siddall International
Parc Innolin
3 Rue de Golf 3370
Bordeaux
Merignax
Tel: +33 556 347 551

LILLE
ABBEY NATIONAL
Les Arcades de Flandre
70 Rue Saint Sauveur
59800 Lille
Tel: +33 320 181 818
www.abbey-national.fr

NICE
Simone Paissoni
22 Avenue Notre Dame
06000 Nice
Tel: +33 493 629 495

PARIS
HSBC Private Bank France
117 Ave Champs Elysées
F–75008 Paris
Tel: +33 144 861 861
www.hsbc.com

GERMANY
BERLIN
Berliner Bank
Hardenbergstr. 32
10623 Berlin
Tel: +49 302 45500
www.berliner-bank.de

FRANKFURT
Deutsche Bank
Tel: +49 699 1000,
0207 545 8000
www.db.com

MUNICH
Bayerische Landesbank
Brienner Str. 18
80333 München
Tel: +49 892 17101
www.bayernlb.de

HONG KONG
HSBC
Aberdeen Centre Branch
Shop 2, G/F, Site 1
Aberdeen Centre
Aberdeen
Hong Kong Island
Tel: +85 227 483 322
Fax: +85 225 530 173

IRELAND
DUBLIN
Anglo-Irish Bank
Dublin Head Office
Stephen Court
18/21 St. Stephen's Green
Dublin 2
Tel: +35 316 162 000
Fax: +35 316 162 488
Email:enquiries@
angloirishbank.ie

ITALY
FLORENCE
Gruppo Banca CR Florence
Viale Matteotti, 20
Firenze
Tel: +39 552 614 772

MILAN
Banca Popolare di Milano
Via L.Montegani, 2
Milan
Tel: +39 800 100 200

ROME
Bank of Rome
Via Roma, 142 0330
Acquapendente
01021 Rome
Tel: +39 848 690 405

JAPAN
TOKYO
Kookmin Bank Tokyo Branch
Yurakucho Denki Bldg,
N,14F,1–7–1
Yurakucho, Chiyoda-ku
Tokyo 100
Tel: +81 332 013 411
Fax: +81 232 013 410
Email:
kookmin@ma.kcom.ne.jp

LUXEMBOURG
LUXEMBOURG
ABN Amro Bank
46 Avenue JF Kennedy
1855 Luxembourg
Tel: +35 22 6071
www.abnamro.lu

NETHERLANDS
AMSTERDAM
Commerzbank NV
2501 Strawinskylaan
1077ZZ Amsterdam
Tel: +31 205 574 911

NEW ZEALAND
AUCKLAND
New Zealand
National Bank
Manukau City
Shop 1
Westfield Manukau City
Cnr Great South Road & Wiri
Station Road
PO Box 76051
Auckland
Tel: 0800 181 818

CHRISTCHURCH
New Zealand
National Bank
665 Colombo Street
PO Box 336
Christchurch
Tel: 0800 181 818
Fax: +64 336 46082

WELLINGTON
New Zealand
National Bank
88 Lambton Quay
188 Lambton Quay
PO Box 1393
Wellington
Tel: 0800 181 818
Fax: +64 449 86169

SOUTH AFRICA
Standard Bank of
South Africa
Customer Contact Centre
Tel: 0860 123 000
Tel: +27 112 994 701
Email: information@
standardbank.co.za

CAPE TOWN
Standard Bank of
South Africa
15 Adderley Street
Cape Town
Tel: +27 086 010 1341
Fax: +27 021 465 1875

DURBAN
Standard Bank of
South Africa
369 West Street
Durban
Tel: +27 086 010 1341
Fax: +27 313 042 494

JOHANNESBURG
Standard Bank of
South Africa
CNR Finch and Reier Road
Atlasville
Johannesburg
Tel: +27 011 395 1712
Fax: +27 011 395 1130

PRETORIA
Standard Bank of
South Africa
67 Gerrit Maritz Street
Pretoria
Tel: +27 125 200 220

SPAIN
Halifax International Ltd
PO Box 664
Halifax House
31–33 New Street
St. Helier Jersey, JE4 8YW
Channel Islands
Tel: 01534 613500

Lloyds TSB
Serrano 90
28006 Madrid
Tel: +34 915 209 980

USA
ARIZONA
Northern Trust
19432 RH Johnson Boulevard
Sun City West
AZ 85375–4420
Tel: +1 602 468 4400

BOSTON
Gannet Welsh
and Kotler LLC
222 Berkeley Street, 1500
Boston Massachusetts 02116
Tel: +1 212 495 1784

FLORIDA
The Bank of Florida
110 East Broward Boulevard
Fort Lauderdale
Florida 33301
Tel: +1 954 653 2000

NEW YORK
The Bank of New York Inc.
1 Wall Street
New York 10286
Tel: +1 212 495 1784

Builders and decorators

AUSTRALIA
ADELAIDE
Fairmont Homes Pty Ltd
21–24 North Terrace
Adelaide
South Australia 5000
Tel:+61 881 13112
Email: sales@
fairmonthomes.com.au

MELBOURNE
Porter Davis Prestige
163 Princes Highway
Hallam Victoria 3803
Tel: +61 387 861 200
Fax: +61 387 861 300
E-mail: info@
barrettgroup.com.au

PERTH
Metrostyle
69 Walters Drive
Osborne Park
Western Australia, 6017
Tel: +61 920 29200
Fax: +61 920 29201
Email: sales@metrostyle.net.au

SYDNEY
Sydney Extensions
and Designs
ABN 92 086 626 002
1/3 Gibbes Street
Chatswood NSW 2067
Tel: +61 298 822 448
Fax: +61 298 823 225
Email: info@
sydneyextensions.com

BELGIUM
ANTWERP
Amber & Partners NV
75 Boomsesteenweg
2610 Antwerp
Tel: +32 382 05909
www.amberbouwfonds.be

BRUSSELS
Conceptimo SA
4 Paviljoenstraat
1000 Brussels
Tel: +32 224 50250

CANADA
TORONTO
Danosh Construction Inc.
Mount Albert
Ontario
L0G 1MO
Tel: +1 905 473 6883

DUBAI
DUBAI
Al Naboodah Contracting
LLC
PO Box 4588
Dubai
Tel: +97 146 60272

FRANCE
Brit Consulting
29 Rue de Verdun
Tregeux
Côtes D'Armor
Tel: +33 623 863 021
www.britconsulting.com

Mark LaTour
11220 Rieux-en-Val
France
Tel: +33 468 200 294
www.diyinfrance.com

GERMANY
FRANKFURT
Treibs Bau GmbH
Heinrichstr 9–11
60327 Frankfurt
Tel: +49 697 500 100
www.treibs.de

MUNICH
ABS Alpa-Bau-Service GmbH
Nymphenburger Str. 111
80636 München
Tel: +49 891 211 0825
www.gmbh-abs.de

HONG KONG
Constructive Creation
Co. Ltd
Peddler Building
Central District
Tel: +85 225 238 691

IRELAND
DUBLIN
SMP Builders
13 Chapel Grove
Balbriggan
Co. Dublin
Tel: +35 387 777 0608

ITALY
BRESCIA
Irxes 95 SRL
Via aldo Maro 5
25100 Brescia
Tel: +39 302 420 316
www.irces95.it

JAPAN
TOKYO
Daioh Construction Co.
5–26–8 Higashi-oi
Shinagawa-ku
Tokyo
Tel: +81 334 711 431

LUXEMBOURG
LUXEMBOURG
Agence Immobilière Infralux
4 Rue de Hesperange
1731 Luxembourg
Tel: +35 249 18811
Email: infraluxconstruction@pt.lu

NETHERLANDS
AMSTERDAM
Mammoet Tapijten BNV
43 Sierplein
1065LN Amsterdam
Tel: +31 206 172 090

ROTTERDAM
Aantrekker LJ Den
95 Nieuwe Crooswijkseweg
3034PN Rotterdam
Tel: +31 104 136 270
www.aantrekker.com

NEW ZEALAND
AUCKLAND
AC Mason Ltd
PO Box 13–370
Onehunga
Auckland
Tel: +64 963 69795
Email: acmasoncont@xtra.co.nz

CHRISTCHURCH
David Magill Builder Ltd
PO Box 6028
Upper Riccarton
Christchurch 4
Tel: +64 334 93582
Email: magillbuilders@
signature.co.nz

WELLINGTON
Fendalton Construction Ltd
Unit 11, 5 Wakefield Street
Petone, Wellington
PO Box 48–163 Silverstream
Tel: +64 456 68940
Email: fendalton_construction
@paradise.net.nz

SOUTH AFRICA
CAPE TOWN
Batir Construction CC
39 Aristea Avenue
Cape Town
Tel: +27 219 133 017

SPAIN
BARCELONA
Construcciones y
Edificaciones SA
171 Provença
08036 Barcelona
Tel: +34 934 547 084

BENIDORM
Tellerola SL
2 Puente
03500 Benidorm
Tel: +33 965 852 504

MALAGA
Mastercare Associates
Calle Poeta Salvador Rueda 75
Los Boliches
29640 Fuengirola
Malaga
Tel: +34 670 034 245

USA
ARIZONA
AE Pete Lewis
& Sons Builders
1530 West Dunlap Avenue
Phoenix
85021 Arizona
Tel: +1 623 584 0484

BOSTON
Elite Builders Inc.
23 Oaklawn Street
New Bedford
MA 02744
Tel: +1 508 996 1000
www.elitebuildersma.com

CALIFORNIA
AAA United Builders Inc.
Tel: +1 866 222 8202
www.aaaunitedbuildersinc.ve
rizonsupersite.com

FLORIDA
Aaron Alexis Corporation
18800 Northwest 2nd Avenue
Miami, Florida, 33301
Tel: +1 954 895 0101

NEW YORK
Gothic Builders
400 East 70th Street
New York
10001 NY
Tel: +1 212 861 9881
www.gothicbuilders.com

WASHINGTON DC
EROC builders
1010 Wisconsin Avenue
Northwest
Washington DC 20007
Tel: +1 202 965 4441

Car hire

AUSTRALIA
MELBOURNE
Ascot Car Rental
399 Elizabeth Street
Melbourne
VIC, 3000
Tel: +61 800 887 007
Email: melbourne-city
@ascotcarrental.com.au
www.ascotcarrental.com.au

SYDNEY
Getabout Oz
810 George Street
Sydney NSW 2000
Tel: +61 800 656 899

BELGIUM
BRUSSELS
Avis
The Victoria Building
Harbour City, Salford Quays
Manchester, M5 2SP
Tel: 0870 606 0100

Hamou Abdelkader
207 Rue Dieudonné Lefèvre
1020 Bruxelles
Tel: +32 473 641 673
www.cherataxtransport.com

CANADA
Avis
The Victoria Building
Harbour city, Salford Quays
Manchester, M5 2SP
Tel: 0870 606 0100

CHINA
Avis
The Victoria Building
Harbour City, Salford Quays
Manchester, M5 2SP
Tel: 0870 606 0100

DUBAI
Avis Rent-a-Car
PO Box 6591 Dubai
Tel: +97 142 52121

FRANCE
Avis
The Victoria Building
Harbour City, Salford Quays
Manchester, M5 2SP
Tel: 0870 606 0100

Hertz Car Hire
23 Broadwater Road
Welwyn Garden City
Hertfordshire, AL7 3BQ
Tel: 0170 331 433

GERMANY
Internet Rental Car Group
5, Puerto Paraiso, Local 27
29680 Estepona, Malaga
Tel: 0870 240 1625
Fax: +34 952 884 666
info@rentalcargroup.com
www.germanycar.net

HONG KONG
Hertz Car Rental
Unit 1206
Queens Road Central
Hong Kong
Tel: +85 225 251 313
www.hertz.com

IRELAND
Anycarhire.com
Tel: 0870 720 0159
www.anycarehire.com/
car-hire/ireland.htm

ITALY
Anycarhire.com
Tel: 0870 720 0159
www.anycarehire.com

JAPAN
Hertz Car Rental
Aoyama Street
Shibuya
Tokyo
Tel: +81 800 2000

LUXEMBOURG
Anycarhire.com
Tel: 0870 720 0159
www.anycarehire.com/
car-hire/luxembourg.htm

NETHERLANDS
**Budget Chauffeur
Drive BV 1/15**
8 Modemstraat
1033RW Amsterdam
Tel: 0206 314 721
Email: info@chauffeurdrive.nl
www.chauffeurdrive.nl

NEW ZEALAND
AUCKLAND
AVIS Rent-a-Car
Auckland Airport
Mangere – AKL
Terminal Building
Auckland
tel: +64 927 57239

CHRISTCHURCH
A Basic Car Rental
31 Moorhouse Avenue
Christchurch
Tel: +64 336 50339
Fax: +64 336 50379
www.abcrentals.co.nz

WELLINGTON
Avis Rent a Car
Wellington Airport – WLG
Terminal Building
Wellington
Tel: +64 480 21088

SOUTH AFRICA
Avis Cape Town
Cape Town
International Airport
Tel: +27 219 340 330

SPAIN
MALAGA
**Barrio Moreno Maria
del Carmen**
8 Rguez Vega
28025 Madrid
Tel: +34 915 250 324

Helle Hollis Car Rental
Malaga Airport
Avda Garcia Morato 14
29004 Malaga
Tel: +34 952 245 544

USA
Avis Los Angeles
9217 Airport Blvd
90045 Los Angeles
Tel: +1 310 646 5600

Avis Phoenix
Sky Harbour
International Airport
PO Box 21007
85034 Phoenix
Tel: +1 602 273 3222

Avis Washington DC
Ronald Reagan
National Airport
20001 Washington DC
Tel: +1 703 419 5815

Currency converters

Caxton FX
2 Motcomb Street
London SW1X 8JU
Tel: 0845 658 2223
Email: sales@caxtonfx.com
www.caxtonfx.com

CMC PLC
66 Prescott Street
London E1 8HG
Tel: 0800 093 3633
Email: info@cmcforex.co.uk

Conti Financial Services
204 Church Road
Hove, East Sussex
BN3 2DJ
Tel: 0800 970 0985
www.mortgagesoverseas.com

Currencies4Less
160 Brompton Road
Knightsbridge
London, SW3 1HW
Tel: 0207 594 0594
Email: info@
currencies4less.com
www.currencies4less.com

Currencies Direct
Hanover House
73–74 High Holborn
London, WV1V 6LR
Tel: 0207 813 0332
Email: london@
currenciesdirect.com
www.currenciesdirect.com

Currency Solutions
Tel: 0208 850 2266

Currency UK
1 Battersea Bridge
London, SW11 3BZ
Tel: 0207 738 0777

Escape Currency
Escape House
45 Buckingham Street
Bucks, HP20 2NQ
Tel: 01296 339 811
Email: sales@
escapecurrency.com
www.escapecurrency.com

Foreign Currency Direct
The Old Malt House
Currencies Court
5 The Broadway
Old Amersham
Buckinghamshire, HP7 0HL
Tel: 0800 328 5884
Email: sales@currencies.co.uk
www.ukcurrencies.co.uk

FX Solutions
FX Solutions House
4 Victoria Works
Fairway, Petts Wood
Kent, BR5 1EG
Tel: 01689 601111
www.fxsolutions.co.uk

Halo Financial Ltd
5 Port House
Plantation Wharf
London, SW11 3TY
Tel: 0207 3505474
www.halofinancial.com

HIFX plc
59–60 Thames Street
Windsor
Berkshire, SL4 1TX
Tel: 01753 859 159
www.hifx.co.uk

ISXFX
869 Romford Road
London, E12 5JY
Tel: 0208 911 9553
Email: info@isxfx.com
www.isxfx.com

MoneyCorp
100 Brompton Road
Knightsbridge
London, SW3 1ER
Tel: 0207 589 3000
Email: enquiries@
moneycorp.com
www.moneycorp.com

Secure Currencies Ltd
363A Crofton Road
Locksbottom
Orpington
Kent, BR6 8NR
Tel: 01689 860 007
www.secure-currencies.com

SGM FX
Prince Rupert House
64 Queen Street
London, EC4R 1AD
Tel: 0207 778 0234

Sterling Exchange Ltd
45 Ludgate Hill
London, EC4M 7JU
Tel: 0207 329 9977
www.sterlingexchange.co.uk

Worldwide Currencies Ltd
1st Floor, Newman House
Leonard Road
Bromley
Kent, BR1 1RJ
Tel: 0208 464 5888
Email: info@
worldwidecurrencies.com

Financial services

1–2 Call Finance Limited
19 Bentalls Centre
Colchester Road
Heybridge
Essex, CM9 4GD
Tel: 01621 843 599

**Blevins Franks Financial
Management**
Barbican House
26–34 Old Street
London, EC1V 9QQ
Tel: 0207 336 1000
www.blevinsfranks.com

Camelot Realty
150 Minories
London, EC3N 1CS
Tel: 0207 264 2162

Charles Hamer
87 Park Street
Thame
Oxfordshire, OX9 3HX
Tel: 01844 218 956

Conti Financial Services
204 Church Road
Hove
East Sussex, BN3 2DJ
Tel: 01273 772811
Email: enquiries@contifs.com
www.mortgagesoverseas.com

Euronext.liffe
Cannon Bridge House
1 Cousin Lane
London EC4R 3XX
Tel: 0207 623 0444
www.liffe.com

Fralex
4 Wimpole Street
London, W1G 9SH
Tel: 0207 323 0103

Frank Hitchcock
Highfield House
White Horse Road
Holly Hill, Meopham
Kent, DA13 0UB
Tel: 01634 245 511

K2 Consulting
44 Avenue Road
London, N12 8PY
Tel: 0208 922 7880
Email: ktwoconsulting
@aol.com

MFS Partners
Grosvenor House
47 Alma Road
Plymouth
Devon, PL3 4HE
Tel: 01752 664 777

Montford International PLC
Home Farm
Shere Road
Albury
Guildford
Surrey, GU5 9BL
Tel: 08000183571
www.miplc.co.uk

Templeton Associates
3 Gloucester Street
Bath, BA1 2SE
Tel: 01225 422 282

The 4less Group PLC
160 Brompton Road
Knightsbridge
London, SW3 1HW
Tel: 0207 594 0525
www.the4lessgroup.com
Email: ah@currencies4less.com

UK EXPAT Ltd
Holly Bank
Chalkhouse Green Road
Kidmore End
South Oxfordshire, RG4 9AU
Tel: 0118 924 2724
www.ukexpat.net

AUSTRALIA
MELBOURNE
**Australian Financial
Services**
87 York Street
South Melbourne
VIC 3205
Tel: +61 396 822 566
Email: info@afsl.com.au
www.afsl.com.au

SYDNEY
Fin Investment Solutions
Suite 8, level 3
88 Pitt Street
Sydney
NSW 2000
Tel: +61 292 390 011
www.finsolutions.com.au
gcaredes@finsolutions.com.au

BELGIUM
JD Financial Services
Koestraat 2
9940 Evergem
Tel: +32 494 500 406

CANADA
TORONTO
Freedom 55 Financial
110–330 University Avenue
Toronto
Ontario
M5G 1R8
Tel: +1 416 366 2971
www.freedom55financial.com

VANCOUVER
Freedom 55 Financial
Suite 1200
111 West Georgia Street
Vancouver
Tel: +1 604 685 6521
www.freedom55financial.com

CHINA
BEIJING
**Changsheng Fund
Management Co.**
Beijing
Tel: +86 106 468 9198

DUBAI
DUBAI
KPMG
PO Box 3800 Dubai
Tel: +97 143 10222

FRANCE
LILLE
Abbey National
Les Arcades de Flandre
70 Rue Saint Sauveur
59046 Lille Cedex
Tel: +33 320 181 818

PARIS
Porter & Reeves
5 Rue Cambon
75001 Paris
Tel: +33 142 615 577

GERMANY
FRANKFURT
**AIG Financial Advisor
Services SA**
Gervinusstr. 18–22
60332 Frankfurt
Tel: +49 69 719 100

MUNICH
Allianz
Knorrstr. 20
80807 München
Tel: +49 89 304 052
www.allianz.de
Email: frank.jendrzytza@
allianz.de

HONG KONG
**HSBC Trinkaus Investment
Management Ltd**
Room 1402, Henley Building
5 Queens Road Central
Hong Kong
Tel: +85 222 402 688
Email: hiatri@hkstar.com

IRELAND
DUBLIN
Power Lynch & Associates
81 Lr. Kilmacud Road
Sillorgan
Co. Dublin
Tel: +35 212 100 004
www.powerlynch.com

ITALY
ROME
BNF SRL
Vl. Giulio Cesare 128
00192 Roma
Tel: +39 637 00087
www.bnf.it

Gestit Services
Via Zoe Fontana 220
00131 Roma
Tel: +39 641 780 098
www.gestitservices.it

JAPAN
TOKYO
**American Express Financial
Advisors Japan**
Landmark Plaza
1–6–7 Shiba Koen
Minato-Ku, Tokyo
Tel: +81 354 700 940

LUXEMBOURG
LUXEMBOURG
Deloitte SA
Rte. D'Arlon 3
8009 Strassen
Luxembourg
Tel: +35 242 1241

NETHERLANDS
DGA Financieel Adviseurs
De Ruyterstr. 24
4335GM Middelburg
Tel: +31 800 022 1415
www.direktgeldadvies.nl

NEW ZEALAND
AUCKLAND
**Future Plan
Financial Services**
26 William Pickering Dve
Albany, Auckland
Tel: +64 941 41882

WELLINGTON
Crest Financial Brokers
Lower Hutt Office
Level 4, Crest House
92–100 Queens Drive
Tel: +64 456 04595
Email: crest@crestbrokers.co.nz

SOUTH AFRICA
CAPE TOWN
Financial Administrators
Picbel Parcadd
Strand Street
Foreshore
Cape Town
Tel: +27 124 180 704

PRETORIA
Abacus Financial Services
58 Middle Hill Road
Pretoria
Tel: +27 126 676 163

SPAIN
ALICANTE
**Lee Hodges
Financial Services**
Box 382
Ctra Cabo la Nao 71–6
03730 Jávea
Alicante
Tel: +34 965 771 500
Email: leehodges@wanadoo.es
www.lhfs-online.com

MALAGA
**Henry Woods Investment
Management**
Calle Azorin 4
296000 Marbella
Malaga, Spain
Tel: +34 965 771 500

USA
BOSTON
**Adviser Investment
Management**
42 Pleasant Street
Watertown MA 02472–2316
Tel: +1 617 926 3582

CALIFORNIA
Skadden
525 University Avenue
Suite 1100
Palo Alto
California 94301
Tel: +1 650 470 4500
www.skadden.com

NEW YORK
Sierra Financial Advisers
900 3rd Avenue
New York
NT 10022–4728
Tel: +1 212 610 2600

WASHINGTON DC
Skadden
1440 New York Avenue NW
Washington DC 20005
Tel: +1 202 371 7000
www.skadden.com

Insurance

AUSTRALIA
MELBOURNE
CGU Insurance
Tel: +61 213 1532
Email: mail@cgu.com.au
www.cgu.com.au

SYDNEY
**Rose Stanton
Insurance Brokers**
11/299 Pacific Hwy North
Sydney, NSW 2060
Tel: +61 299 576 090
Email: sroseins@roseins.com.au
www.rosestanton.com.au

BELGIUM
**ACE European Group
Limited VBR**
9 Rue Belliard
1040 Bruxelles
Tel: +32 251 69711
Email: info.uk@ace-ina.com
www.aceeurope.com

CANADA
**Allstate Insurance
Company of Canada**
27 Allstate Parkway, Suite 100
Markham, Ontario L3R 5P8
Tel: +1 905 477 6900
www.allstate.ca

CHINA
Allianz Dazhong
16F China Merchants Tower
161 Lujiazui Road
Shanghai 200120
Tel: +86 215 879 8828
www.allianzdazhong.com

DUBAI
**Royal International
Insurance**
PO Box 1076 Dubai
Tel: +97 143 10535

FRANCE
**Insurance for
Homes Abroad**
28 Waterloo Street
Weston-Super-Mare
Tel: 01934 424 040

PARIS
Agence Tredinnick
12 Rue Dupy
16100 Cognac
Tel: +33 545 824 293

**Anglo French
Underwriters**
25 Rue de Liege
75008 Paris
Tel: +33 144 707 100

Lloyds of London
4 Rue des Petits Peres
75002 Paris
Tel: +33 142 604 343

GERMANY
**Insurance for
Homes Abroad**
28 Waterloo Street
Weston-Super-Mare
Tel: 01934 424 040

**Schofield's Holiday
Home Insurance**
Trinity House
7 Institute Street
Bolton, Lancashire
Tel: 01204 365 080
www.schofields.ltd.uk

HONG KONG
**American International
Assurance Co.**
AIA Building
1 Stubbs Road
Hong Kong
Tel: +85 228 321 800
www.aia.com.hk

IRELAND
123.ie
Suite 3, The Mall
Beacon Court
Sandyford
Dublin 18
Tel: + 35 318 502 22123
Email: info@123.ie

Sogecore Ireland Ltd
10, Mount Street Lower
Dublin 2
Tel: +35 316 619 100
Email: butler@sogecore.ie
www.captive-management.
com/europe_ireland.html

ITALY
Andrew Copeland Group
230 Portland Road
Woodside
London, SE25 4SL
Tel: 020 865 62544

JAPAN
X-Pat
5F Nikko Building
3–2–11 Minamihonmachi
Chuo-Ku
Osaka
Tel: +81 662 810 878
www.x-pat.net

LUXEMBOURG
**Agence D'Assurance
Flener Steve**
131 av. de Luxembourg
4940 Bascharage
Tel: +35 226 502 525

NETHERLANDS
Andrew Copeland Group
230 Portland Rd
Woodside
London, SE25 4SL
Tel: 0208 656 2544

Semmoh JF
1319 Pieter Calandlaan
1069RE Amsterdam
Tel: +31 206 671 011
www.sfa.nl

NEW ZEALAND
AUCKLAND
Auckland City Brokers
PO Box 56–082
Dominion Road
Mt Eden
Tel: +64 963 86206

CHRISTCHURCH
KSL Financial
Freepost 760
Christchurch
Tel: +64 336 54460
Fax: +64 337 72367

WELLINGTON
Crest Financial Brokers
Lower Hutt Office
Level 4, Crest House
92–100 Queens Drive
Tel: +64 456 04595
Email: crest@crestbrokers.co.nz

SOUTH AFRICA
Allianz Insurance Ltd
33 Baker Street
Rosebank
Johannesburg 2107
Tel: +27 112 804 300
www.allianz.co.za

SPAIN
**Insurance for
Homes Abroad**
28 Waterloo Street
Weston-Super-Mare
BS23 1LN
01934 424 040

MADRID
ACE Insurance SANV
13 Fco. Gervas
28020 Madrid
Tel: +34 915 563 600

MALAGA
Knight Insurance Brokers
Edif. Lance del Sol 10, 1a
Avda. Jesus Santos, Rein s/n
Los Boliches
29640 Fuengirola
Malaga, Spain
Tel: +34 9 52 66 05 35

USA
FLORIDA
All Purpose Insurance
1206 N Mills Avenue
Orlando Florida 32803
Tel: +1 407 855 5992

Sihle Insurance Group
871 Douglas Avenu
Altamonte Springs
Florida 32714
Tel: +1 407 869 0962

Language
services

BELGIUM
Linkword Languages
54 Mansel Street
Swansea, SA1 5TE
Tel: 01792 462 002
www.linkwordlanguages.com

CHINA
**School of Oriental and
African Studies**
Thornhaugh Street
Russell Square
London, WC1H 0XG
Tel: 0207 898 4888
Emai:languages@soas.ac.uk
www.soas.ac.uk

FRANCE
NICE
Idiom
4 Boulevard de Cimiez
Nice
Tel: +33 493 926 090
www.idiom.fr

PARIS
British Institute in Paris
9–11 Rue de Constantine
75007 Paris
Tel: +33 144 117 373

Linkword Languages
54 Mansel Street
Swansea, SA1 5TE
Tel: 01792 462 002
www.linkwordlanguages.com

Promolangues
8 Rue Blanche
75009 Paris
Tel: +33 142 851 945

GERMANY
**Commercial Language
Training**
Derbyshire
Tel: 01629 732 653
Email: info@
languagetraining.com

Linkword Languages
54 Mansel Street
Swansea, SA1 5TE
Tel: 01792 462 002
www.linkwordlanguages.com

ITALY
Linkword Languages
54 Mansel Street
Swansea, SA1 5TE
Tel: 01792 462 002
www.linkwordlanguages.com

Timothy Petrocchi
84 St Andrews Road
Portslade, BN41 1DE
East Sussex
Tel: 01273 412 933
Mobile: 07718 826832
Email: tim.petrocchi@
btinternet.com

JAPAN
Linkword Languages
54 Mansel Street
Swansea, SA1 5TE
Tel: 01792 462 002
www.linkwordlanguages.com

LUXEMBOURG
Linkword Languages
54 Mansel Street
Swansea, SA1 5TE
Tel: 01792 462 002
www.linkwordlanguages.com

NETHERLANDS
Linkword Languages
54 Mansel Street
Swansea, SA1 5TE
Tel: 01792 462 002
www.linkwordlanguages.com

SPAIN
BBC Languages
Room A3022
Woodlands, 80 Wood Lane
London, W12 0TT
Tel: 0208 433 3135

Brian Treneman
Puerta del Sol
Freepost
Lon 295
Bristol, BS1 6FA
Tel: 0800 833 257

Linkword Languages
54 Mansel Street
Swansea, SA1 5TE
Tel: 01792 462 002
www.linkwordlanguages.com

Legal advice and solicitors

Ashley Law
30–32 Staines Road
Hounslow
Middlesex, TW3 3LZ
Tel: 0500 104 106
Email: enquiries@
ashleylaw.co.uk
www.ashleylaw.co.uk

Baily Gibson
5 Station Parade
Beaconsfield
Bucks, HP9 2PG
Tel: 01494 672 661
Email: beaconsfield@
bailygibson.co.uk
www.bailygibson.co.uk

James Bennett and Co. Solicitors
Nightingale House
Brighton Road
Crawley
West Sussex, RH10 6AE
Tel: 01293 544 044

Bennett and Co.
144 Knutsford Road
Wilmslow
Cheshire, SK9 6JP
Tel: 01625 586 937
Email: internationallawyers
@bennett-and-co.com
www.bennett-and-co.com

Blake Lapthorn
Holbrook House
14 Great Queen Street
London, WC2B 5DG
Tel: 0207 430 1709

Champion Miller and Honey Solicitors
15 High Street
Tenterden
Kent, TN30 6JT
Tel: 01580 762 251
Email: cmhspain@aol.com

De Pinna Notaries
35 Piccadilly
London, W1J 0LJ
Tel: 0207 208 2900
Email: info@depinna.co.uk
www.depainna.co.uk

Fox Hayes
Bank House
150 Roundhay Road
Leeds, LS8 5LD
Tel: 0113 209 8922

International Property Law Centre
Unit 2 Waterside Park
Livingstone Road
Hessle, HU13 0EG
Tel: 01482 350 850
Email: internationalproperty
@maxgold.com
www.international
propertylaw.com

John Howell and Co.
English Solicitors and
International Lawyers
The Old Glass Works
22 Endell Street
Covent Garden
London, WC2H 9AD
Tel: 0207 420 0400
www.europelaw.com

MB Law
King Charles House
King Charles Croft
Leeds, LS1 6LA
Tel: 0113 242 4444

Taylors
The Red Brick House
28–32 Trippet Lane
Sheffield, S1 4EL
Tel: 0114 276 6767

AUSTRALIA
Andersons Solicitors
185 Victoria Square
Adelaide, SA5000
Tel: +61 882 386 666

Michell Sillar McPhee
Level 3
Allendale Square
77 St Georges Terrace
Perth, WA 6000
Tel: +61 892 256 066
Email: mjm@msm.com.au
www.msm.com.au

BELGIUM
Billiet & Co. Lawyers
Avenue Louise 148 bte. 2
B–1050 Brussels
Tel: +32 264 33301
Email: info@billiet-co.be
www.billiet-co.com

CANADA
Brawn Douglas H Barrister & Solicitor
15245 Russell Avenue
White Rock
Vancouver
British Columbia
V4B 5CE
Tel: +1 604 542 5344

Singer, Kwinter Barristers & Solicitors
1033 Bay Street
Suite 214
Toronto
Ontario, M55 3A5
Tel: +1 416 961 2882
www.singerkwinter.com

CHINA
Allen & Overy
Unit 518, Tower 2
Bright China Chong
An Building
7 Jianguomennei Dajie
Doncheng district
Beijing
Tel: +86 106 510 2368
www.allenovery.com

DUBAI
Berrymans Solicitors & Legal Consultants
PO Box 9204 Dubai
Tel: +97 143 064 768

FRANCE
PARIS
Conseil Supérieur du Notariat
31 Rue du General Foy
75008 Paris
Tel: +33 144 903 000
www.notaires.fr

GERMANY
Baker and McKenzie
Rechtsanwälte
Bethmannstr 50–54
60311 Frankfurt
Tel: +49 692 99080
www.bakernet.com

HONG KONG
Liau, Ho & Chan Solicitors and Notaries
6F United Chinese
Bank Building
31–37 Des Voeux Rd Central
Hong Kong
Tel: +85 225 212 486
Email: admin@lhc.com.hk
www.lhc.com.hk

IRELAND
Thomas Byrne & Co. Solicitors
78 Walkinstown Road
Dublin
Tel: +35 31450 3633
Email: tbyrne@
thomasbyrnesolicitors.com

ITALY
Coudert Brothers
Viale Liegi 28
Rome 00198
Tel: +39 068 841 713
www.coudert.com

JAPAN
Wada LATS
3–5–3–1402 Nishi-Shinjuku
Shinjuku-Ku
Tokyo
Tel: +81 333 457 977
www.wada-lats.com

LUXEMBOURG
Mr Jacques Wolter
11 Avenue Guillame
1651 Luxembourg
Tel: +35 226 442 644

NETHERLANDS
Blenheim
Blenheim Tower
Westerdoksdijk 40
1013AE Amsterdam
Tel: +31 205 210 100
www.blenheim.nl

NEW ZEALAND
AUCKLAND
Stevenson Campbell Lawyers
National Bank Building
65 Clyde Road
Browns Bay
Tel: +64 947 70388
Email: baylaw@baylaw.co.nz

CHRISTCHURCH
Clark Boyce
104 Victoria St Christchurch
Tel: +64 337 94420

WELLINGTON
Gilbert Swan
49 Boulcott Street
PO Box 10–530
Wellington
Tel: +64 447 20165
www.gilbertswan.co.nz

SOUTH AFRICA
Erwee Attorneys
9 Urvin Street
Musina 0900
Tel: +27 515 343 394

SPAIN
All About Spain
104 Corn Exchange
Fenwick Street
Liverpool, L2 7QL
Tel: +44 151 236 6058
Email: info@
allaboutspain.co.uk
www.allaboutspain.co.uk

John Howell and Co.
English Solicitors and
International Lawyers
The Old Glass Works
22 Endell Street
Covent Garden
London, WC2H 9AD
Tel: 0207 420 0400
www.europelaw.com

ALMERIA
Mar Salas Pradas
Casas Almeria
Urb. Costa Fleming
04600 Huercal-Overa
Almeria, Spain
Tel: +34 450 134 434

MADRID
Adarve Corporacion Juridicia
Calle Francisco de Riojas 2
Madrid, Spain
Tel: +34 915 913 060

MALAGA
Viva Costa
Apartado de Correos 228
29740 Torre del Mar
Malaga, Spain
Tel: +34 495 251 3648

USA
FLORIDA
Baker and Hostetler
Sun Trust Center, Suite 2300
200 South Orange Avenue
Orlando
Florida 32801 3432
Tel: +1 407 649 4000
Email: infor@bakerlaw.com

Beggs and Lane
501 Commendencia Street
PO Box 12950
Pensacola
Florida 32801 3432
Tel: +1 850 432 2451

Medical services

AUSTRALIA
Department of Health
GPO Box 9848
Canberra ACT 2601
Tel: +61 262 891 555
www.health.gov.au

BELGIUM
Institut Medical Edith Cavell
Rue Edith Cavell 32
1180 Brussels
Tel: +32 234 04040

CANADA
Health Canada
A.L. 0900C2
Ottawa K1A 0K9
Tel: +1 613 957 2991
Email: info@hc-sc.gc.ca
www.hc-sc.gc.ca

CHINA
Center for Disease Control for China
27 Nan Wei Road
Beijing 100050
PRC
Tel: +86 106 302 2960
www.chinacdc.net.cn

DUBAI
Al Moussa Medical Centre
Tel: +97 143 452 999

FRANCE
Clinique du Louvre
17 Rue des Prêtres
Saint-Germain l'Auxerrois
75001 Paris
Tel: +33 148 626 712

GERMANY
Bürgerhospital Frankfurt-am-Main
Nibelungenallee 37–41
60318 Frankfurt-am-Main
Tel: +49 691 500 281

HONG KONG
Medical Web
Tel: +85 225 783 833
Email: hkmw@
medicom.com.hk
www.medicine.org.hk

IRELAND
Mater Hospital
Tel: +35 318 032 000

ITALY
Hospital San Raffaele
Via Olgettina 60
Milan
Tel: +39 022 6431
www.sanraffaele.org

JAPAN
National Hospital Organisation
Osaka National Hospital
2–1–14 Hoenzaka
Chuo-Ku
Osaka City
Osaka
Tel: +81 669 421 331

NEW ZEALAND
Hills Road Medical Centre
196 Hills Rd Shirley
Christchurch
Tel: +64 338 53015

Radius Health Group Limited
Ground Floor
12 Viaduct Harbour Ave
Auckland
Tel: +64 935 31160
Email: reception@
radiushealth.co.nz

Wellness Consultants Ltd
Level 4
Williams & Adams building
72–82 Taranaki Street
PO Box 14–405
Wellington
Tel: +64 480 17395

SOUTH AFRICA
Groote Schurr Hospital
Tel: +27 21 761 6202

SPAIN
Aycke OA Smook MD
Euroclinica Rncon
Calle Severo Ochoa 6
03503 Benidorm, Spain
Tel: +34 966 830 849

BUPA International
Apartado de Correos 16
29120 Alhurin El Grande
Malaga, Spain
Tel: +34 952 491 115

Morgan Price International Healthcare
2nd Floor, Bush House
Queen's Square
Attleborough
Norfolk, NR17 2AF
Tel: 01953 458 040

USA
Department of Health
Orlando
Florida 32801
Tel: +1 407 836 2600

Mortgage brokers

Alexander Hall
32 Grosvenor Square
Mayfair
London, W1K 2HJ
Tel: 0207 659 8916
Email: info@
alexanderhall.co.uk
www.alexanderhall.co.uk

Balla Brokers
29 Victoria Street
Douglas
Isle of Man, IM1 2LG
Tel: 0800 652 4410
Email: enquiry@
ballabrokers.com
www.ballabrokers.com

Bennet Sebastian
www.bennetsebastian.com
Email: bsebastian@cfl.rr.com

Commercial and Domestic Mortgages
Willow Tree Cottage
Gloucester Lane
Mickelton
Gloucester
Gloucestershire, GL55 6RP
Tel: 01386 430 000
Email:geoff.hemmings@
btopenworld.com
www.commercialand
domesticmortgages.co.uk

Conti Financial Services
204 Church Road
Hove
East Susex, BN3 2DJ
Tel: 0800 970 0985
Email: enquiries@
conti-financial.com
www.overseasandukfinance.com

CTD Mortgages Ltd
PO Box 267
Christchurch
New Zealand
Tel: +64 332 39887
Email:enquiries@ctd.co.nz

European Mortgage Company
10 Atlanta Boulevard
Romford
Essex, RM1 1TB
Tel: 01708 749 494

First Mortgage Service
Kingstons House
15 Coombe Road
Kingston
Surrey, KT2 7AD
Tel: 0800 689 0077

HIFX PLC
59–60 Thames Street
Windsor
Berkshire, SL4 1TX
Tel: 01753 859 159
www.hifx.co.uk

International Mortgages
PO Box 118
Elan House
Berwick upon Tweed
TD15 1XA
Tel: 870 787 5100
Email: info@
internationalmortgages.net

International Mortgage Plans
101 Benedict Street
Glastonbury
Somerset, BA6 9NQ
Tel: 01458 835 302
www.internationalmortgage
services.com

International Property Network
Tel: 01733 206 628
Email: property@
yourmoneynow.com
www.international-
mortgage-network.com

JD Mortgages
PO Box 28784
London, E18 1XY
Tel: 0208 532 2933

Kevin Sewell Mortgages
7a Bath Road Business Park
Devizes
Wiltshire, SN10 1XA
Tel: 01380 739 198

Mortgages Downunder
Email: info@
mortgagesdownunder.co.uk
Tel: +61 754 505623
www.mortgagesdownunder.
co.uk

Mortgages in Spain
PO Box 146
Ilkley, W Yorkshire
LS29 8UL
Tel: 0800 027 7057

Norton Finance
Norton House
Mansfield Road
Rotherham
South Yorkshire, S60 2DR
Tel: 0800 929 100
Email: applications@
norton-finance.co.uk
www.nortonfinance.com

Offshore Lending
Sunnycrest
Somerset Road
Douglas
Isle of Man, IM2 5AE
Tel: 01624 611 915
Email: enquiries@
offshorelending.co.uk
www.offshorelending.co.uk

Triple Independent Financial Services
4 Aynsley Close
Desborough
Kettering
Northamptonshire
NN14 2YD
Tel: 01536 506 475

Pet transportation

Air Animal Pet Moving Services
4120 West Cypress Street
Tampa
Florida 33607–2358
Tel: +1 813 879 3210
www.airanimal.com
Email: petmover@
airanimal.com

Airpets Oceanic
Willowslea Farm
Spout Lane
Stanwell Moor
Staines
Middlesex, TW19 6BW
Tel: 01753 685 571

Animal Airlines
35 Beatrice Avenue
Manchester, M18 7JU
Tel: 0161 223 4035

Animal Airlines
Adlington
Cheshire
Tel: 01625 827 414

Animal Inn
Dover Road
Ringwould
Deal
Kent, CT14 8HH
Tel: 01304 373 597

Animals Away
1613 w.ainsworth dr.
Phoenix, AZ 85086
Tel: +1 800 492 7961
Email: animalsaway2
@cox.net
www.animalsaway.com

Animals by Air Ltd
World Freight Terminal,
Manchester Airport,
Manchester, M90 5PL
TeL: 0161 436 2777

Chilworth Pet Exports/Kennels
Lordsworth Lane
Chilworth
Southampton, SO16 7JG
Tel: 02380 766 876

Global Animal Transport
14439 W. Grandifloras Road
Canyon Country, California
Tel: +1 661 298 9760
Email: Info@
globalanimaltransport.com

Par Air Services Livestock Limited
Warren Lane, Stanway
Colchester
Essex, CO3 0LN
Tel: 01206 330 332
email: parair@btconnect.com
www.parair.co.uk

Pet Travel Scheme Helpline
Department for Environment
Food and Rural Affairs
Area 201, 1a Page Street
London, SW1P 4PQ
Tel: 0870 241 1710

Pet Travel Services
24 Coulston Street
Dunfermline
Fife, KY12 7QW
Tel: 01383 722 819

Popular Pets Pet Transporters
415 Lower Styx Rd
Spencerville
Christchurch
New Zealand
Tel: +64 398 13698

Skymaster Air Cargo
Room 15
Building 305
Cargo Terminal
Manchester Airport
M90 5PY
Tel: 0161 436 2190

Transfur
19 Dean Close
Salisbury Green
Southampton
SO31 7TT
Tel: 01489 588 072

World Freight terminal
Manchester Airport
M90 5PL
Wel: 0870 833 8020
Email: animalsbyair.co.uk
www.animalsbyair.co.uk

World Moving
5 Saunders Place
Avondale
Auckland
New Zealand
Tel: +64 9 820 6060
Email: sales@
worldmoving.co.nz

Property services

NEW ZEALAND
CHRISTCHURCH
TLC Property Management
100A Riccarton Road
Christchurch.
Tel: +64 334 88966
Email: tlcprop@xtra.co.nz

WELLINGTON
KPM Property Management
Key Property Management Ltd
Mreinz
PO Box 6032
Wellington
Tel: +64 480 18123
www.keyproperty.co.nz

SPAIN
Spanish Property Insight
Mark Stucklin
Tel: +34 687 721 131
www.spanishproperty
insight.com

MALAGA
Abacus Property Management
Residential El Coto
Avda. De Mijas
29649 Mijas Costa
Malaga, Spain
Tel: +34 952 586 653

USA
FLORIDA
All American Management
PO Box 3056
Winter Park
Florida 32790
Tel: +1 407 834 7600
Email: aam@aampm.com
www.aampm.com

Recruitment

Executives on the Web Ltd
Cathedral House
Beacon Street
Lichfield
Staffordshire, WS13 7AA
Tel: 0845 009 2 009
www.executivesontheweb.com

Global Vision International
Arnwell Farmhouse
Nomansland
Wheathampstead
St Albans
Herts, AL4 8EJ
Tel: 0870 608 8898
Email: info@gvi.co.uk
www.gvi.co.uk

Hays Personnel
www.haysworks.com

KFK Recruitment
5 St Vincent Place
Glasgow, G1 2DH
Tel: 0141 248 4818
www.kfkrecruitment.com

Manpower
www.manpower.com

Randstad
www.randstad.com

Travel Tree
90 Long Acre
Covent Garden
London, WC2E 9RZ
Tel: 0870 350 3033
Email: info@traveltree.co.uk
www.traveltree.co.uk

The Work and Travel Company
Rick Lyne
45 High Street
Tunbridge Wells
Kent, TN1 1XL
Tel: 01892 516 164
Email: richard.lyne@
worktravelcompany.co.uk
www.worktravelcompany.co.uk

World Challenge Expeditions
2 Chandos Road
London, NW10 6NF
Tel: 0208 728 7200
www.world-challenge.co.uk

Removals

AUSTRALIA
1st Move International Removals Limited
International House
Unit 5B Worthy Road.
Chittening Industrial Estate
Avonmouth
Bristol, BS11 0YB
Tel: 0117 982 8123
info@shipit.co.uk
www.shipit.co.uk

Anglo Pacific International
Units 1 & 2 Bush Industrial Estate
Standard Road
North Acton
London, NW10 6DF
Tel: 0208 965 1234
Email: removals@
anglopacific.co.uk
www.anglopacific.co.uk

Eagle Relocations
Units 3 & 4 Lodge Lane
Great Blakenham
Ipswich
Suffolk, IP6 0LB
Tel: 01473 832 700
www.eaglegroup-online.com

BELGIUM
Crown Relocations
19 Stonefield Way
Ruislip, HA4 0BJ
Middlesex
Tel: 0208 839 8000
www.crownrelo.com

Dolphin Movers Ltd
2 Haslemere Business Centre
Lincoln Way
Enfield
Middlesex, EN1 1TE
Tel: 0208 804 3232
Email: sales@
dolphinmovers.com
www.aerofreight.co.uk

CANADA
Eagle Relocations
Units 3 & 4
Lodge Lane
Great Blakenham
Ipswich
Suffolk
IP6 0LB
Tel: 01473 832 700
www.eaglegroup-online.com

Removals and Storage Solutions
Codham Hall
Codham Hall Lane
Brentwood
Essex
CNM13 3JT
Tel: 01277 204 422
www.removalsstorage
solutions.co.uk

CHINA
Crown Relocations
19 Stonefield Way
Ruislip
HA4 0BJ
Middlesex
Tel: 0208 839 8000
www.crownrelo.com

Excess International Movers
4 Hannah Close
Great Central Way
London
NW10 0UX
Tel: 0208 324 2066
Email: sales@
excess-baggage.com
www.excess-baggage.com

DUBAI
Eagle Relocations
Units 3 & 4
Lodge Lane
Great Blakenham
Ipswich
Suffolk
IP6 0LB
Tel: 01473 832 700
www.eaglegroup-online.com

United Movers International
Tel: 0208 965 5225
Email: info@unitedmovers.es
www.unitedmovers.co.uk

FRANCE
Anglo French Removals
Invicta Works
Farleigh Lane
Barming
Maidstone
Kent, ME16 9LX
Tel: 01622 679 004

F & N Worldwide Removals
Unit 14 Autumn Park
Dysart Road Grantham
Lincolnshire, NG31 7DD
Tel: 01476 579 210

French Connection
The Old Vicarage
Leigh, Sherborne
Dorset, DT9 6HL
Tel: 01935 812 222

Henry Johnson Ltd
5 Rue Jacques Kable
75018 Paris
Tel: +33 146 079 439

GERMANY
Crown Relocations
19 Stonefield Way
Ruislip
HA4 0BJ
Middlesex
Tel: 0208 839 8000
www.crownrelo.com

Excess International Movers
4 Hannah Close
Great Central Way
London
NW10 0UX
Tel: 0208 324 2066
Email: sales@
excess-baggage.com
www.excess-baggage.com

HONG KONG
Anglo Pacific International
Units 1 & 2
Bush Industrial Estate
Standard Road
North Acton
London, NW10 6DF
Tel: 0208 965 1234
Email: removals@
anglopacific.co.uk
www.anglopacific.co.uk

Doree Bonner
International House
Kennet Road
Dartford
Kent, DA1 4QN
Tel: 0208 303 6261
Email: moving@
dbonner.co.uk
www.doreebonner.co.uk

IRELAND
Dolphin Movers Ltd
2 Haslemere Business Centre
Lincoln Way
Enfield
Middlesex, EN1 1TE
Tel: 0208 804 3232
Email: sales@
dolphinmovers.com
www.aerofreight.co.uk

United Movers International
Tel: 0208 965 5225
Email: info@unitedmovers.es
www.unitedmovers.co.uk

ITALY
Crown Relocations
19 Stonefield Way
Ruislip
HA4 0BJ
Middlesex
Tel: 0208 839 8000
www.crownrelo.com

Eagle Relocations
Units 3 & 4 Lodge Lane
Great Blakenham
Ipswich
Suffolk
IP6 0LB
Tel: 01473 832 700
www.eaglegroup-online.com

JAPAN
Anglo Pacific International
Units 1 & 2 Bush
Industrial Estate
Standard Road
North Acton
London, NW10 6DF
Tel: 0208 965 1234
Email: removals@
anglopacific.co.uk
www.anglopacific.co.uk

Removals and Storage Solutions
Codham Hall
Codham Hall lane
Brentwood
Essex, CNM13 3JT
Tel: 01277 204 422
www.removalsstorage
solutions.co.uk

LUXEMBOURG
Crown Relocations
19 Stonefield Way
Ruislip
HA4 0BJ
Middlesex
Tel: 0208 839 8000
www.crownrelo.com

Excess International Movers
4 Hannah Close
Great Central Way
London
NW10 0UX
Tel: 0208 324 2066
Email: sales@
excess-baggage.com
www.excess-baggage.com

NETHERLANDS
Crown Relocations
19 Stonefield Way
Ruislip
HA4 0BJ
Middlesex
Tel: 0208 839 8000
www.crownrelo.com

Doree Bonner
International House
Kennet Road
Dartford
Kent, DA1 4QN
Tel: 0208 303 6261
Email: moving@
dbonner.co.uk
www.doreebonner.co.uk

NEW ZEALAND
AUCKLAND
World Moving
5 Saunders Place
Avondale
Auckland
Tel: +64 982 06060
Email: sales@
worldmoving.co.nz

CHRISTCHURCH
The Moving Company
119 Buchanans Road
PO Box 16 165, Hornby
Tel: +64 334 26286
Email: info@
themovingcompany.co.nz
www.themovingcompany.co.nz

WELLINGTON
21 Peterkin Street
Lower Hutt
PO Box 38 081
Wellington
Tel: +64 457 78200
Email: info@
themovingcompany.co.nz
www.themovingcompany.co.nz

SOUTH AFRICA
Dolphin Movers Ltd.
2 Haslemere Business Centre
Lincoln Way, Enfield
Middlesex, EN1 1TE
Tel: 0208 804 3232
Email: sales@
dolphinmovers.com
www.aerofreight.co.uk

Eagle Relocations
Units 3 & 4 Lodge Lane
Great Blakenham
Ipswich
Suffolk, IP6 0LB
Tel: 01473 832 700
www.eaglegroup-online.com

SPAIN
Eagle Relocations
Units 3 & 4 Lodge Lane
Great Blakenham
Ipswich
Suffolk, IP6 0LB
Tel: 01473 832 700
www.eaglegroup-online.com

Gil Stauffer
Unit 5 Powergate
Chase Road
Park Royal
London, NW10 6PW
Tel: 0208 965 4560
www.gil-stauffer.com

Union Jack International Removals
Calle Campelle
Nave 9
Pol Ind la Calla
03509 Finestrat
Alicante
Tel: +34 966 812 403

USA
Arrowpak International Removals
National and
International Sales
12 Roman Way
Godmanchester
Huntingdon
Cambridgeshire
PE 29 2LN
Tel: 01480 453 115
Email: sales@arrowpaksl.com

Surveyors

AUSTRALIA
Arie Cafe & Associates
4 Marna Court
Noble Park
Victoria 3174
Tel: +61 397 945 952
Email: acafurv@blaze.net.au

Chris Minchin
87 Third Avenue
Joslin SA 5070
Tel: +61 414 832 746

BELGIUM
Draps Edouard-V
268 Boulevard Emile
Bockstael
1020 Brussels
Tel: +32 242 79892

De Smet & Cie
212 Harenberg
1130 Brussels
Tel: +32 475 809 429

CANADA
AW Hooker Associates Ltd
2896 South Sheridan Way
Oakville, Ontario
L6J 7G9
Tel: +1 905 829 9436
www.awhooker.com

BMC Construction Layout Services Ltd
18 Ivybridge Drive
Brampton
Ontario
L6V 2X2
Tel: +1 905 457 5061

FRANCE
Burrows-Hutchinson
11 Rue du Parc
56160 Ploerdut
Tel: +33 297 394 553

GERMANY
Engel & Volkers Immobilien GmbH
Stadthausbrücke 5
20355 Hamburg
Tel: +49 403 61310

HONG KONG
South China Surveys Ltd
Hing Yip Comm Centre
272–284 Des Voeux
Road Central
Hong Kong
Tel: +85 225 459 396

IRELAND
Patterson Kempster & Shortall
24 Lower Hatch Street
Dublin
Tel: +35 316 763 671

ITALY
Geometric Giovanni Pesare
Via Vercelli 19
00182 Roma
www.teicon.it

NETHERLANDS
Bravenboer & Scheers BV
4538AR Temeuzen
Tel: +31 115 687 000

NEW ZEALAND
CKL Surveying & Planning
8 Manukau Road
Epsom
Auckland
Tel: +64 952 470 29
www.ckl.co.nz

SOUTH AFRICA
Advisors in Construction Investment
Fortunes Gate
Marabou Avenue
Johannesburg
Tel: +27 117 941 953

SPAIN
Christopher Morris
5 Claremont Hill
Shrewsbury
Shropshire, SY1 1RD
Tel: 01743 241 615

USA
Alpha Surveyors Inc.
7421 SW 163rd Pl
Miami
Florida 33193
Tel: +1 305 382 9390

Meridian Surveying and Mapping
5245 Ramsey Way
Fort Myers
Florida 33907
Tel: +1 239 275 8575

Swimming pools

AUSTRALIA
Jansen Swimming Pool Construction
Talle Ponds
54 Syndicate Road
Tellenudgera Valley
QLD 4228
Tel: +61 755 338 147

Swimming Pool Construction Co.
693 Glenhuntly Road
Caufield South
VIC 3162
Tel: +61 398 762 987

DUBAI
A Technologies
PO Box 18400
Dubai
Tel: +97 148 873 344

FRANCE
AB Piscines Ltd
11 Rue André Pichon
24340 Mareuil
Tel: +33 553 566 887

London Swimming Pool Company
138 Replingham Road
London, SW18 5LL
Tel: 0208 874 0414

Transaqua
60 Cours Reverseaux
17100 Saintes
Tel: +33 546 972 584
Email: transaqua@wanadoo.fr
www.transaqua-piscines.com

ITALY
Myrtha Pools
Via Solferino 27
46043 Castiglione d'Stiviere
Tel: +39 376 94261
www.piscinecastiglione.it

NEW ZEALAND
AUCKLAND
Exotic Pools
Tel: +64 927 38883
Email: ExoticPools@
xtra.co.nz

CHRISTCHURCH
Swimjoy
480B Moorhouse Avenue
Christchurch
Tel: +64 334 35505
Email: info@swimjoy.co.nz
www.swimjoy.com

WELLINGTON
Cascade Swimming Pools
PO Box 57–006
Mana Porirua
Tel: +64 423 38451

SOUTH AFRICA
CAPE TOWN
Anthony Pools
34 Kings Road
Brooklyn
Cape Town
Tel: +27 2151 16056

PRETORIA
Pretoria Poola
253 Lynchwood Road
Brooklyn
Pretoria
Tel: +27 123 620 533
www.ptapools.co.za

SPAIN
MALAGA
Marbella Pool Services
Calle Pablo Ruiz Picasso
Conh. Los Boquerores
Local 1
29670 Cortijo Bianco
San Pedro Alcantara
Malaga, Spain
Tel: +34 952 781 939

USA
FLORIDA
Aquamarine
Swimming Pool Co.
13217 Automobile Blvd
Clearwater
Florida 33762
Tel: +1 727 299 9600

Tax specialists

UK EXPAT Ltd
Holly Bank
Chalkhouse Green Road
Kidmore End
South Oxfordshire
RG4 9AU
Tel: 0118 9242724
www.ukexpat.net

Montford International PLC
Home Farm
Shere Rd
Albury
Guildford
Surrey, GU5 9BL
Tel: 0800 018 3571
www.miplc.co.uk

AUSTRALIA
Alpha Tax Aid
14 The Kingsway
Wentworthvillle
NSW 2145
Tel: +61 290 313 354

Income Tax Experts
81 Dundas Court
Phillip
AACT 2606
Tel: +61 266 282 2202

BELGIUM
Accova BVBA
373 Rayymond Delbekestraat
2980 Zoersel
Tel: +32 338 01780
www.accova.be

CANADA
International Tax
Services Group
5001 Yonge Street
North Tork
Ontario
M2N 6P6

CHINA
Dezan Shira
China Resources Building
8 Jianguomenbei Avenue
Beijing
Tel: +86 108 519 2001
Email:chris@dezshira.com
www.dezshira.com

DUBAI
PricewaterhouseCoopers
PO Box 11987 Dubai
Tel: +97 143 13888

FRANCE
Anthony & Company
11 Villantipolis
473 Route des Dolines
06560 Valbonne
Tel: +33 493 657 624

ASD (Alimex Sud-Sarl)
16, Place des Arcades
06250 Mougins
Tel: +33 492 380 805

GERMANY
Arnold, Oliver &
Kröger, Klaus
Hausbachstr. 74
22765 Hamburg
Tel: +49 403 891 480

HONG KONG
Dezan Shira
12/F VIP Commercial Centre
120 Canton Road
Tsimshatsui
Hong Kong
Tel: +85 223 766 339
Email: eddie@dezshira.com
www.dezshira.com

ITALY
GM Corporation
46 v. Semetelle
84012 Angri
Tel: +39 815 135 176
www.gmgroup.info

NEW ZEALAND
AUCKLAND
Auckland Taxation
Service Ltd
311 Manukau Road
Epsom
Auckland
Tel: +64 962 31730
Email:atls@xtra.co.nz

CHRISTCHURCH
Canterbury Taxation
Service Ltd
Cnr Wordsworth & Colombo
Sts Sydenham Christchurch
Tel: +64 336 65776

WELLINGTON
Tax Planning Services Ltd
Level 8
75 Ghuznee Street
PO Box 2106
Wellington
Tel: +64 480 16602

SOUTH AFRICA
Rennol Tax Services
75 Voortrekker Road
Edenvale
Tel: +27 114 530 383

SPAIN
API Official Valuations
Tax Adviser
Apdo. Correos 2
Avda. de Madrid 10
Moraira
Tel: +34 965 744 057

Just Tax
57 London Road
High Wycombe
Bucks
HP11 1BS
Tel: 0800 716 961

USA
British American Tax
8 Forest View
London E11 3AP
Tel: 0208 989 0088
Email: liz@
britishamericantax.com

Travel — air

AUSTRALIA
British Airways
Tel: 0870 850 9850
www.ba.com

Qantas
Qantas House
395 King Street
Hammersmith
London, W6 9NJ
or
PO Box 4357
Melbourne
Victoria 3001
Tel: 0845 774 7767
www.qantas.co.uk

Singapore Airlines
Tel: 0870 608 8886
www.singaporeair.com

Virgin Atlantic
Tel: 0870 380 2007
www.virgin-atlantic.com

BELGIUM
British Airways
Tel:08708 509850
www.ba.com

Ryanair
Tel: 0871 246 0000
www.ryanair.com

SN Brussels Airlines
Tel: 0870 735 23 45
www.flysn.com

VLM
Flemish Airways
Tel: 0207 476 6677
www.vlm-airlines.com

CANADA
Air Canada
Tel: 0871 220 1111
www.aircanada.com

Alitalia
Tel: 0870 544 8259
www.alitalia.com

British Airways
Tel:08708 509850
www.ba.com

CHINA
AirChina
Tel: 0207 630 0919
www.air-china.co.uk

British Airways
Tel:0870 850 9850
www.ba.com

Finnair
Tel: 0870 241 4411
www.finnair.com

KLM
Tel: 0870 243 0541
www.klm.com

Singapore Airlines
Tel: 0870 608 8886
www.singaporeair.com

DUBAI
Bangladesh Biman
Tel: 0207 629 0252
www.bimanair.com

British Airways
Tel:0870 850 9850
www.ba.com

Emirates
Tel: 0870 243 2222
www.emirates.com

Gulf Air
Tel: 0870 777 1717
www.gulfairco.com

Royal Brunei Airlines
Tel: +673 221 2222
www.bruneiair.com

FRANCE
Air France
Terminal 2 Heathrow Airport
Hounslow
Middlesex
TW6 1ET
Tel: 0845 0845 111

Air France
2 Place de la Porte Maillot
75017 Paris
Tel: 08453 591 000
www.airfrance.co.uk

Air Littoral
www.airlittoral.com

Air Lib
www.airliberte.fr

BMI
Tel: 0870 6070 555
www.flybmi.com

Britannia Airways Ltd
Luton Airport Luton
Bedfordshire
LU2 9ND
Tel: 0870 607 6757
Tel: 01582 424155

British Airways
Tel:0870 850 9850
www.ba.com

Easyjet
Tel: 0871 244 2366
www.easyjet.com

Flybe
Tel: 0871 700 0535
www.flybe.com

Ryanair
Tel: 0871 246 0000
www.ryanair.com

GERMANY
Air Berlin
Tel: 0870 738 8880/
+49 1805 737 800
www.airberlin.com

British Airways
Tel: 0870 850 9850
www.ba.com

Cirrus Airlines
Tel: +49 6893 800 400
www.cirrus-world.de

Easyjet
Tel: 0871 244 2366
www.easyjet.com

EU Jet
Tel: 0870 414 1414
www.eujet.com

European Air Express
Tel: 01293 596 600
www.eae.aero

Fly Niki
0870 738 8880
www.flyniki.com

Germania Express
Tel: +49 1805 737 100
www.gexx.de

German Wings
Tel: 0870 252 1250/
+49 1805 955 855
www.23.germanwings.com

Hapag Lloyd Express
Tel: 0870 606 0519
www.hlx.com

Lufthansa
Tel: 0208 750 3460/
+49 1805 838 005
www.lufthansa.co.uk

Ryanair
Tel: 0871 246 0000
www.ryanair.com

HONG KONG
British Airways
Tel:0870 850 9850
www.ba.com

Cathay Pacific
Tel: 0208 834 8888
www.cathaypacific.com

Lufthansa
Tel: 0870 8377 747
www.lufthansa.com

Virgin Atlantic
Tel: 0870 380 2007
www.virginatlantic.com

IRELAND
Aer Lingus
Tel: 0845 084 4444
www.aerlingus.com

Ryanair
Tel: 0871 246 0000
www.ryanair.com

ITALY
Alitalia
Tel: 0870 544 8259
www.alitalia.co.uk

BMI
Tel: 0870 6070 555
www.flybmi.com

British Airways
Tel:0870 850 9850
www.ba.com

Easyjet
Tel: 0871 244 2366
www.easyjet.com

Jet 2
Tel: 0871 226 1737
www.jet2.com

Ryanair
Tel: 0871 246 0000
www.ryanair.com

JAPAN
All Nippon Airways
Tel: 0870 837 8866
www.anaskyweb.com

British Airways
Tel:0870 850 9850
www.ba.com

Japan Airlines
Tel: 0845 774 7700
www.jal-europe.com

Korean Air
Tel: +800 0656 2001
www.koreanair.eu.com

Lufthansa
Tel: 0870 8377 747
www.lufthansa.com

LUXEMBOURG
British Airways
Tel: 0870 850 9850
www.ba.com

Luxair
Tel: 0800 3899 443
www.luxair.lu

VLM
Flemish Airways
Tel: 0207 476 6677
www.vlm-airlines.com

NETHERLANDS
British Airways
Tel:0870 850 9850
www.ba.com

Easyjet
Tel: 0871 244 2366
www.easyjet.com

KLM
Tel: 0870 507 4074
www.klm.com

Ryanair
Tel: 0871 246 0000
www.ryanair.com

NEW ZEALAND
Air New Zealand
Tel: 0800 028 4149
www.airnewzealand.co.uk

British Airways
Tel:08708 509850
www.ba.com

Qantas
Tel: 0845 774 7767
www.qantas.co.uk

Singapore Airlines
Tel: 0870 609 9996
www.singaporeair.com

United Airlines
Tel: 0845 844 4777
www.unitedairlines.co.uk

SOUTH AFRICA
Air France
Tel: 0845 0845 111
www.airfrance.com

British Airways
Tel:0870 850 9850
www.ba.com

KLM
Tel: 0870 507 4074
www.klm.com

South African Airways
Tel: +27 119 785 313
www.flysa.com

SPAIN
Air Europa
24 Goodge Place
London, WIT 4SW
Tel: 0870 777 7709

Bmibaby
Tel: 0870 264 2229
www.bmibaby.com

British Airways
Tel: 0870 850 9850
www.ba.com

Easyjet
Tel: 0871 244 2366
www.easyjet.co.uk

Flybe
Tel: 0871 700 0535
www.flybe.com

Iberia
Tel: 0845 601 2854
www.iberia.com

Jet2
Tel: 0871 226 1737
www.jet2.com

Monarch
Tel: 0870 0405 040
www.flymonarch.com

MyTravelLite
Tel: 0870 156 456
www.mytravellite.com

Ryanair
Tel: 0871 246 0000
www.ryanair.com

ThomsonFly
Tel: 0870 1900 737
www.thomsonfly.com

USA
American Airlines
Miami International Airport
Miami
Florida 33159
Tel: +1 800 433 7300

British Airways
Tel:0870 850 9850
www.ba.com

Continental Airlines
Tel: 0845 607 6760
www.continental.com

Delta
Tel: 0800 414 767
www.delta.com

Northwest/KLM
Tel: 0870 507 4074
www.nwa.com

United Airlines
Tel: 0845 844 4777
www.united.com

Virgin Atlantic Airways
6025 NW 18th Street
Miami
Florida 33126
Tel +1 305 743 1940

Travel – coach

AUSTRALIA
Greyhound Buses
111 Franklin Street
Adelaide
GPO Box 2585
Brisbane, QLD 4001
Tel: +61 746 909 950
Email: info@
greyhound.com.au
www.greyhound.com.au

BELGIUM
Eurolines
52 Grosvenor Gardens
Victoria
London
SW1W OAU
Tel 0870 808080

CANADA
Greyhound Buses
Pacific Central Station
1150 Station Street
Vancouver
BC V6A 4C7
Tel: +1 604 683 8133
www.greyhound.ca/en

FRANCE
Eurolines
52 Grosvenor Gardens
Victoria London
SW1W OAU
Tel: 0870 808080

GERMANY
Berlin Linien Bus
Tel: +49 308 619 331
www.berlinlinienbus.de

Eurolines
Tel: 0870 514 3219
www.eurolines.co.uk

Gullivers Reisen
Tel: +49 303 110 2110
www.gullivers.de

IRELAND
Eurolines
52 Grosvenor Gardens
Victoria
London
SW1W OAU
Tel: 0870 808 080

ITALY
Eurolines
52 Grosvenor Gardens
Victoria
London
SW1W OAU
Tel: 0870 808 080

LUXEMBOURG
Eurolines
52 Grosvenor Gardens
Victoria
London
SW1W OAU
Tel: 0870 808 080

NETHERLANDS
Eurolines
52 Grosvenor Gardens
Victoria
London
SW1W OAU
Tel: 0870 808 080

NEW ZEALAND
Touring New Zealand Ltd
131 Dodson Valley Road
Nelson
Tel: +64 354 67020
www.touring-
newzealand.com

SOUTH AFRICA
Municipal Bus Service
Pretoria
Tel: +27 123 080 839

SPAIN
Eurolines
52 Grosvenor Gardens
Victoria
London
SW1W OAU
Tel: 0870 808 080

USA
Greyhound Buses
10 N Pearl Street
Jacksonville
Florida 32202
Tel: +1 800 231 2222
www.greyhound.com

Travel – sea

AUSTRALIA
Spirit of Tasmania
Tel: +61 800 634 906

BELGIUM
Hoverspeed
Tel: 0870 240 8070
www.hoverspeed.co.uk

P&O
Tel: 0870 600 0600
www.poferries.com

CANADA
BC Ferries
1112 Fort Street
Victoria
BC
V8V 4V2
Tel: +1 250 386 3431

Harbour Lynx
303–235 Bastion Street
Nanaimo
BC
V9R 3A3
Tel: +1 250 753 4443

FRANCE
Brittany Ferries
Tel: 0870 366 5333
www.brittanyferries.co.uk

Condor Ferries
Tel: 0845 345 2000
www.condorferries.co.uk

Hoverspeed
Tel: 0870 240 8070
www.hoverspeed.co.uk

Norfolkline
Tel: 0870 870 1020
www.norfolkline.com

P&O
Tel: 0870 600 0600
www.poferries.com

SeaFrance
Tel: 0870 571 1711
www.seafrance.com

Transmanche Ferries
Tel: 0800 917 1201
www.transmancheferries.com

GERMANY
DFDS Seaways
Tel: 0870 533 3111
www.dfdsseaways.co.uk

IRELAND
Direct Ferries
Tel: 0870 458 5120
www.directferries.com

ITALY
Italian Ferries
Corso Garibaldi 96/98
Brindisi
Tel: +39 831 590 84012
Email: etabrindisi@
italfer.inet.it
www.italianferries.it

NETHERLANDS
Stenaline
Tel: 0870 570 7070
www.stenaline.co.uk

DFDS Seaways
Tel: 0870 533 3111
www.dfdsseaways.co.uk

P&O Ferries
Tel: 0870 600 0600
www.poferries.com

NEW ZEALAND
**Bluebridge Cook
Strait Ferry**
Waterloo Quay
Wellington, 6001
Tel: +64 447 37289
Email: bookings@
bluebridge.co.nz
www.bluebridge.co.nz

Interislander Ferry
Wellington Railway Station
Bunny Street
Wellington, 6001
Tel: +64 449 83302
Email: info@
interislandline.co.nz
www.interislander.co.nz

SOUTH AFRICA
Auto carrier transport Ltd
25 Doreen Crescent
Hillside
Port Elizabeth
Tel: +27 414 535 682

Cape Point Ferries CC
Simon's Town
Tel: +27 217 861 045

SPAIN
Brittany Ferries
The Brittany Centre
Wharf Road
Portsmouth
Hampshire
PO2 8RU
Tel: 02392 892 239

USA
Carnival Cruise Lines
10440 SW 48th Street
Miami
Florida 33165 5648
Tel: +1 305 554 5954

**Windjammer
Barefoot Cruises**
1122 Port Boulevard
Miami
Florida 33132 2009
Tel: +1 305 329 3742

Travel – rail

AUSTRALIA
Rail Australia
PO Box 445
Marleston Business Centre
Marleston SA 5033
Tel: +61 882 134 592
Email: reservations@
railaustralia.com.au
www.railaustralia.com.au

BELGIUM
Eurostar
Tel: 0870 518 6186
www.eurostar.co.uk

Rail Europe
Tel: 0870 837 1371
www.raileurope.co.uk

CANADA
ViaRail Canada
www.viarail.ca

FRANCE
Eurostar
Tel: 0870 518 6186
www.eurostar.co.uk

Rail Europe
Tel: 0870 837 1371
www.raileurope.co.uk

SNCF
Tel: +33 890 361 010
www.sncf.com

TGV
Tel: +33 892 353 535
www.tgv.com

GERMANY
Deutsche Bahn
Tel: 0870 243 5663/
+49 180 519 4195
www.bahn.de

Rail Europe
Tel: 0870 837 1371
www.raileurope.co.uk

Thalys
Tel: +33 835 3536
www.thalys.com

IRELAND
Rail Europe
Tel: 0870 837 1371
www.raileurope.co.uk

ITALY
Channel Tunnel
Tel: 0870 535 3535
www.eurotunnel.com

Rail Europe
Tel: 0870 837 1371
www.raileurope.co.uk

JAPAN
Japan Rail
www.japanrail.com

LUXEMBOURG
Chemins de Fer
Luxembourgeois
www.cfl.lu

Eurostar
Tel: 0870 5186186
www.eurostar.co.uk

NETHERLANDS
NS Rail
www.ns.nl

Rail Europe
Tel: 08708 371 371
www.raileurope.co.uk

NEW ZEALAND
Tranzscenic
Tel: +64 449 50775
www.tranzscenic.co.nz

SOUTH AFRICA
Spoornet
www.spoornet.co.za

SPAIN

Rail Europe
Tel: 0870 837 1371
www.raileurope.co.uk

USA

Amtrak
Tel: +1 800 872 7245
www.amtrak.com

Utilities

AUSTRALIA
ELECTRICITY
EnergyAustralia
570 George Street
Sydney
NSW 2000
Tel: +61 800 131 535
Email: enquiries@
energy.com.au
www.energy.com.au

Powercor Australia Ltd
Locked Bag 14090
Melbourne 8001
Tel: +61 800 132 206
www.info@power.com.au

GAS
CitiPower
Locked Bag 14090
Melbourne VIC 8100
Tel: +61 800 131 280

EnergyAustralia
570 George Street
Sydney
NSW 2000
Tel: +61 800 131 535
Email: enquiries@
energy.com.au
www.energy.com.au

PHONE
Optus
Tele-communications
Consultants
Tel: +61 800 502 067
www.optus.com.au

BELGIUM
ELECTRICITY
Electrabel
Regentlaan bd du Régent 8
1000 Brussels
Tel: +32 227 44044
www.electrabel.be

PHONE
Telecom Center Belgium
302 Galerie de la Toison d'Or
Gulden Vliesgalerij
1050 Ixelles Elsene
Tel: +32 251 42807

CANADA
Terasen Inc.
1111 West Georgia Street
Vancouver, BC
V6E 4M4
Tel: +1 604 443 6500
Email: websupport@
terasen.com
www.terasen.com

GAS
Union Gas
50 Keil Drive North
PO Box 2001
Chatham
Ontario
Canada
N7M 5M1
Tel: +1 519 352 3100
www.uniongas.com

CHINA
CLP Holdings
(China Light and Power)
1 Jianguomenwai Avenue
Beijing
Tel: +86 106 505 5608
www.clpgroup.com

FRANCE
ELECTRICITY
Electricité de France (EDF)
Tel: +33 058 137 000
www.edf.fr

GAS
Gaz de France
23 Rue Philibert Delorme
75840 Paris Cedex 17
Tel: +33 147 542 020

GERMANY
Energie Baden-
Wuerttembourg AG
Tel:+49 800 999 9966
Email: info@endw.com
www.enbw.com

HONG KONG
China Light and Power
Company Ltd
Tel: +85 226 782 678
www.chinalightandpower.
com.hk

IRELAND
ELECTRICITY
ESB
Lr. Fitzwilliam Street
Dublin 2
Ireland
Tel:+35 318 581 486
www.esb.ie

ITALY
GAS
EDISON SPA
Foro Buonaparte, 31
20121 Milan
Tel: +39 026 2221
Email: infoweb@edison.it

JAPAN
Chubu Electric Power Co.
www.chuden.co.jp

LUXEMBOURG
SUDGAZ
BP 383
L–4004 Esch
Tel: +35 255 66551
Email: contact@sudgaz.lu
www.sudgaz.lu

NETHERLANDS
GAS
EnergieNed
email: icentrum@
energiened.nl
www.energiened.nl

Enerco
www.enerco.nl

PHONE
AMNEZ TELECOM
37 Businesspark Friesland-W
8466SL Nijehaske
Tel: 0513 646 534
Email: info@
amnez-telecom.nl
www.amnez-telecom.nl

NEW ZEALAND
Alpine Energy
www.alpineenergy.co.nz

Contact Energy
PO Box 10742
Wellington
Harbour City Tower
29 Brandon Street
Wellington
Tel:+64 449 94001
www.mycontact.co.nz

TELTRAC Communications
Teltrac Communications Ltd
22 Alloy Street
PO Box 8484
Riccarton
Christchurch
Tel: +64 334 88641
Email: sales@teltrac.co.nz

SOUTH AFRICA
Eskom
Megawatt Park
Maxwell Drive
Sunninghill
Sandtown
Tel: +27 312 045 793
www.eskom.co.za

SPAIN
ELECTRICITY
EDF Ibérica
c/ Alcala 54, 4° Izqda
28014 Madrid
Tel: +34 918 373 900
Fax: +34 918 373 909
Email: hispaelec@
edf-energia.com

GAS
Repsol YPF SA
Paseo de la Castellana, 278
28046, Madrid
Tel: +34 913 488 100
Email: info@repsol.com
www.repsol.com

USA
Duke Energy
Tel: +1 800 873 3853
www.duke-energy.com

Visas and immigration

AUSTRALIA
Australian Migration
Associates Ltd
Carringtom Business Park
Manchester Road
Carrington
Manchester
M31 4DD
Tel: 0161 776 9839
www.australiamigrate.co.uk

Ian Harrop & Associates
Endeavour House
Priory Lane
Burford
OX18 4SG
Tel: 01993 824 111
www.ianharrop.co.uk

Migration Matters
Charwell House
Wilsom Road
Alton
Hampshire
GU34 2PP
Tel: 0870 760 7040
www.migrationmatters.com

The Emigration Group Ltd
Head Office
7 Heritage Court
Lower Bridge Street
Chester
Cheshire
CH1 1RD
Tel: 0845 230 2526
www.emigration.uk.com

Visa Go Emigration
16 Forth St
Edinburgh
Scotland
EH1 3LH
Tel: 0131 477 8585
www.visa-go.com

BELGIUM
Belgian Embassy
103 Eaton Square
London
SW1W 9AB
Tel: 0207 470 3700
Email: uk@diplobel.org
www.diplobel.org/uk

CANADA
Best Place Immigration
1500 West Georgia Street
Suite 1400
Vancouver
BC V6G 2Z6
Tel: +1 604 970 0629
www.bestplace.ca

Visa Go Emigration
16 Forth St
Edinburgh
Scotland
EH1 3LH
Tel: 0131 477 8585
www.visa-go.com

CHINA
British Embassy
11 Guang Hua Lu
Jian Guo Men Wai
Beijing
Tel: +86 106 532 1961
Email: consularmail@
peking.mail.fco.gov.uk
www.britishembassy.org.cn

DUBAI
United Arab
Emirates Embassy
30 Princes Gate
London
SW7 1PT
Tel: 0870 005 6984
Email: information@
uaeembassyuk.net

FRANCE
French Embassy
58 Knightsbridge
London
SW1X 7JT
Tel: 0207 073 1000
Email: presse.londres-
amba@diplomatie.fr
www.ambafrance-uk.org

GERMANY
Embassy of the Federal
Republic of Germany
23 Belgrave Square
London
SW1X 8PZ
Tel: 0207 241 300
Email: mail@german-
embassy.org.uk
www.german-embassy.org.uk

HONG KONG
British Embassy
1 Supreme Court
Road Central
Hong Kong
Tel: +85 229 013 000
Email: consular@
britishconsulate.org.hk
www.britishconsulate.org.hk

IRELAND
Embassy of Ireland
17 Grosvenor Place
London
SW1X 7HR
Tel:0207 235 2171
Email: ir.embassy@
lineone.net
http://ireland.embassy
homepage.com/

ITALY
Italian Embassy
14 Three Kings Yard
Davies Street
London
W1K 4EH
Tel: 0207 312 2200
Email: ambasciata.londra
@esteri.it
www.embitaly.org.uk

JAPAN
British Embassy
No 1 Ichiban-cho
Chiyoda-ku
Tokyo
Tel: +81 352 111 100
Email: embassy.tokyo@
fco.gov.uk
www.uknow.or.jp

LUXEMBOURG
Embassy of Luxembourg
27 Wilton Crescent
London, SW1X 8SD
Tel: 0207 235 6961
Email: embassy@
luxembourg.co.uk

NETHERLANDS
Royal Netherlands
Embassy
38 Hyde Park Gate
London, SW7 5DP
Tel: 0207 590 3200
Email: london@netherlands-
embassy.org.uk
www.netherlands-
embassy.org.uk

NEW ZEALAND
Migration Matters
Charwell House
Wilsom Road
Alton
Hampshire, GU34 2PP
Tel: 0870 760 7040
www.migrationmatters.com

The Emigration Group Ltd
7 Heritage Court
Lower Bridge Street
Chester
Cheshire, CH1 1RD
Tel: 0845 230 2526
www.emigration.uk.com

Visa Go Emigration
16 Forth St
Edinburgh
Scotland
EH1 3LH
Tel: 0131 477 8585
www.visa-go.com

SOUTH AFRICA
High Commission for the
Republic of South Africa
South Africa House
Trafalgar Square
London, WC2N 5DP
Tel: 0207 451 7299
Email: general@
southafricahouse.com
www.southafricahouse.com

SPAIN
Spanish Embassy
39 Chesham Place
London SW1X 8SB
Tel: 0207 235 5555
Email: embespuk@
mail.mae.es
www.cec-spain.org.uk

USA
Migration Matters
Charwell House
Wilsom Road
Alton
Hampshire, GU34 2PP
Tel: 08707 607040
www.migrationmatters.com

Index of agents

Code	Name and contact details
ALL	**AllGrund, Tel: 00 49 700 101 07000** Postfach 10 22, 10 63263 Dreieich, Germany, www.allgrund.com, service@allgrund.com
AOI	**AOI property, AOI real estate co.,Tel: 00 51426 51 1675, 50-1** Nishiterakata-machi, Hachioji city, Tokyo, 192-0153, Japan
APT	**Apartments.com, Tel: 00 1 888 658 7368** 175 W. Jackson Blvd, Chicago, IL 60604, USA, www.apartments.com, feedback@apartments.com
BAY	**Bayleys, Tel: 00 64 930 96020** PO BOX 8923, Symonds Street, Auckland, New Zealand, www.bayres.co.nz
BOL	**Boland Estates, Tel: 0800 032 7847** Calle C Guadalmina, Blq 4, Local 8, San Pedro de Alcántara, Málaga, Spain, www.bolandestates.com, enquiries@bolandestates.com
BOS	**Bosley Real Estate, Tel: 00 1 416 481 6137** 276 Merton Street, Toronto, Ontario, M4S 1A9, Canada, www.bosleyrealestate.com, service@bosleyrealestate.com
CAS	**Casas Almería, Tel: 01367 240013** 35 Coxwell Road, Faringdon, Oxon, SN7 7EB, UK, www.casasalmeria.com, peter@casasalmeria.com
CAT	**Casa Travella Ltd, Tel: 01322 660988, Fax: 01322 667206** 65 Birchwood Road, Wilmington, Kent, DA2 7HF, UK, casa@travella.f9.co.uk
CAZ	**Coldwell Banker Success Realty, Tel: 00 1 602 954 6888** 3113 East Lincoln Road, Phoenix, AZ 85016, USA, www.coldwellbanker.com
CCA	**Coldwell Banker Residential Brokerage, Tel: 00 1 310 777 6200** 301 North Canon Drive, Suite E, Beverly Hills, California, 90210, USA, www.coldwellbanker.com
CDC	**Coldwell Banker Residential Brokerage-Alexandria** Washington Street, 607 South Washington Street, Alexandria VA, 22314, USA, wwwlcoldwellbanker.com
CMA	**Coldwell Banker Residential Brokerage-Brookline** 1375 Beacon Street, Brookline, MA 02446, USA, www.coldwellbanker.com
CNY	**Coldwell Banker Beach West Realty** 880 West Beech Street, Long Beach, NY 11561, USA, www.coldwellbanker.com
COL	**Coldwell Banker Realty, Florida, USA, Tel: 00 1 863 688 8326** www.coldwellbanker.com
DUN	**Duncan Brown at Royal LePage, Tel: 00 1 605 351 3312** Royal LePage Westside, 5970 East Boulevard, Vancouver, BC, V6M 3V4, Canada, www.condovancouver.com/www.royallepage.ca, duncanbrown@royallepage.ca
GPG	**The Global Property Group, Tel: 01457 833083** 94 Langbourne Place, London, E14 3WW, UK, www.thegpg.com, chris.dunkerley@thegpg.com
HOL	**HousingOnline Verhuur BV., Tel: 00 31 20 561 6095** Joop Geesinkweg 999, 1096 AZ Amsterdam, Netherlands, www.housingonline.nl, info@housingonline.nl
ICR	**Immobilière Christine Rossi, Tel: 00 35 244 4401 1** 44, rue de Vianden, L-2680 Luxembourg, www.icr.lu
KIN	**Kingfisher Rentals, Kingfisher Leisure Marketing Ltd, Tel: 00 33 553 407 113** Pelléry, 47370 Thézac, Lot et Garonne, France, www.king-fisher.net
LAT	**Latitudes, Tel: 020 8951 5155** Grosvenor House, 1 High Street, Edgware, Middlesex, HA8 7TA, UK
LIS	**Lisney, Tel: 00 35 316 382 728** 24 St Stephen's Green, Dublin 2, Ireland, www.lisney.com
MAK	**Slettenhaar NVM Makelaars, Tel: 00 31 203 458 585** Amsterdamseweg 414 1181 BT Amstelveen, Netherlands, www.makelaar.com, huis@makelaar.com
MON	**Montreal Real Estate, Tel: 00 1 514 529 1010** Groupe Sutton Immobilia Inc., 785 Mont-Royal est, Montreal, Quebec H2J 1W8, Canada, www.Montreal-Real-Estate.com, GeoPel@Montreal-Real-Estate.com
OCE	**Ocean Estates International, Tel: 00 34 952 811 750** Avenida Julio Iglesias 3, Puerto Banús, 29660 Marbella, Málaga, Spain, www.oceanestates.com, info@ocean-estates.com
OPT	**Opinz Ltd, Tel: 0845 408 4202** Faraday Business Centre, 34 Faraday Street, Dundee, Angus, DD2 3QQ, Scotland, www.opinz.co.uk
ORY	**Oryx Real Estate, Tel: 00 97 143 515 770** Suite 505, 5th floor, Bin Ham Building, PO Box 115431, Dubai, UAE, www.oryxrealestate.com
PAC	**Pacific Property Ltd, Tel: 00 86 106 539 1399** Unit 709, IBM Tower, Pacific Century Place, 2A Worker's Stadium North Road, Chaoyang District, Beijing, PRC, Postal Code: 100027, www.pacificproperty.net
PAM	**Pam Golding International, Tel: 020 7824 9088** 139 Sloane St, London, SW1X 9AY, UK, www.pamgolding.co.za, lscorovich@savills.com
PIE	**Property.ie, MyHome Ltd** 14 Whitefriars, Peters Row, Aungier Street, Dublin 2, Ireland, www.myhome.ie
PPA	**Passepartout Andaluz, Tel: 00 34 661 626 298** Pasaje Brazales s/n Edif., Milenio A 13, 29649 Riviera del Sol, Mijas Costa, Málaga, Spain, www.passepartoutandaluz.com, consult@passepartoutandaluz.com
PRF	**Property Frontiers, Tel: 01908 616461** www.propertyfrontiers.com, enquiries@property frontiers.com
RAY	**Ray White Properties, Tel: 00 612 9262 3700** Level 4, The Landmark, (GPO Box 5200), 345 George Street, Sydney NSW 2000, Australia, www.raywhite.com
RED	**Redcoats Professionals, Tel: 00 64 456 62233** Hutt City Limited, 28 Cornwall Street, Lower Hutt, New Zealand, www.redcoats.co.nz
REL	**Relocation Central, Tel: 00 1 408 969 7700** Santa Clara, CA, USA, www.relocationcentral.com, info@relocationcentral.com
RET	**Real Estate Tokyo, Ken Corporation Ltd (MAP)** 2–7, Nishi-Azabu 1-chome, Minato-ku, Tokyo Japan, www.kencorp.com
RLP	**Royal LePage, Tel: 00 1 604 261 9311** 5970 East Blvd, Vancouver, British Columbia, V6M3V4, Canada, www.royallepage.ca
RRR	**Rural Retreats-Italy, Tel: 00 39 761 434 144, Mob: 00 39 347 727 3708** Via della Scrofa 12, 01017 Tuscania (VT), Italy, www.rural-retreats-italy.com
SHV	**Shanghai Vision, Tel: 020 7072 8629** 9 Carmelite St, EC4Y 0DR, London, UK, UK@ShanghaiVision.com, www.shanghaivision.com
SIF	**Sifex Ltd, Tel: 020 7384 1200** 1 Doneraile Street, London, SW6 6 EL, UK, www.sifex.co.uk
YHS	**Your House In Spain, Tel: 00 34 932 153 110** c/ Mallorca 264, 2, 1, 08008 Barcelona, Spain, www.yhis.com, wboerhof@yhis.com
ZKI	**Zoek Immo (To the Point)** Parkstraat 41, 9700 Oudenaarde, Belgium, www.zoek-immo.be, info@to-the-point.biz

Acknowledgments

Contributors

Mark Horne
Lorraine Kennedy
(Switzerland article)
Natasha Kingston
Hannah Langfield
Jimmy Razazan

Visas

Oonagh Baerveldt, Visa Bureau, oonagh.baerveldt@visabureau.co.uk, 0870 744 7340

Benelux

Christopher C Credo, HousingOnline Verhuur BV., 00 31 20 561 6095
Jeroen Covemaeker, Zoek Immo (To the Point), www.zoek-immo.be
Wouter, Slettenhaar nvm Makelaars, 00 31 20 345 8585

Canada

Tom Bosley & Bill Statten, Bosley Real Estate, 00 1 416 481 6137
George Pelyhe, Montreal Real Estate, 00 1 514 529 1010
Duncan Brown, Royal LePage, 00 1 605 351 3312

China

Joanna Leverett, Shanghai Vision, 0207 0728 629
Tina Scuse and **Neera Dhingra**, VSO, www.vso.org.uk, 0208 780 7226/7526

Dubai

Ray Withers, Property Frontiers, 01908 616 461

Germany

Peter Talkenberger, Allgrund Immobilien, 00 40 799 1010 7000
Julia Lutz, German Embassy Press Department, 0207 824 1358

South Africa

Lyall Scorovich, Pam Golding International, 0207 824 9088
Matthew Allright, Ocean Estates, 00 34 952 811 750

Spain

Ani Boteva Boland, Boland Estates, 00 34 952 88 66 25
Peter Pickett, Casas Almería, 01367 240013
Chris Dunkerley, The Global Property Group, 01457 833 083
Richard Citteur, Passepartout Andaluz, 00 34 66 16 26 298

Willem Boerhof, Your house in Spain, 00 34 93 215 3110
Mark Stucklin, Spanish Property Insight, 00 34 687 721 131

USA

Sarah Jane Smith, Coldwell Banker, 00 1 863 688 8326
Michael Ricciardelli, Apartments.com, 00 1 312 601 5069

Index to advertisers